# The
# Blood
# of
# Abraham

# The
# Blood
# of
# Abraham

JIMMY CARTER

Houghton Mifflin Company / Boston

For Joshua

Library of Congress Catalog Card Number: 86-80194
ISBN 0-395-37722-6
ISBN 0-395-41498-9 (pbk.)

Printed in the United States of America

D 10 9 8 7 6 5 4 3 2 1

Maps by ANCO/Boston

Houghton Mifflin Company paperback, 1986

# Acknowledgments

My partner in writing this book has been Kenneth Stein, associate professor of Near Eastern history at Emory University. In the spring of 1983, Ken joined my wife, Rosalynn, and me in an extensive journey to Egypt, Israel, Jordan, Saudi Arabia, Syria, Lebanon, and Morocco, during which we interviewed many of the statesmen, scholars, and others who contributed greatly to our more current information about the region. He then helped arrange the first consultation at the new Carter Center of Emory University. It was held in November of that same year and was devoted to a definitive analysis of the political, social, and military situation in the Middle East.

Working with President Gerald Ford, my co-chairman in the consultation, Dr. Stein and I identified those persons from each country and from the Palestinian community who could describe most forcefully and accurately the widely varying perspectives on the Middle East. During the private and public sessions in Atlanta, we were able to let the many points of view be expressed without restraint, to encourage open debate and cross-examination, and to prevent any personal vituperation or angry walkouts among the participants.

In early 1984, Ken became director of the Carter Center, and he has devoted his energies and driving commitment to make it an academic focus for research, teaching, and public education.

Throughout the writing of this volume, I have sought Ken's advice and he has been generous with his contributions. He provided me with new material as the manuscript evolved and read the various drafts with a careful historian's eye, for which I am most grateful.

My wife, Rosalynn, shared with me the four years in the White House, the thirteen days at Camp David with Begin and Sadat, and all my journeys to visit the people of the Middle East. It would be impossible to acknowledge adequately her support and valuable perceptions all along the way.

I am grateful to Nan A. Talese at Houghton Mifflin, who helped me take what was just an outline of recent events and expand it into a more complete story of the Middle East — from its ancient past into the uncertain years ahead. She forced me to spend many additional hours of study and research in order to answer her penetrating questions.

William Brink, an editor who worked for ten years each with United Press, *Newsweek,* and the *New York Daily News,* spent a week with me in Plains going over every chapter with his fine editorial pencil and exacting from me additional personal insights. He helped to clarify many of the most confusing questions.

Professor Nadav Safran of Harvard University, a noted author and historian, read the manuscript and offered many suggestions that improved the accuracy and clarity of the text.

My research assistant, Steven Hochman, gave the manuscript its final reading in order to minimize errors, contradictions, imprecisions, and redundancy.

I might add that some repetition is deliberate in order to indicate how the same event seldom has the same impact on the many people who are affected by it. The most unremitting conflicts of the Middle East are not on the battlefields but in the minds of the people who live there. Bred in the most ancient of times, these differences of conviction continue to cause bloodshed even among those who share one fundamental thing: a dream of peace and justice.

# Contents

# Chronology

Events in the Middle East can best be understood if the history of the region is reviewed. Listed below are a few of the important events that have led up to the existing state of affairs.

| | |
|---|---|
| *c. 9000* B.C. | Human beings leave the first archaeological evidence of their presence at Jericho. |
| *c. 3500* B.C. | Urban life develops in Syria-Palestine. Egypt begins its commerce and political involvement in the region. |
| *c. 3000* B.C. | King Menes unifies Upper and Lower Egypt into one nation. |
| *c. 2300* B.C. | Written records in Syria and Egypt describe the continuing struggles between Egypt and other powers and between nomadic tribes and city dwellers. |
| *c. 1900* B.C. | Abraham journeys from Ur to Canaan. |
| *c. 1200* B.C. | Moses leads the Israelites' exodus from Egypt. |
| *c. 1000* B.C. | Saul is anointed as the first king of the Israelites (1022). King David, his successor (1010–970), unites the twelve tribes of Israel and wins control of the fertile lands on both sides of the Jordan River as well as portions of Syria. King Solomon, David's son, builds the first temple in Jerusalem. |
| *c. 930* B.C. | The Israelite nation divides into two weaker kingdoms, Israel (ten tribes in the north) and Judah (two tribes in the south). They survive frequent conflicts with their neighbors until Israel is progressively destroyed by the Assyrians (721–715); |

Judah is destroyed in 587 B.C. by the Babylonians, who take many of the Jews captive. This marks the beginning of the Jewish Diaspora, or dispersion.

*c. 538* B.C.  The Persian conquerors of Babylonia permit the exiled Jews to return to Jerusalem.

*332* B.C.  The Greeks, under Alexander, conquer the region. Hellenistic kingdoms in Egypt and Syria struggle for control. Under all their conquerors, the Jews fight to retain their religious freedom and to protect their holy places.

*167* B.C.  The Jews' revolt results in the establishment of an independent Judea.

*63* B.C.  The Romans take Jerusalem and control Palestine but generally permit freedom of worship.

*c. 4* B.C.  Jesus is born. He is crucified thirty-three years later, after a ministry of three years. Christian churches are established in Palestine, Syria, Asia Minor, and Rome.

A.D. *70*  The Jewish revolt against Rome is put down and the Temple in Jerusalem is destroyed.

*135*  Following further Jewish revolts, the Romans prevail and lay waste to Judea. Many more Jews are exiled into other regions, particularly Eastern and Western Europe.

*313*  With the Edict of Milan, the Roman Emperor Constantine establishes religious tolerance and, as a Christian, strengthens his own religion throughout the empire, which includes Syria and Palestine.

*570*  The Prophet Mohammed is born in Mecca. He establishes the faith of Islam and dies in 632. Within two decades, Moslem rule has spread throughout Syria-Palestine, Persia, Arabia, and Egypt. Some freedom of worship is permitted under Moslem leaders.

*1099*  The First Crusaders take Jerusalem.

*1187*  The Moslems recapture Jerusalem and, except for a fifteen-year interval (1229–1244), retain control of Palestine until the end of World War I.

*1516*  The Ottomans take Syria, Palestine, and then Egypt.

*1861*  Civil war between the Maronite Christians and Druzes in Mount Lebanon leads to French intervention and the establishment of Lebanon as an autonomous district within Syria, under Christian leadership.

*1882*  The first Zionists from Eastern Europe arrive in Palestine, an area that has been under Ottoman rule for more than three centuries. British forces occupy Egypt; they remain there until 1955.

*1897*  The first World Zionist Congress meets in Switzerland.

*1917*  Great Britain, at war with the Ottoman Empire, issues the Balfour Declaration, which promises a Jewish national home in Palestine with respect for the rights of non-Jewish Palestinians. The area is then occupied by about 600,000 Moslems, 75,000 Christians, and 60,000 Jews.

*1922*  The British Mandate, authorized by the League of Nations, is established over Iraq, Palestine, and Transjordan (later Jordan). A French mandate is established for Syria and Lebanon. Zionists object strongly to any limits placed by the British on Jewish immigration and land purchases, while the Arabs in Palestine adamantly oppose concept and development of a Jewish national home. The White Paper on Palestine confirms Great Britain's dual obligation of establishing a Jewish national home in Palestine while protecting the civil and religious rights of the non-Jewish population. The British protectorate over Egypt ends. The autonomous state of Transjordan is established.

*1932*  King Ibn Saud consolidates his hold over the Arabian Peninsula and forms the Kingdom of Saudi Arabia.

*1936*  The Anglo-Egyptian Treaty is signed to complete the independence of Egypt.

*1938*  Oil is produced commercially in Saudi Arabia for the first time.

*1939*  Britain announces severe restrictions on Jewish immigration and land purchases in Palestine.

*1943*  Syria achieves its independence from France.

*1945*  Lebanon becomes independent of France. The Arab League is established; its members pledge co-

|                    | operation to prevent a Jewish state in Palestine. World War II ends, leaving European Jewry decimated by the Holocaust. |
|--------------------|--------|
| *1946*             | The Kingdom of Jordan becomes independent of British rule. |
| *1947*             | After Jewish terrorist attacks against British facilities and personnel and under worldwide pressure to provide a home for the displaced Jews, Britain allows the newly formed United Nations to decide what to do about Palestine. |
| *November 1947*    | Led by the United States and the Soviet Union, the U.N. votes in favor of partitioning Palestine. Now occupied by about 1,000,000 Moslems, 600,000 Jews, and 150,000 Christians, Palestine is divided into Jewish, Arab, and international areas (Jerusalem). The Arab world objects violently to the partition. Most Jews rejoice, but some claim they must have all of Palestine and others oppose any state at all. |
| *May 1948*         | The British Mandate over Palestine terminates and the State of Israel is proclaimed. It is recognized almost immediately by the United States and the Soviet Union. Israel is attacked by its Arab neighbors. |
| *1949*             | Armistice agreements with the Arabs give Israel more land, but the Arabs retain Old Jerusalem. Over the opposition of the other Arab nations, Jordan annexes what is left of the West Bank of the Jordan River and Egypt occupies the Gaza Strip. Israeli elections give the Labor Party control, which it will retain until 1977. The Arab world remains in a technical state of war with Israel. |
| *1952*             | In Egypt, King Farouk is forced to abdicate by young military officers. Eventually, Colonel Gamal Abdel Nasser emerges as President of Egypt and the leader of the Arab world in the 1950s and 1960s. |
| *1953*             | Hussein, at the age of eighteen, becomes King of Jordan. |
| *July 1956*        | The Suez crisis begins when Nasser nationalizes the canal. Having long been denied passage through the Suez Canal and following repeated |

|              | border skirmishes, in October Israel invades Egypt's Sinai and the Gaza Strip and, along with the British and French, occupies the canal area. |
|--------------|---|
| *March 1957* | Under pressure from the U.N., the United States, and the Soviet Union, foreign forces withdraw from all Egyptian territory and the Gaza Strip. U.N. forces are assigned to patrol strategic areas of the Sinai. |
| *February 1958* | Syria and Egypt merge to form the United Arab Republic and maintain a close relationship with the Soviet Union. |
| *1961* | The Syrian-Egyptian merger is dissolved because of Egypt's domineering attitude toward Syria. |
| *June 1964* | The Palestine Liberation Organization is established with the goal of destroying Israel and gaining control over Palestine. Persistent terrorist attacks against Israel are launched. |
| *April–June 1967* | Following Syrian raids on Israeli settlements, Israel attacks Syria. Nasser closes Israel's southern port by blockading the Strait of Tiran and expels the U.N. emergency force in Sinai. Israel launches pre-emptive attacks on the airfields of Egypt, Syria, Iraq, and Jordan. Within six days, Israel occupies the Golan Heights, the Gaza Strip, the Sinai, and the West Bank, including Jerusalem. |
| *August 1967* | At a summit conference in Khartoum, Sudan, the Arab leaders commit themselves to no peace with, no recognition of, and no negotiation with Israel. Full support is pledged to return all of Palestine to the control of non-Jewish Palestinians. |
| *November 1967* | U.N. Security Council Resolution 242 (Appendix 1) is passed and becomes the basis for future peace negotiations. Essentially, it calls for Israel's withdrawal from occupied territories, the right of all states in the region to live in peace within secure and recognized borders, and a just solution to the refugee problem. The Palestinians oppose being defined as refugees; instead they want a political and not just a humanitarian solution to their plight. |
| *December 1969* | After the failure of negotiations between the United States and the Soviet Union, Secretary of State |

|                    | William Rogers proposes basic peace terms between Israel and Egypt, involving the return of the territories occupied by Israel (including the West Bank) but with some modifications. This plan is immediately rejected by all parties except Jordan. Israel has already begun to build military and civilian settlements in the occupied territories. |
| --- | --- |
| *September 1970*   | Civil war erupts in Jordan between the Palestinians and the Jordanians. Syrian forces enter Jordan but retreat in the face of Israeli threats to intervene with help from the United States. President Nasser dies and is succeeded by Anwar Sadat. |
| *February 1971*   | Sadat proposes that with partial Israeli withdrawal from Sinai, Egypt would clear and reopen the Suez Canal. |
| *July 1971*       | Following months of struggle against the Palestinians, who want to use Jordan as a military base against Israel, Jordanian forces destroy the guerrilla bases and force many Palestinian fighters to find a haven in politically weak Lebanon. |
| *July 1972*       | Sadat expels Soviet military advisers from Egypt. |
| *September 1972*  | Israeli athletes are killed at the Munich Olympics by Palestinian terrorists. |
| *October 1973*    | Egypt and Syria attack Israeli forces in the Sinai and Golan Heights respectively. Caught by surprise, Israel nevertheless forces Arab troops farther back toward Damascus and across the Suez Canal. The Arabs embargo oil shipments to the United States and the price of oil is quadrupled. The Soviets threaten direct military intervention to protect the Arab forces. After sixteen days of war, U.N. Resolution 338 (Appendix 2) is passed, confirming Resolution 242 and calling for a peace conference of all the parties to the dispute. |
| *December 1973*   | The Geneva Peace Conference is convened for two days, according to U.N. Resolution 338, with the United States and the Soviet Union as co-chairs and with Egypt, Jordan, and Israel attending. The PLO was not invited and Syria chose not to attend. |
| *January 1974*    | The Sinai disengagement agreement is signed between Egypt and Israel, in effect separating the mil- |

|                     |                                                                    |
|---------------------|--------------------------------------------------------------------|
|                     | itary forces of the two countries and placing U.N. observers between them. |
| *May 1974*          | The Syrian-Israeli disengagement agreement is reached as part of the implementation of U.N. Resolution 338. |
| *October 1974*      | The Arab summit conference at Rabat unanimously proclaims the PLO as the sole legitimate representative of the Palestinian people. PLO leader Yasir Arafat addresses the U.N. |
| *March 1975*        | President Gerald Ford announces a "reassessment" of U.S. policy in the Mideast to pressure Israel to cooperate on the second Sinai withdrawal agreement. Two months later, seventy-six senators urge him to "be responsive to Israel's economic and military needs." |
| *September 1975*    | The second Sinai agreement is signed between Egypt and Israel. The United States promises not to recognize or negotiate with the PLO until the PLO acknowledges Israel's right to exist and accepts U.N. Resolutions 242 and 338. |
| *1976*              | Civil war erupts again in Lebanon, with the Palestinians' seeking to retain freedom of maneuver there, the Moslems' desiring a greater share of political power and economic advancement, and the Christians' striving to preserve their political prerogatives. In June, Assad sends Syrian troops into Lebanon against the Moslem-radical-PLO coalition, with the acquiescence of the United States and Israel. Egypt and Iraq bitterly oppose Syria's intervention at first, but by November the Arab world supports Syria. |
| *Spring 1977*       | President Jimmy Carter meets with the leaders of Israel (March), Egypt (April), Jordan (April), Syria (May), Saudi Arabia (May) to explore possible peace initiatives. |
| *May 1977*          | Menachem Begin is elected Prime Minister of Israel. |
| *August 1977*       | The United States seeks a way of having the Palestinians participate in the Arab delegation in a reconvened Geneva conference on the Middle East. |
| *October 1977*      | The U.S.-Soviet statement on the Middle East (Appendix 3) is issued. |

| | |
|---|---|
| *November 1977* | Sadat visits Jerusalem, followed by the return visit of Begin to Ismailia, Egypt, in December. Talks begin. |
| *January 1978* | A U.S.-Egyptian statement calls for normalized relations between the Arabs and the Israelis, the withdrawal by Israel from the occupied territories, secure and recognized borders, and a resolution of the Palestinian problem in all its aspects, including the rights of the Palestinian people to participate in the determination of their own future. |
| *March 1978* | Responding to PLO attacks, Israel invades Lebanon. The United States urges Israel's withdrawal. A U.N. peacekeeping force replaces the Israelis. Carter delivers to Begin Sadat's ideas for an overall settlement. |
| *July 1978* | Negotiations break down at the Leeds Castle (England) talks between Egypt and Israel; Sadat rejects any further discussions with the Israelis. |
| *August 1978* | Sadat and Begin accept Carter's invitation to negotiate a peace treaty at Camp David. |
| *September 1978* | The Camp David accords (Appendix 4) are signed after nearly two weeks of intensive discussion. |
| *November 1978* | Arabs at the Baghdad summit conference condemn the Camp David agreement and pledge to punish Sadat. |
| *January 1979* | The Shah leaves Iran, and within a few days Khomeini goes there from France. |
| *March 1979* | With talks again stalemated, Carter visits Egypt and Israel to conclude the terms of the peace. The peace treaty is signed in Washington, calling for Israel's withdrawal from the Sinai and normal trade and diplomatic relations between the two countries, including an exchange of ambassadors. The Arab League headquarters are transferred from Cairo to Tunis. |
| *November 1979* | U.S. citizens are seized in Iran. |
| *December 1979* | Soviet troops invade Afghanistan. |
| *January 1980* | Carter proclaims the Persian Gulf critical to U.S. interests and pledges to resist any attempt by an outside power to control it. |
| *September 1980* | The Iran-Iraq war begins. |
| *January 1981* | The hostages in Iran are released. |

| | |
|---|---|
| *June 1981* | Israel bombs and destroys an Iraqi nuclear reactor; Begin is reelected Prime Minister. |
| *August 1981* | Saudi Arabia's Crown Prince Fahd proposes a plan for a Middle East settlement. |
| *October 1981* | Sadat is assassinated; Hosni Mubarak succeeds him as President. |
| *December 1981* | Israel announces the application of Israeli law to the Golan Heights. |
| *April 1982* | In compliance with the peace treaty, Israel returns the remainder of Sinai to Egypt, including oil fields and air bases, and dismantles its settlements. |
| *June 1982* | Israel invades Lebanon, seeking to destroy the PLO and to establish a friendly regime. Begin first promises that Israel will not penetrate deeply, but Israeli forces push on to surround Beirut. |
| *September 1982* | Reagan calls for the implementation of the Camp David accords, with self-rule for the Palestinians in association with Jordan (Appendix 5). Begin rejects this proposal. At a summit meeting in Fez, the Arabs propose their own outline (Appendix 6) for a settlement, which is rejected by Israel, Libya, and radical Palestinians. U.S. Marines enter Beirut to oversee the departure of most PLO fighters to Arab countries and then withdraw. Lebanon's President Bashir Gemayel is assassinated in a bomb blast and is succeeded by his brother, Amin. Hundreds of Palestinians and Lebanese Moslems are massacred at the Sabra and Shatila refugee camps by Phalangist militia forces in an area near Beirut supervised by the Israelis. The American and European peacekeeping forces return to Beirut. Egypt withdraws its ambassador from Israel, protesting Israel's actions in Lebanon. |
| *April 1983* | More than fifty people die in a terrorist bomb attack on the U.S. embassy in Beirut. King Hussein rejects the U.S. request to join the peace talks with Israel and Egypt after failing to obtain assent from the PLO. |
| *May 1983* | Israel and Lebanon sign a withdrawal agreement that is immediately rejected by Syria. The PLO is wracked by internal dissension focusing on Arafat's leadership role. |

*October 1983* Seventy-eight French soldiers and 241 U.S. Marines are killed in suicide bombing attacks in Beirut. Yitzhak Shamir replaces Menachem Begin as Prime Minister of Israel.

*November 1983* The United States and Israel agree to form a committee to explore modes of strategic cooperation. Jordan, Syria, Egypt, and the other Arab nations strongly object.

*December 1983* Arafat and the PLO troops are forced out of northern Lebanon by Palestinian dissidents supported by Syria. Arafat meets with President Mubarak in Cairo, causing great consternation in the radical Palestinian community. The United States praises the visit; Israel condemns it.

*January 1984* The Jordanian parliament, suspended since October 1974, is reassembled by King Hussein and includes Palestinian representatives. Egypt continues its quiet diplomacy to stimulate negotiations.

*February 1984* The United States announces the withdrawal of its Marines from Lebanon. King Hussein and Arafat meet to discuss political options.

*March 1984* Under pressure from Syria, the Lebanese abrogate the May 1983 withdrawal accord with Israel and hold reconciliation talks among the political factions. The violence continues at a reduced level; Israel continues to occupy southern Lebanon; Syria remains in other areas.

*May 1984* The United States supplies Stinger surface-to-air missiles to Saudi Arabia for the defense of its territory against possible attacks from Iran. Twenty-seven Israelis are indicted for engaging in terrorism against Palestinians in the West Bank.

*July 1984* Israeli elections are held, with indeterminate results.

*September 1984* A National Unity government under Prime Minister Shimon Peres is formed to deal with pressing economic problems. Jordan and Egypt reestablish diplomatic relations.

*November 1984* Israeli-Lebanese negotiations begin on the terms for the withdrawal of Israel's forces from southern Lebanon.

*January 1985* Initial withdrawal commenced.

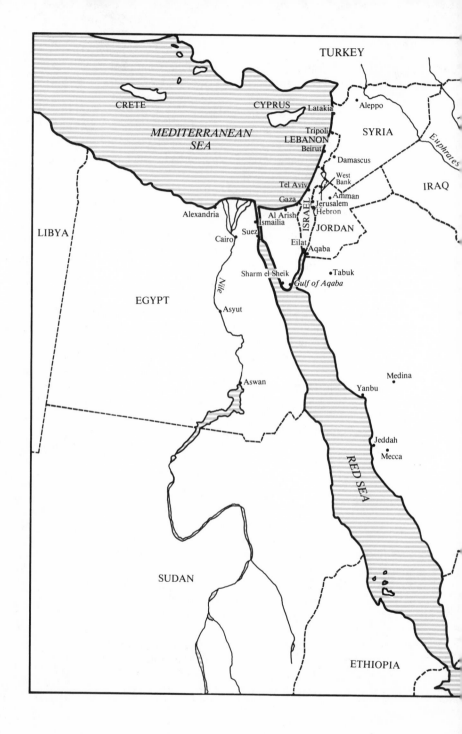

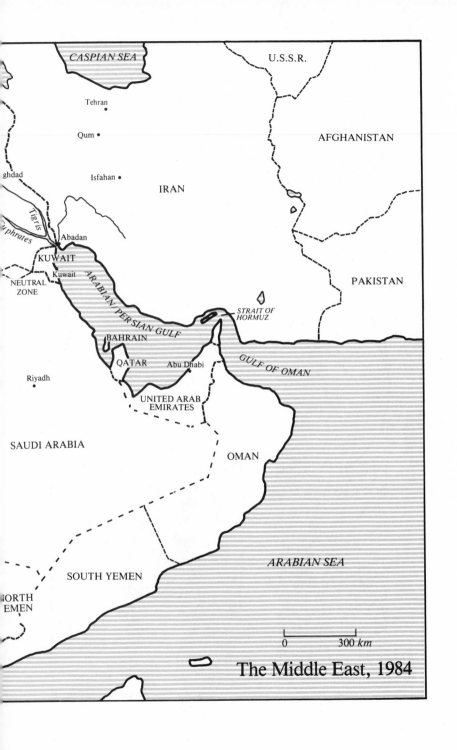

The Middle East, 1984

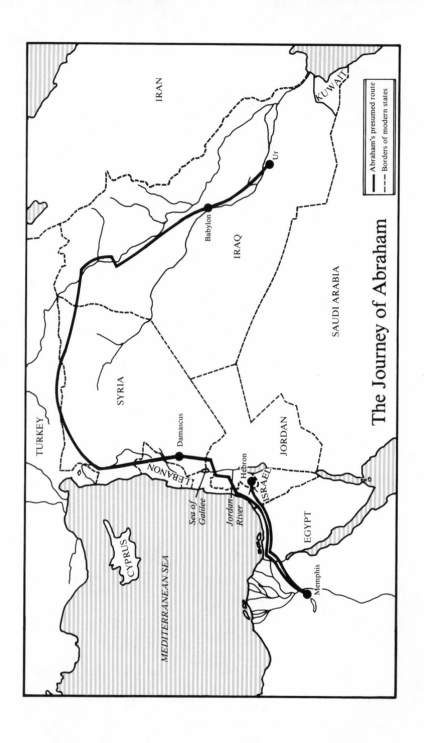

The Journey of Abraham

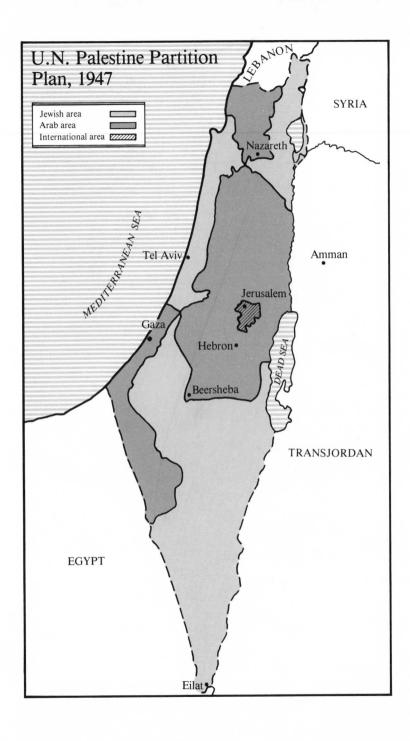

U.N. Palestine Partition Plan, 1947

Jewish area
Arab area
International area

MEDITERRANEAN SEA

LEBANON

SYRIA

Nazareth

Tel Aviv

Amman

Jerusalem

Gaza

Hebron

DEAD SEA

Beersheba

TRANSJORDAN

EGYPT

Eilat

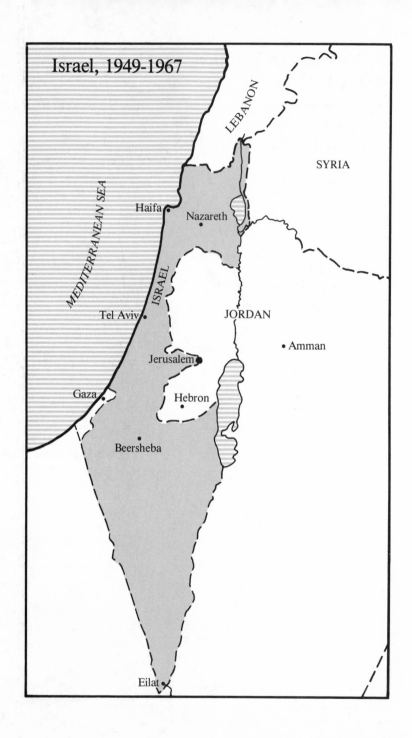

Israel, 1949-1967

MEDITERRANEAN SEA

LEBANON

SYRIA

Haifa

Nazareth

ISRAEL

Tel Aviv

JORDAN

Amman

Jerusalem

Gaza

Hebron

Beersheba

Eilat

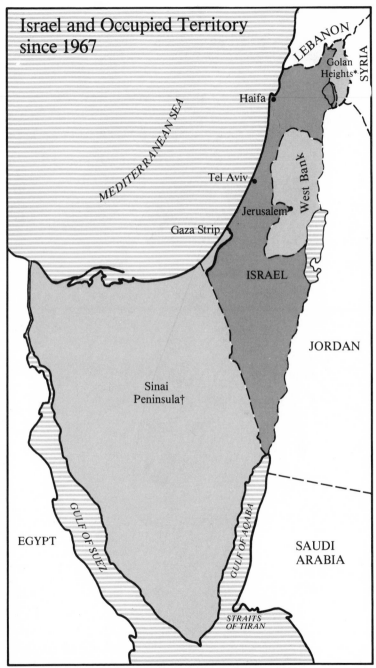

Israel and Occupied Territory
since 1967

LEBANON

SYRIA

Golan
Heights*

MEDITERRANEAN SEA

Haifa

Tel Aviv

West Bank

Jerusalem

Gaza Strip

ISRAEL

JORDAN

Sinai
Peninsula†

GULF OF SUEZ

GULF OF AQABA

EGYPT

SAUDI
ARABIA

STRAITS
OF TIRAN

*A portion of the Golan Heights was returned to Syria in May 1974.
†The Sinai Peninsula was returned to Egypt in April 1982.

# Introduction

THE HISTORY OF the Middle East has been characterized by tremendous suffering and conflict among its peoples. At no time in its recent history, however, has human misjudgment been so tragically the cause of pain as in September of 1982, when hundreds of defenseless people were slaughtered in the Sabra and Shatila refugee camps in Lebanon. It seems that in the historical game of politics and contests for territories, it is almost always the guiltless who die in greatest number.

The tragedy at Sabra and Shatila, and the events leading up to it, vividly demonstrated the complex interrelationships that have so long frustrated those who seek peace in the region. It is important for us to understand more fully this part of the world — to know more about the events of today, its recent history, and its distant past.

In June of 1982, three months before the tragedy, Israeli Prime Minister Menachem Begin had sent his troops into Lebanon, supported by the Lebanese Christian Maronite militia forces (known as Phalangists) and with the seeming acquiescence of Washington. This action was not characteristic of Israeli policy. Previous leaders had refrained from military action except in retaliation against specific terrorist attacks or in response to a direct threat to Israel's security. Within a few days Beirut was surrounded, and during the ten-week siege and bombardment thousands were reported dead and tens of thousands homeless. Begin had achieved one of his major goals when, on the first of September, Yasir Arafat and 12,000 of his Palestine Liberation Organization (PLO) fighters had been driven from Beirut. The American and European peacekeeping forces then left Lebanon, their job of supervising the withdrawal complete. The Israeli leaders and their American supporters were highly gratified at the apparent success of this military venture.

At that time Bashir Gemayel, a Phalangist leader and friend of Israel, was preparing to take office as President of Lebanon. But within days of the withdrawal, President-elect Gemayel was killed by a bomb explosion. Then, in an area of Beirut controlled by the Israelis, the Phalangist troops methodically murdered hundreds of helpless Palestinians and Lebanese Moslems huddled in the Sabra and Shatila refugee camps. During and after the two-day slaughter, many of the victims were secretly buried in mass graves. The final toll was more than 1400 dead and missing, most of them children, women, and the aged. No evidence was presented that PLO troops or militia were among the Palestinians in the camps.

A shocked world responded with condemnation and revulsion. Although the Phalangists had done the killing, the Israeli government leaders were the ones most severely censured. The reaction among the most moderate Arabs was as intense as that of Israel's most virulent enemies. The Egyptians were particularly embarrassed by this ugly result of their peace treaty with Israel and withdrew their ambassador from Tel Aviv. Overnight, the Syrians and their Soviet supporters gained a new opportunity to repair their fortunes and perhaps ultimately to prevail in Lebanon.

Nowhere, however, was the reaction more angry or anguished than in Israel's democratic society. There was a massive uprising among the people and instant demands for a thorough and unrestrained investigation. Opposition leader Shimon Peres referred to "this abominable act which the rabbis said is the absolute antithesis of the traditions of Judaism." Leading Israeli newspapers called for the resignation of Prime Minister Begin, Defense Minister Ariel Sharon, and the military commanders responsible for the Lebanese operation. When Begin's government refused the growing demands for an investigation, almost 400,000 citizens — more than 10 percent of Israel's total population — took to the streets to demonstrate their distress and to demand that those who were guilty be identified and punished. These pressures finally forced Begin to establish a commission to investigate Israel's role in the massacre.

In the meantime, Amin Gemayel, the brother of the slain Lebanese leader, was inaugurated as President. American troops were returned to Beirut as part of a multinational force to bring some semblance of order to the war-torn capital. Instead of remaining neutral, however, the Americans found themselves aligned with Gemayel's Phalangists against a majority composed of Moslems, Druzes, and other Christians.

The events of this month exemplified some of the most disturbing elements of the Middle East disputes:

• Continuing bloodshed caused by the ancient rivalries between the Israelis and Arabs and among the Christians and Moslems.

• The proven power of Israel's military forces in taking territory, but their failure to achieve permanent stability or security in the region.

• The ineffectiveness of the Arab nations in devising or consummating a cohesive policy to deal with Israel's presence among them.

• The surprising permanence of the Egyptian-Israeli peace treaty, but a growing Egyptian belief that it might be contributing to Israeli attacks on other Arabs.

• Misdirected American policy, which enhanced the status of adversaries like Syria and the Soviet Union.

• The growing divisions within Israel itself concerning the wisdom and ultimate consequences of the policies of Begin and his government.

Is there any hope for peace in the Middle East? What caused this series of events just four years after the Camp David peace agreement? I have spent a considerable portion of my public life attempting to answer the first question positively and to understand the answer to the second.

In its broadest definition, the Middle East extends through all the countries that border the southern and eastern coasts of the Mediterranean Sea, from Morocco to Turkey, the Red Sea, the Gulf of Aqaba, and the Persian Gulf. This book deals with that portion of the Middle East comprising the areas most directly involved in the conflict over the future of the Holy Land — Israel and its neighbors (Egypt, Jordan, Syria, Lebanon, and the occupied territories encompassing the West Bank and the Gaza Strip) and Saudi Arabia. The Middle East is perhaps the most volatile and coveted region in the world, one whose instability is almost certainly the greatest threat to world peace.

For centuries, this region has been both a crossroads of trade and a center of conflict for control of the precious land surrounding the holy places of three great monotheistic religions, Judaism, Islam, and Christianity — the faiths of those who share the blood of Abraham. In addition, the Arabian Peninsula contains the largest oil reserves in the free world, fuel upon which other nations of the world depend heavily. The superpowers themselves have made heavy economic, political, and military investments in the Middle East as they have striven to protect their own interests and those of their allies and to expand their influence for the future. As a result of these forces, internal and external, fighting in the region constantly threatens to interrupt the vital supply of oil and deprives an increasingly demanding populace of financial and social benefits that can come only with peace.

To understand the roots of the hatred and bloodshed that still shape the relationships among the people of the region, it is useful to go back to the holy scriptures of ancient times. To a remarkable degree, "the will of God" is the basis for both esoteric debates and the most vicious terrorist attacks among Jews, Moslems, and Christians. God's early promises and how they must now be implemented cause conflict some forty centuries after the patriarch Abraham fathered the Arabs and the Jews in the Holy Land, almost 3000 years since the mighty King David's rule, nearly 2000 years after Jesus brought his revolutionary message to the same land, and 1350 years since the personal ministry of the Prophet Mohammed was ended. Tragically for "the People of the Book" who profess to worship the same God, the scriptures are a source of more difference than agreement, inspiring more hatred than love, more war than peace.

In my discussions of these religious conflicts with President Anwar Sadat of Egypt, he mentioned frequently, and almost casually, the brotherhood of Arab and Jew and how they are both the sons of Abraham. His references to the patriarch caused me to reexamine the ancient biblical story of Abraham and his early descendants, looking at their adventures for the first time from a Jewish, a Christian, and an Arab point of view simultaneously. How could different believers be convinced by the same history that each was God's chosen people?

It is revealing to remember that Abraham's original home, Ur of the Chaldees, was probably in Iraq near where the Euphrates River runs into the Persian Gulf. Following God's directions, Abraham and his family traveled northwest for more than 1200 miles and settled for a while in northern Syria. Then God instructed the patriarch, at the age of seventy-five, to go into the promised land of Canaan (generally, the land between the Jordan River and the Mediterranean Sea), which would forever belong to him and his descendants. They arrived to find a great famine, so Abraham moved his family even farther south, into Egypt. Abraham prospered there, and in time the Pharaoh sent him back to Canaan with increased herds and flocks. Because of his family's great size and wealth, it was decided that they could no longer dwell together, so Abraham permitted his nephew Lot to choose the fertile lands in the Jordan River valley and around the Dead Sea. Abraham took what was left, the hilly regions to the west. He was a wise and good man and God again promised him great blessings, including the land from the Nile to the Euphrates and heirs beyond counting.

Abraham's wife Sarah could not have children, so she gave her husband an Egyptian maid, Hagar, to be his wife. The pregnant Hagar despised Sarah, who then forced the maiden to leave the house. The angel of God found Hagar in the wilderness, told her to return to Abraham's home, and promised her a son and a mul-

titude of other descendants. Abraham was eighty-six years old
when Ishmael was born of Hagar. Thirteen years later, the Lord
made another covenant with Abraham, promising that Sarah
would have a son named Isaac and become the mother of nations,
that He would establish a covenant with Isaac, and that Ishmael
would beget twelve princes and also a great nation. Abraham,
Ishmael, and all the servants and slaves were then circumcised to
seal the agreement, as directed by God. Sarah bore Abraham the
promised son, Isaac, and subsequently she forced Hagar and Ishmael to leave home. This grieved Abraham, but the Bible says
that God continued to bless Ishmael until the end of his days.

Isaac and his wife Rebekah had twin sons, Jacob and Esau,
who were first divided by jealousy but were later reconciled and
united by professions of love because of their blood kinship. After
Sarah's death, Abraham had six other sons by his wife Keturah,
whose descendants make up entire tribes of people who live on in
Lebanon, Syria, Jordan, and Egypt and other North African
countries. He died at the age of one hundred and seventy-five,
and his sons, Isaac and Ishmael, buried him alongside Sarah near
his home in Hebron.

God later told Isaac: "I will make thy seed to multiply as the
stars of heaven, and will give unto thy seed all these countries;
and in thy seed shall all the nations of the earth be blessed." The
Moslems consider themselves descendants of Abraham (Ibrahim)
through Ishmael, but they also revere such biblical figures as
Isaac, Moses, the prophets, and Jesus. A later revelation from
God to Mohammed, through the angel Gabriel, confirmed the
belief in their special blessings from heaven. The Jews share the
blood of Abraham through Isaac and his descendants, but emphasize the special heritage of Jacob.

Jacob was the younger of Isaac's twin sons, but with the help of
his mother he tricked his brother Esau, Isaac's favorite, out of his
father's blessing. Isaac promised Jacob that he would be lord over
his brethren, but when he discovered the trickery, he told Esau
that he must live by the sword and serve his brother, adding that
Esau would later "break Jacob's yoke on his neck."

Jacob's name was changed to Israel at the time of the brothers'
reconciliation, and it was from him that the ancient tribes and the

modern nation got their names. After Israel (Jacob) and Esau buried their father, Isaac, they dwelt together in Canaan until their families became too large and wealthy. Then Esau and his descendants moved farther east into Edom, and Israel stayed in Canaan.

The family of Israel moved to Egypt in a time of severe drought and their descendants became slaves of the pharaohs. After they had lived in this foreign land for 430 years, God guided Moses to deliver the descendants of Israel's twelve sons out of Egypt to freedom. In the twelve tribes of Israel there were 603,550 able-bodied men as well as an uncounted number of priests, women, children, and men who were too old or otherwise unable to go to war.

They were promised Canaan as their home, but because of their sinfulness God forced them to wander in the wilderness until a new generation came. Joshua led them across the Jordan River and established them in the Promised Land. The Israelites struggled against their enemies and were successful when their actions pleased God. About a thousand years after the time of Abraham (and the same interval before the birth of Christ), the twelve tribes were united under King David into a powerful nation. God promised David that because of his faithfulness, his kingdom would be established forever.

However, Moses had made it clear to the Israelites that God's promises always obliged his chosen people to be obedient and faithful to the covenant and divine law. David and his son Solomon had many successors, almost all of them disobedient, under whom the land was ruled as two separate nations, Judah and Israel. Both nations failed to meet God's standards of loyalty and justice and so were destroyed by their enemies, Israel in about 722 B.C. and Judah in about 586 B.C. The Jews were taken into captivity, but some of them subsequently returned to Jerusalem, where they lived under foreign domination but were able to preserve their customs and religious faith.

This brief outline of early biblical history is significant even today as a common foundation for both Judaism and Islam. Jews consider the covenants made by God with Abraham, Isaac, Jacob, and Moses to apply exclusively to them. Moslems also

consider some of this history profoundly significant and derive
from it the justification for their assured place in the eyes of God,
as later revealed to Mohammed. It is also of crucial importance to
Christians of all lands, who know Jesus, the descendant of King
David, as the fulfillment of God's early promises of a permanent
blessing and an unending kingdom among all nations of the
earth. For Christians and Moslems, therefore, the promises of
God are not just for the people of Moses. Christians believe that
Abraham was blessed by God because of his faith, not because of
his race, and that he is the father of all who share his faith in God.

During my long meetings with Prime Minister Begin and even
more with President Sadat, we discussed the three monotheistic
religions and their influence on the ancient and current relationships among people in the Middle East and also on us as individuals — a Jew, a Moslem, and a Christian — searching for peace.
Sadat seemed particularly fascinated with the subject, and he
often referred to his plans to build a holy shrine on Mount Sinai,
so that believers of all three faiths could go there to worship together.

Begin was most interested in the analysis of history, particularly concerning how their faith influenced the Jews of the Diaspora, keeping them unique and united in spite of centuries of
persecution and their fragmentation into minority communities
scattered among many nations. I was familiar with the religious
origin of some of his political commitments concerning the absorption of additional territory into Israel and had noted the
chant of his campaign supporters: "Begin, King of Israel." This
was a modern reminder by the Prime Minister's followers of Israel's ancient glory, when kings led the Jews and when King
David won many military victories and ruled over much of the
region.

Perhaps in deference to my strong and public opposition to his
plans to absorb the entire West Bank and Gaza, Begin rarely referred to any ordainment by God that particular geographical
lines should mark the bounds of his authority. A dedicated stu-
dent of the Bible, on occasion he quoted scriptural passages, such
as "If I forget thee, O Jerusalem, let my right hand forget her
cunning," in order to emphasize why he would not share au-

thority in Jerusalem. I do not recall any occasion, however, when he initiated a discussion about Christianity or Islam or participated in any comparative analysis of religious beliefs. In fact, Sadat's comments on our sharing the blood of Abraham seemed to cause Begin some slight embarrassment.

Like Begin, Sadat was a very devout man. In our private quarters and during our early morning walks at Camp David, he discussed his own Islamic beliefs and was glad to answer my numerous questions. In preparing for the Middle East peace discussions, I had made a brief study of the Koran, which made my discussions with Sadat much more meaningful, but he knew a great deal more about Judaism and Christianity than I knew about his faith.

Judaism and Islam have a profound effect on the governments and public policy in Israel and the Arab countries. Israel is a Jewish state, established as a homeland for the Jews, who uniquely have automatic citizenship when they arrive in Israel. Even those Jews who do not otherwise observe their religious faith often predicate their support for Israel's more controversial policies on the holy scriptures. Their social and political way of life is influenced by the deep traditions of Judaism.

Islam also is more than a religion. The words of the Prophet Mohammed are a guide for tribal and family existence — how to treat friends and enemies, guests in one's home, those who harm their neighbors or who have a legal dispute. Along with other traditions passed down from Mohammed, the Koran is a binding force in that it provides the Arab nations with a common language and culture and, except for Lebanon, a common state religion from which basic laws are derived. This melding of government and religion tends to promote a sense of unity among Islamic nations and between Israel and Jews around the world that is largely missing in predominantly Christian countries today.

Despite the common language, customs, and religion, and regardless of the desire of influential and prosperous leaders for harmony and unity of purpose, the Islamic world is still torn by strife that is not limited to combat with Israel. The terribly destructive war between Iran and Iraq has been a serious threat to the peace of their neighbors. Revolution has been a constant possibility in nations with large ethnic and religious minorities who are not compatible with the ruling elite. The Iranian revolution and Lebanese political disharmony took place against a background of such competing groups seeking to enhance their power and prestige. Differences in religion, race, and place of origin all contribute to the political tensions omnipresent in the region, not only within the Arab nations but also among the citizens of Israel.

However, the basic cause of continuing bloodshed in the region is the struggle for land. With their swift victory in the 1967 war, the Israelis tripled the amount of land they controlled at the expense of Egypt, Jordan, the Palestinians, and Syria, and for several years Israel lived with almost absolute confidence in its military invincibility. Then, in October of 1973, came the surprise attack by Syria and Egypt. Israel's defenses eventually proved adequate, but the Arab forces did well enough to restore their psychological sense of equity. They regained sufficient pride and self-confidence to permit the Egyptian and Syrian leaders to accept limited withdrawal agreements with Israel, even though the Israelis continued to occupy substantial portions of their territory.

The 1973 war also changed America's role in the Middle East. After helping to negotiate the terms of the cease-fire, the United States was identified as a mediator that might be accepted by both Israelis and Arabs. The war made it clear that overwhelming Israeli military power could not, by itself, ensure or force the peaceful resolution of differences.

By the time I was elected President in 1976, I felt that the leaders in the region might welcome further initiatives from the United States to reach the goal of peace. U.N. Security Council Resolution 242 had been adopted in November 1967, calling for the exchange of territories for peace, the sovereignty and independence of all states in the region, an end to belligerency, a solution to the refugee problem, and outside help in resolving outstanding differences and in ending the almost constant conflict (Appendix 1). This resolution was to be the basis for all future peacemaking efforts, but it was rejected by the Palestinians because it did not acknowledge any of their claims to a homeland or their right to form a nation. U.N. Resolution 338 came at the end of the 1973 war; it demanded an immediate cease-fire and suggested a procedure for negotiations under the joint chairmanship of the two superpowers (Appendix 2).

And, in a roundabout way, new attitudes in Israel and among its neighbors had already begun to take shape. The Israeli leaders had seen proof of the U.S. commitment to their nation's security while most other Western powers stayed neutral at best. In the face of President Gerald Ford's "reassessment" of our Middle East policy in 1975, designed to put pressure on Israel, its supporters in the United States had flexed their political muscle, and seventy-six U.S. senators signed a letter cautioning the President about any action that might deprive Israel of its military or economic needs. The Israelis were justifiably confident of their own military strength and of the support of the United States, both in the White House and especially in the Congress.

President Sadat had already broken Egypt's strong ties to the Soviet Union, and he believed the United States could be trusted to protect both Israeli and Arab interests in a time of crisis. He had also proven himself quite willing to negotiate with Israel indirectly, using the American President and secretary of state as mediators. There was strong evidence that Egypt was inclined to withdraw from the persistent conflict with Israel if favorable conditions could be gained, and Sadat had proven that both he and his country had the strength to withstand any condemnation from other Arabs that resulted from such negotiations.

Syria's President Hafez al-Assad, however, was not willing to deal with Israel on a bilateral basis. He had acceded to the cease-fire terms with Israel very reluctantly at the end of the 1973 war, and he had supported the key U.N. resolutions only with strong provisos. In December 1973, he had not attended the two-day negotiating session held in Geneva under U.N. Resolution 338.

By 1976, the Jordanians had been relegated to a minor role in shaping policy in the region, for they had lost control of the West Bank in the 1967 war. They had stayed relatively aloof from the 1973 war and therefore from the negotiating process, and at the Arab summit conference in Rabat in October 1974 the PLO under Yasir Arafat was recognized unanimously as the sole legitimate representative of the Palestinian people. At a minimum, the

PLO wanted the West Bank and Gaza to be an independent Palestinian nation, not subservient to any foreign sovereignty. The Rabat decision severely reduced King Hussein's authority to bargain with Israel even over the status of Jordan's lost territories in the West Bank and, in the process, tended to radicalize the disputes involving this land and its people.

During the disengagement negotiations after the 1973 war, Secretary of State Henry Kissinger and President Ford had made a secret commitment that our country would not recognize or negotiate with the PLO until the Palestinian leaders recognized Israel's right to exist and accepted U.N. Resolutions 242 and 338. Under the circumstances, this was unacceptable to the PLO, and for all practical purposes the Palestinians as represented by the PLO were eliminated as negotiators with either the United States or Israel. This combination of events left the occupied territories without an Arab voice at the potential bargaining table from either its own Palestinian inhabitants or from Jordan.

Meanwhile, across the Persian Gulf, the seeds of rebellion were being germinated in Iran, by the autocratic rule of the Shah, by a rising demand for more personal benefits from the nation's oil wealth, and by the adverse reaction of conservative religious leaders to the Shah's rapid moves toward a Western and secular society. The fundamentalist Shia Moslems were especially critical of growing equality for women and non-Moslems, the absence of Islamic influence in the government, foreign commercial agreements concerning Iran's oil and agricultural products, and the brutal oppression by state police of those who demonstrated publicly against the Shah's policies.

During the mid-1970s, there was no serious thought within our own intelligence agencies or among the political leaders of Europe or the Middle East that the Shah would actually be overthrown. However, because of reports of increasing violence in Iran, when the Shah made his first visit to Washington in November 1977, I spoke to him about the need to address the revolutionary forces against him, among both Iranian students in the United States and the demonstrators on the streets of Iran. The Shah discounted these activities as "a few communists and their sympathizers," who had no legitimate complaints and no popular support. He insisted that the imprisonment of his vocal critics and gunfire from his police into demonstrating crowds were the best ways to stamp out the dissension. Indeed, the Shah went so far as to suggest that the Western leaders might well emulate his toughness, lest our permissive democratic principles open floodgates of public protests that could not be controlled.

As President, I had to confront this multiplicity of factors in the Middle East, but there were indications that reconciliation was possible. Israel and its Arab neighbors were technically at war, but the region was fairly stable. There was continuity of leadership in all the major countries in the area. Sadat gave signs that he might be ready for further negotiations, Syrian troops maintained a semblance of stability in Lebanon, and the successful Saudi efforts to smooth over dissension among the Arab leaders signaled to the United States and others that further steps toward peace would be acceptable to them. Although the Palestinians were still excluded from any peace talks, it was possible that this barrier might be circumvented through King Hussein of Jordan. Israeli elections were forthcoming early in 1977, and it was hoped that a stronger ruling coalition would be formed with enough popular support to take some bold diplomatic moves in negotiating for peace.

I was willing to participate personally in this task, if necessary, and in rapid succession during my first few months in office I had long discussions with Israel's Prime Minister Yitzhak Rabin (March), President Anwar Sadat of Egypt (April), King Hussein of Jordan (April), Syria's President Hafez Assad (May), Crown Prince Fahd of Saudi Arabia (May), and finally Israel's newly elected Prime Minister Menachem Begin (July). After all these meetings, I was determined to proceed with our efforts for peace. Most of the Arab leaders were supportive but reluctant to become involved directly in any early negotiations. Only Sadat and Begin were willing to join me in substantive discussions concerning the basic issues of land, Israel's right to exist in peace with its neighbors, and Palestinian rights.

Some major advances were made in September 1978 at Camp David and during follow-up negotiations, leading to a peace treaty between Egypt and Israel in 1979, but subsequent events made further progress impossible. The Jordanians and Palestinians have refused to join the talks that would implement the pledges made to the West Bank and Gaza Palestinians, the commitments made at Camp David concerning the occupied territories and rights of the Palestinians have not been honored, and Israel's invasion of Lebanon in 1982 further undermined any progress toward peace.

With this stalemate in the peace process, the involvement of outside powers and their alignment with the various Middle Eastern factions have become increasingly important. The contention for influence among Eastern and Western nations in the region is nothing new. More than a thousand years before Abraham, outside forces struggled almost continuously along the eastern shores of the Mediterranean Sea, either for their own commercial or political benefit or to deny the area's advantages to an adversary. More recently, during the four centuries leading up to World War I, this seacoast area was mostly under the control of the Turks as part of the Ottoman Empire. An exception was Egypt, where French and then British influence had prevailed since the opening of the Suez Canal in 1869.

Victorious in World War I, the British and French were free to divide the Ottoman territories between themselves. Under a League of Nations mandate, French rule was recognized over Syria and Lebanon, while the British retained effective control in Egypt, Iraq, the newly created Transjordan, and Palestine. Subsequently the Arab and Jewish populations strove for sovereignty in Palestine, but ultimate political control remained in London.

The two European powers were under an obligation to the League of Nations and to the indigenous populations to promote development toward independence in all these countries. Palestine was considered a hopeless case, because there was no chance that the Arabs or the Jews could agree on a government that would include the other. Furthermore, the British had to deal with the equivocal Balfour Declaration, which called for "the establishment in Palestine of a national home for the Jewish people" without "prejudice to the civil and religious rights of the existing non-Jewish communities," a dilemma still confronting the region.

The advent of World War II found the British and French still dominant in the Middle East, but rising nationalist fires burned in every area. The Nazis did everything possible to fan these flames, but with limited success. Even after France fell, the Vichy forces were quickly replaced by the British in Lebanon and Syria. An independent Saudi Arabia remained neutral until late in the conflict, then declared war on Germany. In Iran, Reza Shah Pahlevi quite early aligned himself with the Axis but was then deposed by the British and the Russians. With Allied support, his son Mohammed Reza Pahlevi replaced him on the throne in 1941, ruling until he was overthrown by the revolution in 1979, almost thirty-eight years later.

By 1945, therefore, at the end of the war, British influence was dominant throughout the area. The Soviets attempted — unsuccessfully — to occupy northern Iran permanently, and the struggle for influence between the Soviet Union and the Western nations soon became a major factor in the political life of the entire region. Syria and Lebanon achieved independence after the end of the war. Great Britain gave the responsibility for Palestine to the United Nations and in 1948 withdrew all its forces from the region, leaving behind what became a divided Jerusalem, the new State of Israel, the West Bank as part of Jordan, and the Gaza Strip occupied by Egypt.

Europe's influence in the Middle East faded steadily after World War II and was practically eliminated by an aborted effort of France and Great Britain, with Israel's help, to seize the Suez Canal from Egypt in 1956. Soviet and American influence then increased, filling the political vacuum that was created. In the 1970s, however, there was a rekindling of interest, and new alignments were formed between the countries of Europe and some areas of the Middle East because of one major reason: oil. A nervous Europe's need for assured supplies of energy solidified an attitude that was more balanced toward the Arab-Israeli conflict in general and more attuned to the Palestinian dimension of the conflict in particular. All these trends were demonstrated quite vividly during the October 1973 war between Israel and its Arab neighbors, when none of the European countries would permit the United States to refuel its aircraft taking supplies to Israel during the latter days of the conflict. This was a clear break with the United States and Israel, a show of unanimity by the Europeans on behalf of the Arab nations.

But this renewed interest and activity between Europe and the Middle East can be misleading. None of these nations or even a united European community has the power or influence to replace the United States as a principal force for peace in the area. Furthermore, even if the Arabs and Israelis would accept the Europeans as worthy mediators, there is little likelihood that any of them would invest a significant portion of their limited political resources in the highly charged atmosphere of the region, because their own citizens would probably not support this effort over an extended period of time. The Arab world still looks to the European countries, particularly to the permanent members of the U.N. Security Council (Britain and France), to be even-handed in their policies concerning the Arab-Israeli conflict.

What are the Soviet interests in the Middle East, and how do they differ from those of the United States? Like some of the Western European nations, the Soviet Union's proximity has long caused its history to be intertwined with that of the Middle East, while the United States, 5000 miles away, has until modern times remained aloof from the area's internal affairs. The Soviets share borders with Turkey, Iran, and Afghanistan and claim the same regional interests in Syria, Iraq, Lebanon, and the Arabian Peninsula as the United States does in Central America.

With the history of Soviet doubt about the reliability or friendship of its neighbors, it is no surprise that the unstable Middle East has become a primary concern to them. They fear any undue Western presence and influence in the region, and they worry about the spillover of an Islamic resurgence into the southern portions of the vast Soviet landmass, where a Moslem minority makes up 20 percent of the total population.

Practical benefits and ideology both play a role in the Soviets' designs on the region, as shown by their aggressive manner in luring the Egyptians and the Syrians to their corner in the 1950s. Their December 1979 invasion of Afghanistan can be seen both as a defensive move in establishing another subservient state on their southern border and as an ideological impulse in expanding Marxist-Leninist doctrine. Regardless of their ultimate goals or motives, there is no doubt that the Soviets will make every effort to retain and expand their foothold in the Middle East.

However, because of competitive Western forces and the Moslems' natural aversion to atheistic communism and fear of internal subversion, Soviet influence in the region remains limited. The Arabs know the pronounced tendency among the Soviets to move in and attempt to establish a puppet government, safely subservient to their interests, in order to protect their "security." In spite of these contrary factors, the Soviets now have long-term Friendship and Cooperation treaties with Iraq, Ethiopia, Afghanistan, North and South Yemen, and Syria.

Another motive for the Soviet presence in the Middle East is Moscow's quest for parity with the United States in the area. They want to have their own clients, like elements of the PLO, Syria, Libya, and others, just as we have our friends in Israel, in Egypt, and in some moderate Arab nations like Jordan and those in the Arabian Peninsula. Also, they do not want to be excluded from any peacemaking process, which is why they supported the 1973 Geneva conference and the 1977 U.S.-Soviet declaration (Appendix 3).

Finally, although the Soviets are interested in greater influence in the region and are sometimes willing to encourage dissension, they have not directly interfered with oil production, seized oil fields, or interdicted tanker transports. They can "keep the pot boiling" by using local rivalries, national animosities, and the Arab-Israeli conflict for their own ends. There is substance to the contention that the Soviet Union "needs" Israel so that the Arab world's antagonism to the Jewish state will increase its dependence upon Moscow for arms and political support.

There is no doubt that the U.S.-Soviet hostility and competition aggravate an already intractable situation in the Middle East. The freeze in relations and the termination of most negotiations between the United States and the Soviet Union in the last few years have not made it easier to find areas of agreement that might end the impasse in the Middle East peace process. At least Israel and the United States are convinced that any involvement by the Soviets in the next round of discussions would add an extra element of dispute and complexity. The Israelis and many Arabs simply do not trust the Soviets and, in spite of the imbalance of American diplomacy toward Israel, the United States is still considered by the Arab leaders who will acknowledge Israel's existence as the most likely outside power to bring to the region a new stability and a next step toward the reconciliation of differences. The prospects for peace will be dismal or nonexistent if the United States neglects this duty, and the Soviets will continue to benefit from the American default.

At this writing (January 1985), Israeli troops are still in southern Lebanon, the West Bank, Gaza, and the Golan Heights. The Egyptian ambassador remains withdrawn from Israel and a tenuous "cold peace" prevails between the two countries. King Hussein's inclination to revive the peace process and to negotiate on behalf of the Palestinians is still being frustrated by lack of support from the PLO and moderate Arab leaders. The United States suffered a costly and embarrassing defeat in Beirut, and Syria's President Assad has emerged as the unchallenged external force in Lebanon.

At best, there is now a stalemate in the Middle East that is constantly exacerbated by policies, statements, and actions on all sides that feed distrust and misunderstanding. In spite of its current impotence in the area, the United States still has fairly good relations with some of the countries involved, notably Israel, Egypt, and Saudi Arabia. However, U.S. ties with Syria and Lebanon continue to be strained, Jordan has lost confidence in Washington's commitment to the peace process, and official relations with the Palestinians as a people are still nonexistent.

Sometimes, under equally difficult circumstances, American officials have been able to bring disputing parties together and on occasion have had limited success: the sponsorship and support of U.N. Resolutions 242 and 338, Kissinger's shuttle diplomacy under Presidents Nixon and Ford leading to the two Sinai disengagements, and the Camp David accords and the Egyptian-Israeli peace treaty.

U.S. goals in the Middle East have been often stated but as often misunderstood. They are easy to enumerate (but extremely difficult to accomplish):

• Israel and its Arab neighbors to be secure and living in peace.

- Each nation to be autonomous, free of external intervention.
- The Palestinians of the West Bank and Gaza to be given their legitimate rights, including self-determination.
- Israel to withdraw from occupied territories.
- A fully sovereign and independent Lebanon, with all foreign forces withdrawn.
- The Middle East to be free of superpower confrontation.
- Minimal Soviet interference in the affairs of the region.
- An end to the war between Iran and Iraq, with their former national frontiers restored.
- Economic prosperity and a good life for the people of the region.

These goals seem reasonable and well balanced even to most people in the Middle East. Why, then, is it so difficult — seemingly impossible — to bring peace to the region? It is obvious that the people in every nation want an end to the bloodshed and suffering. What prevents their leaders from even going to the negotiating table? The contending parties believe in the rightness of their cause, and some of them are willing to face death rather than change their position or even to admit the legal existence of their adversaries. They act with absolute certainty that they are carrying out the will of God. Most of the facts are not in dispute. So how could there possibly be such sharply conflicting views among people in the same region?

Only by listening to the voices in each nation and by examining more closely the history of the people themselves is it possible to approach the answers to these questions.

# Israel

M Y FIRST VISIT to Israel was in May 1973 at the invitation of General Yitzhak Rabin, one of the heroes of the Six-Day War of 1967, who was soon to become a member of the Israeli cabinet. He had visited us at the Georgia governor's mansion while he was an envoy to Washington.

Rosalynn and I had long been interested in the area through our weekly Bible study, so we welcomed the opportunity to visit the exciting new democracy of Israel after completing a trade mission to several European countries on behalf of the State of Georgia.

As governor, I was an official guest of Prime Minister Golda Meir, but I had few duties and we considered this part of our trip a vacation. The Israeli government furnished us with an old Mercedes station wagon, a driver, and a young guide, and we were encouraged to choose our own itinerary.

In preparing for this trip, Rosalynn and I had pored over maps and reviewed both the ancient and modern history of Israel. I was torn between the pleasure of visiting the Christian holy places I had longed to see since I was a child and the knowledge that I should be preparing for a future career. (At the time, my plans were known only to a small group of people and would not be revealed for another eighteen months, when I announced my candidacy for President of the United States.) So our choice of how to spend the precious days in Israel was a series of compromises.

Each of my mornings in the Jerusalem area began quite early, with a walk before sunrise through the old city. I wanted to see it come to life when few tourists were about, and to catch a flavor of how it might have been two thousand years earlier, when Jesus strolled the same streets. We visited the small bakeries where delicious loaves of bread were prepared for the market in large open ovens, sipped coffee or tea in the small shops, and watched the vendors arrange their wares for the unfolding day. I had long talks with some American archaeologists who were involved in the excavation of the biblical City of David, trying to complete as much of their work as possible during the cooler hours of the day. They described how the detritus of past civilizations had constantly raised the level of the streets on an average of about one foot a century. They were digging at a thirty-foot depth, and they showed me a few Roman coins of King Herod's day that had been found about twenty feet below the surface.

This made it easier for us to understand why the urban sites we visited in Jerusalem, Bethlehem, Hebron, Jericho, and Nazareth were often so different from what we had expected. They seemed buried, closed in, tinseled, and highly commercial, not simple and primitive as we had imagined. Only when we traveled in the open spaces and saw the Mount of Olives, the Garden Tomb, Cana, Mount Carmel, the Sea of Galilee, the Mount of Beatitudes, Capernaum, Bethsaida, and the Jordan River did we feel that we were looking at the country as it might have appeared in biblical times.

Throughout our travels we found the country to be surprisingly relaxed. On our entire trip we saw only a handful of men in uniform, mostly directing traffic at some of the busier intersections. Also, there seemed to be an easy relationship among the different kinds of people we met, including Jews and Arabs.

After visiting the Church of the Nativity and the subterranean dwellings in Nazareth that were said to typify those where Jesus lived, we enjoyed an exciting and somewhat boisterous lunch with the Moslem mayor, the Christian deputy mayor, the Jewish mayor of Upper Nazareth, and a number of their family and friends. For several hours we ate prodigious quantities of lamb that had been roasted whole, a stew that we scooped up with our fingers, fruit, vegetables, and bread; we also drank a lot of spirits and later the thick black coffee typical of the region.

We were intrigued with how the officials of Nazareth were striving to increase tourism and promote economic progress, and in the afternoon we went over to the new city to meet some of the recent immigrants from the Soviet Union, who seemed to be arriving in a steady stream. The paint was hardly dry when each family moved into their new apartment, and there were plans to build three thousand more units to house those yet to come. The mayor said that up to a hundred factories around metropolitan Nazareth would provide jobs for both the old and new residents. Immigration had boomed following Israel's great victory in the 1967 war, reaching its highest level the year we were there. Some of the longtime citizens complained about the special treatment being given to the newcomers, but these dissident voices were not widespread or persistent. We talked to several of the Soviet settlers; they were quite proud that they had begun studying Hebrew from the first day in their new homes.

Later we visited several kibbutzim (collective farms or settlements) near the Sea of Galilee and then far south in the Negev desert region. At Ayelet Hashahar, in northern Galilee, we were told that the Jewish settlement was already fifty-four years old. As a farmer, I was interested to learn that they grew apples and were able to keep them in cold storage for sale almost year round and that their cows were milked three times daily (instead of the usual two milkings) to increase the production and the profits.

This community of several hundred permanent residents was also a tourist center and accommodated many visitors from the United States and other countries. It was the Sabbath, and we asked if we could attend the worship service. At the appointed time we entered the synagogue and stood quietly just inside the door. There were only two other worshipers. When I asked if this was typical, our guide gave a wry smile and shrugged his shoulders as if it was not important either way.

One day we ate "Peter's fish" for lunch at Ein Gev, on the shore of the Sea of Galilee, and then ascended the Golan Heights to a kibbutz at Mevo Hamma. There we found much more of a pioneer spirit, and we were impressed by the quiet dedication of the young families who farmed together. They seemed to share everything and were quite proud of their hard manual labor and the absence of worldly goods in their homes.

The kibbutz leaders took us to the steep western slope overlooking Galilee to show us the gun emplacements that had been built and used by the Syrians against the Israelis during the 1967 war. From that vantage point we could see the small villages along the lake shore, the homes below in the valley, the automobiles on the roads, and the tractors cultivating the fields. They looked quite vulnerable; it seemed that they could almost be hit by a rock thrown from where we were standing, certainly by a rocket or a shell. It was obvious why the control of this site was so important to Israel.

As we stood together, the young Israelis spoke with growing fervor, as though debating an absent adversary. One by one, the small group of men and women explained that Israel was surrounded by powerful enemies determined to destroy their fragile nation. Palestinian terrorists, they said, were being sheltered across the border and supported and dispatched by other Arabs on frequent raids against defenseless Israeli settlers. The Syrians, in particular, were attempting to form a united bloc of Arab states with the avowed purpose of driving the Israelis into the sea. The strength of Israel was being tested every day and must never be found wanting.

Our Israeli hosts reported proudly that kibbutzim like theirs were making productive farms out of desert lands in other occupied Arab territory, helping to sustain the Israeli economy. They said that agriculture was Israel's most important industry, with oranges second only to polished diamonds as the largest export. Their commitment was to do their own work, not to hire any helpers. This was an exciting part of the spirit of Israel. There were not many settlers in the occupied territories, but these people were convinced that their own kibbutz was valuable both economically and militarily, and they were determined to stay. They made it clear to us that they never intended to have enemy guns firing down from these cliffs again.

To get a clearer understanding of Israel's military capability, I had asked to observe some naval facilities, to learn about its training program for the citizen army, and to have as thorough a briefing as possible on the relative strength of Israel and its Arab neighbors.

We visited Mount Carmel to see where the prophet Elijah had demonstrated God's miraculous power before King Ahab and the prophets of Baal (1 Kings 18). Then we descended to the navy base at Haifa and went to sea on one of the missile boats. Our hosts were very proud that the vessels had been spirited so deftly from the French at Cherbourg despite the post-1967 arms embargo against Israel. These boats were fast and efficient, and a good portion of their crews were women.

From the seacoast we drove east and then down through the West Bank, staying as close as we could to the Jordan River. All our lives we had read about this river, studied and sung about it, so we visualized a mighty current with almost magical qualities. We were amazed. In fact, it was not as large as many of the tributary creeks that flow into the smaller rivers of Georgia. The stream was naturally small, and we learned that much of the water was diverted from the headwaters of the stream to irrigate Israeli land; this had been one of the prime causes of the animosity between Israel and its neighbors.

As we drove south, barbed wire and roadblocks kept us away from the river's banks and out of a relatively narrow security zone, but we could often see Jordan in the distance. At the Allenby Bridge, near Jericho, we watched for a while as streams of people moved back and forth between the two countries. The Israeli officials told us that here, at the river crossing, only routine security checks were made. During the last three years, they said, more than three quarters of a million Arabs had visited Israel legally. With a wink, one of the guards said that they could only estimate how many illegal visitors there had been, but that some of them (referring to captured terrorists) had never been able to return home to Jordan.

At Bethel, a few miles north of Jerusalem and still in the occupied territories, we attended a graduation ceremony at a training camp for Israeli soldiers. This facility had been used by the Jordanians for the same purpose before the Six-Day War. The commanding officer, who had been given basic training by the U.S. Marines, said that he used some of the most severe techniques for developing the physical and mental capabilities of his troops. He had also been stationed briefly at a military base near my own home in Georgia, and on the spur of the moment he asked me to participate in the graduation ceremonies. The soldiers stood rigidly at attention while their names were called, one by one. Then each graduate ran at top speed to the reviewing stand, where the commander delivered a diploma and I presented a "Sword of the Spirit" — a Bible.

Our final military visit was with Major General Eliahu Zeira, the chief of Military Intelligence. Using photographs, maps, and charts, he described the formidable array of Arab tanks and planes that were marshaled against Israel. He emphasized the need for a much greater supply of weapons from the United States, but he and other military commanders had an air of absolute confidence. Again and again they referred to the 1967 war, and they left no doubt that they were thoroughly prepared for any eventuality. Although only 5 percent of the Israeli military personnel were kept in uniform, they said, their intelligence was excellent and their mobilization time very brief. (Within five months, on Yom Kippur, they were to be shocked by the surprise attack from Egypt and Syria.)

I talked privately with some of the Israeli cabinet members, and they invited us to attend an evening debate in a large auditorium. Prime Minister Golda Meir and other political and military leaders were to discuss some of the issues being addressed by the government, for the benefit of a large radio audience.

I noticed No Smoking signs around the auditorium, which everyone was obeying except the Prime Minister. But our guide explained: "We have a choice to make. Either have no signs and everyone smoking or have signs and have one person smoke. We decided that one person smoking wouldn't be too bad."

We listened with fascination to Abba Eban, Chaim Bar-Lev, and Yitzhak Rabin, who were speaking in English. The atmosphere was buoyant with a sense of success and prosperity. I recorded some of the private and public comments that indicate the attitudes prevailing in the springtime of 1973:

"The United States is our only important friend."

"The Russians now want peace in the Middle East. They cannot afford another major defeat of their Arab allies."

"The Europeans are obsessed with economics. France is our worst enemy in the Common Market — moralistic to a fault."

"Although we do a lot of trading there, buying diamonds for our jewelry industry, South Africa cannot go on as it is."

On the subject of whether to keep a large portion of the West Bank: "The size of our nation is overemphasized; partition is desirable. Arabs are incompatible with us; they have no loyalty to the Israeli flag. Israeli Arabs are the fastest growing community on earth. They are now 35 percent west of the Jordan and will grow to more than half."

"No one should fear the Arabs. They have been beaten badly and will have to sue for peace."

"The Arab oil weapon is not a real threat. They need dollars more than the world needs their oil."

"Israel receives 90 percent of its oil needs from the Sinai and Iran. We have no foreseeable problems in obtaining enough fuel."

"Nixon never broke his promises, but we would vote for Senator Scoop Jackson."

When asked why the Israelis did not depend more on the United Nations to address their problems:

"We would turn to the U.N. if there were thirty-nine Jewish nations and one Arab."

Rosalynn and I ended our stay in Israel by visiting Prime Minister Golda Meir to thank her for extending to us the hospitality of her country. She was not pressed with state business that morning, so we stayed for an extended talk. When she asked if we had any concerns, I replied that there was one of a religious nature that I hesitated to mention. I knew that she had been born in America and that neither she nor the key members of her cabinet were known to be devout Jews. With a smile she encouraged me to go on, and I told her about the sabbath service at Ayelet Hashahar and a general absence of religious interest among the Israelis. I commented that during biblical times, the Israelites triumphed when they were close to God and were defeated when unfaithful.

She laughed aloud and agreed with me, but added that this was
not a matter of concern to her because there were certainly
enough "orthodox" Jews around. She was referring to the religious Jews in the Israeli parliament, who were sometimes a real
thorn in her side. She added, "If you attend a session of the
Knesset, you will see them in action and will know they have not
lost their faith." With Israel's system of elections, which necessi-
tates a coalition of parties to form a ruling majority, the minority
religious parties had an influence far exceeding their numerical
strength.

Neither Mrs. Meir nor I realized it then, but a member of one
of the larger minority parties was destined to play a major role in
her country's history, and much of his political strength would
come from his deep fundamentalist convictions, based on a rigid
interpretation of the scriptures. In 1973, Menachem Begin was
the leader of the Herut party, which had only 22 percent of the
Knesset seats. Within four years he would be Prime Minister of
Israel.

After a while she asked if there were others in our party. We
told her that my press secretary, Jody Powell, and a Georgia state
patrolman were outside and would like very much to meet her, so
she invited them in. Throughout our visit she smoked continuously, and she finally noticed Jody looking hungrily at her ciga-
rette. She offered him one and he timidly took it, remarking,
"This is the first time I've ever bummed a smoke from a Prime
Minister." She indicated the absence of a health warning on the
package and said, "You will notice, young man, that Chester-
fields are not a danger to your health in Israel."

Although we had heard news reports about aerial skirmishes
between Israel and Egypt over the Sinai (and were somewhat
concerned that our travels might be restricted), we found
throughout Israel a glow of security, pride, prosperity, confidence, and harmony. We left the Middle East convinced that Israel's military forces were invulnerable, and that they would have
to be kept strong to defend the small nation against its Arab
neighbors. We did not visit any Arab country or have any personal contact with the Palestinians of the West Bank and Gaza.
At that time, few Americans were asking any difficult questions.

The Israelis were dominant, the Arabs subdued, and the political and military situation seemed destined to remain perfectly stable. But in Cairo and Damascus, and possibly in Moscow, secret plans for war were already well under way.

For me there is no way to approach or enter Israel without thinking first about the Bible and the history of the land and its people. The names and images have long been an integral part of my life as a Christian, but many of them took on a new and entirely different significance when I became President of the United States and joined in life-or-death negotiations to resolve some of the twentieth century's problems. It is rare indeed to find the distant past so intertwined with the immediate present, not just for historians and theologians in their classrooms and studies but for statesmen in the halls of government and military commanders on the field of battle.

In Israel, the study of the scriptures has a unique significance in that the Bible and its derivative interpretations have a profound role in defining the secular life of the nation. Although the majority of Israelis are not particularly religious, many of those who are have joined political parties that require the governing coalition to endorse certain religious practices in return for their support. Religious beliefs are debated most fervently in the Knesset, and governments may stand or fall on the political allegiance of a few elected representatives whose interests are narrowly focused on precise interpretations of the scriptures. The recent trend has been for the religious groups to draw a sharper distinction between themselves and the major parties and to become more nationalistic and militant. An ultraconservative minority takes a contrary position, seeing the establishment of the secular State of Israel as a violation of God's commandments.

Israel is the focal point of the religious disputes, but the Jews of many other nations observe closely and sometimes become directly involved. However, any differences among them on these or other issues are greatly overshadowed by their united support of Israel. Of the 14 million Jews in the world, about 6 million live in the United States, perhaps 2 to 3 million in the Soviet Union, and 3.5 million in Israel. There are about a half million Jews in

both Great Britain and France and a little more than that in Latin
America. The rest are scattered among numerous other nations.
This provides a core of strong support for Israel in many places,
because no matter what their citizenship, with few exceptions
Jews throughout the world are deeply committed to Israel's sur-
vival and prosperity.

They know very well that 4 million Palestinians, supported by
hundreds of millions of Moslems everywhere and by friends and
allies of the Arab nations, claim the right to a nation on the same
land. This is a fearsome prospect for those dedicated to the pres-
ervation and prosperity of the tiny nation. They realize that the
inherent conflict has deep, almost unshakable roots, with many
Jews and Palestinians claiming the most admirable traits for
themselves but characterizing the others as either imperialists or
terrorists. The superpowers are not excluded from this adversarial
alignment, the United States giving strong support to the Israelis
and the Soviet Union attempting in every way to cement further
its relationships with the peoples of the Arab world.

There are some interesting differences and similarities between
the Jews and the Palestinian Arabs. Since the time of King David,
the concept of a Jewish nation has been kept alive, even though
the Jewish people have been scattered among the nations of the
world. Only a small remnant managed to survive in Palestine
under its numerous conquerors. Christian and Moslem Arabs
continued to live in this same land, but with no hope or even
thought of establishing a separate and independent nation. Their
concern was with family and tribe and, for the Moslems, the
broad world of Islam. Strong ideas of nationhood only began to
take shape among the Arabs during the last fifty years, after they
saw the Zionists immigrate to Palestine, buying tracts of land for
permanent homes. In their struggles for self-determination, sometimes with the shedding of blood, the Jews and Arabs lived as
uneasy neighbors under British domination until after the Second
World War and the establishment of the State of Israel.

When I travel in the Middle East there is one persistent impression: the difference in public involvement in shaping national
policy. In a few of the Arab countries with more authoritarian
leadership, it is almost fruitless to seek free expressions of opinion

from private citizens, even among business leaders, journalists, and scholars in the universities. Only in Israel, a democracy with almost unrestricted freedom of speech, can one hear a wide range of opinion concerning the disputes among Palestinians, other Arabs, Israelis — and often between Israelis and distinguished guests.

In March 1979, when I visited Egypt and then went on to Israel to conclude the peace treaty between the two countries, I was asked to stop at the entrance to Jerusalem to receive the official welcome from Mayor Teddy Kollek and the senior rabbi of the city. As we approached the site, the Israeli security officer reported that I would probably be bombarded with eggs and vegetables by some demonstrators who opposed the peace process. There were umbrellas, he said, to be opened to protect me if necessary. As we drove up and I emerged from the limousine, I turned to wave to the large crowd across the street. They were well within throwing range, and some of them seemed quite angry. A wide variety of banners and placards were held aloft, most of them in English and negative in tone; the most prominent of all was one that read WELCOME, BILLY'S BROTHER. All of us Americans laughed and the tension was broken. We ate the ceremonial bread and salt without incident, and I continued on my way to see the Prime Minister.

On another visit, when I addressed the Knesset, it was a shock to observe the degree of freedom permitted the members of the parliament in their relatively undisciplined exchanges. Although I concluded my remarks with few interruptions, it was almost impossible for either the Prime Minister or the opposition leader to speak. Instead of being embarrassed by the constant interruptions and by the physical removal of one of the members from the chamber, Prime Minister Begin seemed to relish the verbal combat and expressed pride in how unrestrained the shouted argument was. During an especially vituperative exchange, he leaned over to me and said proudly, "This is democracy in action."

With the exception of sometimes excessive military censorship, this freedom of expression pervades the news media, and in private discussions in Israel there is a notable desire to explore every facet of domestic and international political life. Only among some of the Israeli Arabs is there an obvious reluctance to speak freely, caused by the natural suspicion of a minority group that does not have strong and independent political status. Also, there are strict Israeli prohibitions against political activity by the Palestinian Arabs in the occupied territories.

Although important disagreements exist among opposing political leaders in the Israeli debates, the differences pale into relative insignificance when questions of Israel's security are concerned. Then the Jews close ranks; a common religion, a shared history, and memories of horrible suffering bind them together in a strength and cohesion unequaled in the Middle East or perhaps anywhere in the world.

In assessing the attitudes of Israelis toward their region and its future, there is no way for any thinking human being to ignore the Jewish experience of the past. Jews suffered for centuries the pain of the Diaspora, compounded by persistent racial persecution in almost every nation in which they dwelt.

In Europe, despite their remarkable contributions to the social, scientific, and economic development of their communities, many Jews were killed and others driven from place to place by Christian rulers. Although not given the same rights as Moslems, both Christians and Jews who remained in the Islamic Middle East as minorities often fared better than non-Christians in Christendom, because the Prophet Mohammed commanded his followers to recognize in Judaism and Christianity the common origins of their faith, to honor their prophets, and to protect their believers.

More benevolent rule finally came to Western Europe with the Enlightenment of the nineteenth century, and the unique identity of the scattered Jews was threatened as they began to lose the cohesion that had come with persecution and to accept assimilation into the Christian and secular societies of that time. But almost three fourths of all the Jews were living in Eastern Europe, where their suffering continued, and it was there that the seeds of Zionism were nourished. Although the vast majority of European emigrants went to the United States, increasing demands were heard for the establishment of a Jewish state in their ancient homeland — both to escape their oppressors and to fulfill the ancient biblical prophecy.

In 1880, there were only 30,000 Jews in Palestine scattered among 600,000 Moslem and Christian Arabs, but from this time on each phase of persecution in Europe brought a wave of Zionist settlers. Large groups arrived in Palestine in the 1880s, just before and after World War I, and again in the late 1920s. By 1930, their numbers had grown to more than 150,000, a figure that more than doubled again in the next ten years.

The Arabs in Palestine became more and more alarmed and fought politically and militarily against these new settlers in their midst, but beyond this issue they could agree on little else and dissipated their strength and influence by contending among themselves. After World War I, various plans were proposed to resolve these disputes between the Jews and the Arabs, but they were always rejected by one or the other side, most often by both. The British, who succeeded the Ottoman Turks as rulers of Palestine, attempted to minimize the bloody disputes by restricting the immigration of Jews to the Holy Land, despite desperate appeals from those who faced increasing threats and racial abuse in Europe.

And then came the indescribable horror of the Holocaust, which at the time was accepted or ignored by many people in the earth's civilized nations, including the United States. Only when the facts were impressed more clearly on the consciousness of a deeply mortified world community was action taken to bring to a climax the fervent and untiring efforts of the Zionist movement to form the State of Israel. This was the culmination of the Jews' never-ending dream to establish and live under a government of their own choice in their biblical homeland. The victory over almost insurmountable odds and the undying memories of the tragic past color and shape the attitude of world Jewry. And the possibility of a vulnerable and isolated Israel, bereft of strong allies and exposed to a phalanx of implacable Arab foes, has forged the commitment of the nation to an invulnerable defense in spite of the political and economic sacrifices that may be required.

The final United Nations partition proposal in November 1947 was acceptable to a majority of the Jews, but the Arab forces objected to the legal usurpation of any of the land on which the Palestinians had lived for centuries. The Palestinian Arabs began to intensify their armed attacks against the Jews, and fierce fighting erupted between the neighbors. The following year, in May, the British forces withdrew and Israel declared itself an independent state. At that point Arab troops from Egypt, Lebanon, Syria, Transjordan, and Iraq joined the Palestinians in attacking the new nation.

Like the Israelis, some of the Arab troops had fought with the Allies against the Axis powers. They had inherited weapons from their European overlords, and some of them had had good training. However, the Egyptians, Syrians, Lebanese, and Iraqis were struggling to establish viable governments and still divided among themselves. Their separate national forces were not well coordinated, and there was some doubt about their specific objectives. With the exception of Jordan, the governments of Israel's neighbors were torn with dissension, and several were soon overthrown by coups or revolution.

The Jews, in contrast, were fighting for their very lives and the existence of their new nation, and their forces were cohesive, better trained, well led, and highly motivated. With Soviet support, the Israelis were able to get modern arms from Czechoslovakia, which helped them finally to prevail. The war ended in 1949 with armistice agreements signed between Israel and the proximate countries. Iraq, not contiguous to Israel, played only a minor role in the combat and never bothered to participate in the concluding armistice negotiations.

One of the most significant elements of the documents signed in 1949 was Israel's acceptance of the principle of a divided Palestine and the agreement that King Abdullah of Jordan would control what is now known as the West Bank. At that time, the Palestinians had no effective capability of forming a separate nation, and the Jordanians wanted as much territory as possible on the west bank of the Jordan River. Therefore, no serious consideration was given to establishing an independent state for the Palestinians while their desired homeland was being divided among Jordan, Israel, and Egypt.

The state of war between Israelis and Arabs caused many Jews to flee from the Arab countries to Israel. At the same time, Palestinian refugees from Israel and the West Bank were being scattered more broadly throughout the weakened countries. From all sides, the Palestinians launched guerrilla attacks to harass the Israelis, who were attempting to cultivate land, establish new homes, and proceed with the business of strengthening the infrastructure of their new nation. These attacks precipitated repeated retaliatory raids from Israel against the host nations that were giving support and encouragement to the Palestinians. These kinds of border skirmishes continued during the succeeding years.

In 1956, Israel launched an attack against Egypt and was immediately joined by France and Great Britain in an attempt to take the Sinai and the Suez Canal from Egypt. Israel's goal was to break the long-standing Egyptian maritime blockade against Israel, to neutralize the Sinai as a launching area for military attacks against Israeli settlements, to return control of the canal to the European powers, and to force the Egyptians to give diplomatic recognition to Israel. In the face of President Gamal Abdel Nasser's ineffective defense the military strike was successful, but both the United States and the Soviet Union mounted a concerted effort in the United Nations, and international political pressure forced the invaders to withdraw. Israel was successful, however, in winning U.N. guarantees of a largely demilitarized Sinai with a peacekeeping force therein as well as the right of navigation through the Straits of Tiran. This war let the Arabs know that Israel would not hesitate to use its powerful military force to secure its borders and protect its interests. The Suez attack also intensified their perception of Israel as an alien force in their midst, still supported by the colonial powers of the West.

Except for spasmodic border raids, there followed ten years of relative peace, but it became increasingly clear that both sides were preparing for another war. Israel and Egypt were arming themselves as rapidly as possible and conducting frequent military maneuvers, and the rhetoric of hatred was promoting in the people a conviction that war was inevitable. Finally, in 1967, President Nasser expelled the United Nations peacekeeping force, remilitarized the Egyptian Sinai, and imposed a blockade on Israeli shipping in the Tiran Straits.

These actions were a powerful blow to Israel's economic existence and a military threat that could not be ignored. Taken as a whole, they were clearly recognized as an adequate cause of war. Despite frantic efforts by the United Nations, the United States, and other Western powers to prevent another outbreak of hostilities, the Israeli cabinet in early June decided to launch preemptive strikes against Syria and Egypt. War erupted and, despite Israel's warnings to Hussein, the Jordanian forces attacked Israel. In six days, the Israeli air and land forces were successful beyond all expectations. Israel's forces moved west through the Gaza Strip and the arid Sinai desert to the Suez Canal, east to occupy the West Bank, and northeast to take the Golan Heights. With this startling victory, a sense of pride and euphoria spread through Israel.

However, there was strong international reaction, and new alignments of opposition and support emerged. The Soviets broke diplomatic relations with Israel and offered almost unlimited aid to the Arabs. Israel's strong ties with some of its European friends were seriously weakened as many nations joined in the condemnation of its expansion into Arab lands. At the same time, the commitment of the United States to Israel grew, and military and financial assistance was increasingly forthcoming.

Within Israel itself there was considerable opposition to retaining the captured territories, but the prevailing attitude among the Israeli leaders was that the occupied lands, excluding some still undefined parts of the West Bank, should be kept and traded for a secure peace with the Arabs.

The efforts within Israel to prepare for this exchange of land for peace revealed political alignments that were to become increasingly significant in later years. The most notable plan was put forward by Yigal Allon, a war hero and cabinet minister. In general terms, Allon proposed that Israel keep a strip of relatively uninhabited land on the West Bank, next to the Jordan River, and establish fortifications and scattered settlements there as a defense against a possible surprise attack from the east. The areas north and south of Jerusalem, heavily populated by Palestinians, would be retained by the Arabs as part of Jordan and connected geographically to Jordan by a corridor through the area surrounding Jericho. The plan was roundly condemned by Menachem Begin, then a leading opposition member of the Knesset, and others who were determined to retain the entire West Bank as part of Israel. Subsequently, King Hussein also rejected the entire concept of dividing the West Bank.

In fact, all the neighboring Arab nations refused to negotiate on Israeli terms. During the succeeding months the Egyptians continued to pound Israeli forces in the Sinai, and Israel's air force responded with effective raids on Cairo and other cities. The Soviets provided antiaircraft weapons to the Egyptians and even deployed some of their own fighter planes against those of Israel, but they made little impact on the Israelis' powerful punitive strikes deep into Egypt.

At the same time, Palestinian guerrillas, especially in Jordan, were encouraged by other Arabs to continue their attacks across the border, and terrorist acts were committed against Israelis throughout the world. The Israelis withstood the raids and were not intimidated by the threats of terrorism, but they were deeply concerned by a simultaneous development on the broader political scene. The Palestine Liberation Organization, which had been founded in 1964, was becoming a dangerous military force and a powerful political entity, able to arouse strong support in international forums from the Arabs, the Soviet Union, most Third World countries, and some Europeans.

Preoccupied with consolidating their hold on the West Bank and Gaza and continuing to build their own economy, the Israelis were caught completely by surprise in October 1973, when President Anwar Sadat of Egypt orchestrated a simultaneous attack by his forces across the Suez Canal and a Syrian thrust into the Golan Heights. Well armed with Soviet weapons, the Arabs were at first successful, but Israeli tenacity and additional military supplies from the United States eventually turned the tide.

With Israeli forces still pushing forward, the two superpowers used their influence to bring about a cease-fire, and negotiations began for withdrawing the opposing troops from direct confrontation. The United States was the key mediator, with Secretary of State Henry Kissinger shuttling among the nations, seeking agreement.

In December 1973, the foreign ministers of the United States, the Soviet Union, Israel, Egypt, and Jordan met in Geneva in accordance with U.N. Resolution 338 (Appendix 2). Their goal was to forge disengagement agreements that would end the October 1973 war formally and lay a foundation for other peace talks in the future. Syria refused to attend, and the PLO leaders were not invited. Subsequently, however, with the United States still acting as intermediary, agreements were consummated between Israel and both Egypt and Syria to permit an end to the combat and to stabilize the line between the countries, with Israeli forces still occupying the Sinai and the Golan Heights. These agreements made the United States the virtual guarantor of compliance and further increased its commitment to Israel.

Following a second disengagement agreement between Israel and Egypt in September 1975, there was a period of relative dormancy in international negotiations. However, a national election was approaching in Israel. The results of the Israeli election of December 1973 portended what was to happen in 1977, but few people recognized or believed the evidence. In 1973 the Labor Alignment membership in the Knesset, under Prime Minister Golda Meir, dropped by five, while the Likud (formerly Herut) members, led by Menachem Begin, increased by thirteen. Labor still had a plurality, and was able to form a coalition government by involving enough minor parties.

Mrs. Meir resigned in 1974, and Yitzhak Rabin succeeded her as the Prime Minister. In May 1977, however, the election yielded a new leader. The Likud gained four more Knesset members while the Labor Alignment lost another nineteen. The Likud formed a new government, and Menachem Begin became Prime Minister, emerging as a bold and forceful leader.

Begin's surprising victory ended the uninterrupted domination of the Labor party since Israel's independence. It is interesting to note that Begin's Herut party was formed partially out of a pre-state terrorist organization. Sharp controversy developed within Herut and between Begin and other Israeli leaders about Israel's rights to the whole of historic Palestine. Now, however, Begin had put together a majority coalition that insisted, as he had in 1949, that the land in Gaza and on both banks of the Jordan

River belonged rightfully to the State of Israel and should not be exchanged for a permanent peace agreement with the Arabs. Public opinion varied widely, but there was no doubt in 1977 that a more hawkish attitude had been generated in the government of Israel. Begin had not changed; Israel had.

Although many factors influenced the outcome of the election, age and ethnic differences strongly favored the Likud over the Labor Alignment. Oriental Jews (known as Sephardim), whose families had come from Asia and Africa, gave the Likud coalition parties a two-to-one margin in 1977. These Jews from Islamic nations were inclined to support a much more militant policy in dealing with the problems of the Palestinian Arabs. Also, the Sephardim were generally near the bottom of the economic ladder and resented the more prosperous and sophisticated Jewish immigrants from Europe and America (known as Ashkenazim), who had furnished almost all of Israel's previous leaders. Although Begin was not one of them by birth, his philosophy and demeanor were attractive to the Sephardic voters. The Sephardic families had a higher birth rate than the Ashkenazim and now, with their children, formed a majority of the Jews in Israel. Their support was an important factor in giving the leadership of Israel to the Likud coalition.

But the character of Menachem Begin was a major factor in the victory. A charismatic leader and spellbinding speaker, he was able to convince many Israelis of his personal courage and his steadfastness in pursuing the political goals for Israel from which he had never deviated. He cast himself as a champion of the downtrodden Sephardic voters and put forward simplistic answers to complex questions about peace and war, religion, the Palestinians, finance, and economics. Begin's messages were easy to understand. He had a clear idea of when he might yield and what he would not give up in negotiations with his Arab neighbors and the United States. His promises to consumers were also very attractive (and ultimately almost catastrophic to Israel's economic system).

Menachem Begin was born in Poland of Polish parents. After the country was overrun by Germany, his parents and brother died at the hands of the Nazis. Begin fled to the Lithuanian sector of the Soviet Union, where he was arrested and sent to Siberia for his unacceptable political activity as a Zionist. After about a year in prison, including some time in solitary confinement, Begin was released and was able to go to Palestine in 1942.

There he became the leader of a militant underground group called the Irgun, which espoused the maximum demands of Zionism. He fought with every weapon available against the British, who characterized him as the preeminent terrorist in the region. A man of personal courage and single-minded devotion to his goals, he took pride in being a "fighting Jew." The self-portrait of Israel's new Prime Minister was of a man who would readily resort to violence to achieve goals in which he believed.

In January of 1977, I had taken the oath of office as President of the United States. In April, President Sadat had come to Washington for a state visit. The first night, after the official banquet, we went upstairs to the living quarters in the White House. During a long, private conversation, Sadat told me plainly that he was willing to take significant steps toward peace, and we discussed some of the specific elements of possible direct negotiations in the future: Israel's permanent boundaries, the status of Jerusalem, free trade and open borders between the two nations, even full diplomatic recognition and the exchange of ambassadors.

After Begin was elected a month later, his press statements reiterated his earlier beliefs, including his commitment to expand Israel's borders to both sides of the Jordan River. However, when he came to Washington to meet with me, I found him quite willing to pursue the major goals that I had discussed with Sadat. The presumption then was that another Geneva conference would be convened, with all the disputing parties in the Middle East in attendance and with the United States and the Soviet Union as cochairs.

In November 1977, Sadat made a dramatic peace initiative by going directly to Jerusalem. Begin received Sadat graciously and listened with apparent composure while the Egyptian President spelled out to the Israeli Knesset the maximum demands of the Palestinians and of Israel's Arab neighbors. Subsequently the leaders met again in Egypt, but it was soon obvious that they were unlikely to make any further progress toward peace.

The following year I invited the two men and their key advisers to Camp David in September for two weeks of concentrated negotiations. My goal was to have the Israelis and Egyptians meet in a secluded place, away from the press, so that they could come to understand the compatibility of many of their goals and the advantages to both nations in resolving their differences. We would have to address such basic questions as the Israeli withdrawal from the occupied territories, Palestinian rights, Israel's security, an end to the Arab trade embargo and open borders between Israel and Egypt, the rights of Israeli ships to transit the Suez Canal, and the many issues concerning Jerusalem. In the process, we hoped to achieve a permanent peace between the two countries based on full diplomatic recognition as confirmed by a bilateral peace treaty.

Begin and Sadat were personally incompatible, and we decided after a few unpleasant encounters that they should not attempt to negotiate with each other. Instead, I worked with each of them separately or with their representatives. Although it was more difficult for me — I had to go from one negotiating session to another — there were advantages in that it eliminated the rhetoric and personal arguing between the two leaders.*

Begin had come to Camp David intending to work out a statement of general principles for a peace agreement, then to leave to subordinates the task of resolving the more difficult issues. It was soon obvious that he was much more interested in discussing the Sinai than the West Bank and Gaza. After detailed negotiations began, Begin spent the best part of his energy on the minute details of each proposal, the specific language of each sentence or phrase. The other key members of the Israeli team, Foreign Minister Moshe Dayan, Defense Minister Ezer Weizman, and Attorney General Aharon Barak, desired as full an agreement as possible with the Egyptians, and they were often able to convince Begin that a particular proposal was beneficial to Israel.

Sadat was the most forthcoming member of the Egyptian delegation. His general requirements were that all Israelis leave

* For a fuller description of the Camp David negotiations, see Jimmy Carter, *Keeping Faith: Memoirs of a President* (New York: Bantam, 1982), pp. 319–403.

Egyptian soil in the Sinai and that any bilateral agreement be based on a comprehensive accord involving the occupied territories, Palestinian rights, and Israel's commitment to resolve peacefully any further disputes with its neighbors. He most often left the details of the negotiations to others.

On several occasions, either Begin or Sadat was ready to terminate the discussions and return home, but we finally negotiated the Camp David accords, including the framework of a peace treaty between the two nations. The two leaders and their advisers even agreed upon this carefully worded paragraph on the most sensitive issue of all, the Holy City:

> Jerusalem, the city of peace, is holy to Judaism, Christianity, and Islam, and all peoples must have free access to it and enjoy the free exercise of worship and the right to visit and transit to the holy places without distinction or discrimination. The holy places of each faith will be under the administration and control of their representatives. A municipal council representative of the inhabitants of the city shall supervise essential functions in the city such as public utilities, public transportation, and tourism and shall ensure that each community can maintain its own cultural and educational institutions.

At the last minute, however, after several days of unanimous agreement, both Sadat and Begin decided that there were already enough controversial elements in the accords, and requested that this paragraph be deleted from the final text. The Camp David accords were signed in September 1978 (Appendix 4).

It was obvious to us that both sides had made commitments that would not be easy to implement. Some of the concessions made by Begin were highly unpopular with his closest political associates in Israel, such as accepting in writing "the legitimate rights of the Palestinians," but he went forward courageously to gain Knesset approval for the withdrawal of all Israelis from the Sinai. On the other hand, he soon proved to be unwilling to carry out the more difficult commitments concerning full autonomy for the Palestinians and the withdrawal of Israeli military and civilian governments from the West Bank and Gaza. Sadat also faced condemnation from his fellow Arabs, who imposed severe but ultimately unsuccessful diplomatic, economic, and trade sanctions against Egypt in an attempt to isolate and punish him.

Despite these problems, the peace treaty itself between Israel and Egypt, based on the Camp David accords, was concluded and signed at the White House in March 1979. Since then, the terms of the treaty have been observed by both parties.

Neither the Jordanians nor any Palestinians were willing to participate in the subsequent peace talks to help implement the Camp David agreements concerning Palestinian rights and the West Bank and Gaza. This rejection and the persistent refusal of the Palestinians and most other Arabs to acknowledge the legitimacy of Israel's statehood have confirmed the Israelis' fears that their existence would again be threatened as soon as their adversaries could accumulate enough strength to mount a military challenge. In turn, this conviction precipitated a very hard line among the leaders of the Likud government, expressed most clearly by the Prime Minister in the West Bank in May 1981: "I, Menachem, son of Ze'ev and Hana Begin, do solemnly swear that as long as I serve the nation as Prime Minister, we will not leave any part of Judea, Samaria, the Gaza Strip or the Golan Heights."* Unfortunately, this statement contravenes the basic terms of the Camp David accords.

From Begin's point of view, the peace agreement with Egypt was the significant act for Israel; the references to the West Bank and Palestinians were to be finessed. With the bilateral treaty, he removed Egypt's considerable strength from the military equation of the Middle East and thus gave the Israelis renewed freedom to pursue their goals of fortifying and settling the occupied territories and removing perceived threats by preemptive military strikes against some of their neighbors.

Under Begin's leadership, in 1981 the Israelis launched an air strike that destroyed an Iraqi nuclear reactor, announced the "annexation" of the Golan Heights, and escalated their costly effort to build Israeli settlements in the West Bank. Then, in 1982, came the full-scale invasion of Lebanon. All these acts were widely condemned in the Arab world, and the Israeli people themselves

---

* Judea and Samaria are the names Begin uses for the West Bank.

were divided over the wisdom of this militant policy. They were particularly distressed because of the high rate of casualties among the Israeli troops in Lebanon. Only in Washington did the Israeli government find relatively consistent support.

Israel has proven that it has one of the most powerful military forces in the world. Regardless of who launched the first attacks that precipitated the five wars between 1948 and 1982, the Israelis have deployed more troops and have ultimately managed to prevail over their adversaries. However, the victories have been very costly — in both financial and human terms. After each war, both sides have plunged into a new arms race. Israel has had to borrow heavily, and approximately two thirds of its gross national income is now being spent on defense and servicing the national debt. Many thousands have died in the wars, and each time that Israel has occupied and retained more territory, large numbers of Christian and Moslem Arabs have either been displaced from their homes or put under military rule. This relocation of so many people has continued to exacerbate an already serious military confrontation, intensified the fear, hatred, and alienation on both sides, and made more and more difficult the ultimate reconciliation that must come before peace, justice, and security can prevail in the region.

None of the wars has resolved any of the basic causes of continuing conflict. In my travels to Israel since leaving the White House, and in extensive meetings with Israeli scholars and political leaders as well as in conversations with many ordinary Israeli citizens, I see over and over a reluctance to face the troubling question of what to do about the Palestinians. Many choose to pretend they do not exist. In one discussion with some friends near Caesarea, for instance, an eloquent Israeli widow became somewhat emotional as she said, "I have lived in this community for more than thirty years and have never visited the West Bank. To me that is a different world. In fact, there is an Arab village just a few miles from here, but I have never had any contacts or conversations with any of them. I'm not sure I'll ever want to." The distance between Jewish and non-Jewish Israelis is increasing.

Another basic question is land, specifically the West Bank and Gaza. During most of the period of the British Mandate, when the area was controlled from London, Jews had ample opportunity to purchase land where they desired. They reasonably chose to concentrate on the less populated, more cultivable coastal and valley regions, and it was within those boundaries that Israel was created. However, the security and ideological motivations of more recent years, as well as the offer by the government of inexpensive and convenient apartments in the suburban areas around Jerusalem, have encouraged an increasing number of Israelis to settle in the West Bank. This is one basis of the Arab-Israeli dispute and is, in the opinion of most American officials, both contrary to international law and a serious obstacle to peace.

These two major issues illustrate the obvious complexity and intransigence of the issues involved. However, I still believe that peace is possible and that a strong plurality or even a majority of Israelis are now willing or in the future might be prepared to accept terms for an agreement that could also be tolerable to most of their Arab neighbors.

Although almost all the leaders in Israel's major political parties are convinced that a strong and continuing Israeli presence must be retained in the West Bank, many of them believe that Israel will benefit if the Palestinian question can be resolved without perpetuating military rule over the 1.4 million non-Jews. Including those Arabs who live in Israel itself, more than one half of all the Palestinians on earth now live under Israeli authority, and perhaps half a million non-Palestinian Arabs are under Israel's dominion in southern Lebanon.

The occupation of southern Lebanon contributes further to political dissension in Israel. In recent political debates, many Israeli leaders have declared the 1982 invasion and occupation of Lebanon to be a political disaster, and the continuation of military confrontation and the concerted absorption of occupied territories to be counterproductive in the search for regional stability and a permanent peace. They have blamed the loss of overseas support and an increase in the emigration of Jews from Israel on their government's departure from the idealism of its earlier leaders, on economic woes, and on the nonretaliatory use of force against Lebanon. These voices brought about a degree of moderation in both major parties in the 1984 elections, including commitments to withdraw Israeli occupation forces from Lebanon as soon as practicable.

Regardless of what is decided concerning Lebanon, the key issue still being debated in Israel is what to do about the West Bank and Gaza and the people who live there. None of the options is very attractive for Israel:

• Withdrawal as specified in U.N. Resolution 242 and as envisioned in the Camp David accords, including self-determination for the Palestinians at least to the extent of full autonomy in the territories under some kind of confederation with Jordan. This action has been strongly opposed by Menachem Begin and his followers, and such a decision would have doubtful political support in Israel without strong and forceful leadership.

• A forcible annexation of the area and its legal absorption into Israel, which would give large numbers of non-Jewish citizens the right to vote and live as equals under the law. Any official action to take the occupied territories would directly violate the Camp David accords, on which the Egyptians consider the peace treaty to be based, and at the same time would result in the establishment of a dual or binational society, with the two million Palestinians composing 40 percent of its inhabitants and destined to grow to 50 percent by the end of this century — whether or not they are granted the basic rights of citizenship. In either case, Israel would likely be further isolated and condemned by the international community, with no remaining chance to end hostilities with any appreciable part of the Arab world.

• Continuing military occupation of the Palestinian land with possible legal absorption after the Arab population has been substantially reduced by emigration. With or without legal annexation, full citizenship would not be granted to the Palestinians. Many believe that this is the basic policy followed by the Likud government. Its opponents in Israel deride the racist connotation of prescribing permanent second-class status for the Palestinians.

• Some form of shared sovereignty, perhaps with Jordan, or a division of the land into small communities, with equal rights for all those dwelling in the area. This would involve either granting independence to the Palestinians or giving equal authority to Jews and Arabs in small locations scattered throughout the occupied territories. Administration would be very difficult, but not impossible if Israelis, Jordanians, and Palestinians ever decide to cooperate.

The most attractive option — and one that might ultimately be acceptable as a basis for peace — is the first: granting genuine autonomy and the right of self-determination to the Palestinians within most of the West Bank and Gaza areas, provided substantial demilitarization of the area occurs and there are adequate guarantees that Israel's and Jordan's security will not be threatened. Some association between this Palestinian "homeland" and Jordan would be preferable and probably necessary. These basic principles of the Camp David accords, as interpreted by the United States, by the Egyptians, and by many Israelis, provide the best foundation for further progress.

During the 1984 election campaign, the Labor Alignment pledged to reverse some of the Likud policies in order to reinvigorate the peace process. However, its failure to win a clear victory forced the formation of a National Unity government in September, with the Likud still playing an almost equal role. Under such circumstances, it is likely that the power of some of the more extreme leaders will be magnified and that vigorous or innovative action by the government in international affairs will be difficult or impossible. Yet there is a hopeful sign in the agreement between the two parties not to change the sovereignty of the West Bank and Gaza at least for now.

The full range of opinions can be heard in Israel about the proper path to peace, justice, and prosperity. One of the participants in this internal debate is Peace Now, a vocal group organized at the time of the Camp David negotiations. During my most recent visit to Israel, I invited its leaders to meet with me to explain the substance of their beliefs. They claimed to have organized the massive demonstrations against the Israeli invasion of Lebanon in 1982, and said that some of their most active members were officers and men of the Israel Defense Forces.

They told me that they endorsed the Camp David process as the best approach to peace, provided its character as an interim arrangement was honored, and believed that Palestinian representatives should be welcomed to the negotiating table on an equal basis with members of other national groups. They had no intention of forming a separate political party, but would endorse and support candidates who most nearly represented their views.

I am sure that there is considerable diversity among the supporters of the Peace Now movement, but the leaders espoused an Israeli policy that included a strong military capability, close relations with the United States, partial withdrawal from and demilitarization of the occupied territories, equal rights for all the inhabitants of Israel, no Israeli rule over other peoples, a halt to all settlement activity, a national existence for the Palestinians compatible with the security of Israel, and peace negotiations with all interested parties without obstructive preconditions. One of them stated, "I am afraid that we are moving toward a government like that of South Africa, with a dual society of Jewish rulers and Arab subjects with few rights of citizenship. The West Bank is not worth it."

Although many of these individual points have wide acceptance, the Peace Now views in their totality are too dovish for most Israeli political leaders. When I later questioned some of the more liberal leaders of the Labor Alignment, even they seemed to be somewhat nervous about any public relationship with the Peace Now movement, but they said that the group was having an effect on the news media and on the general public.

In the spring of 1983, two years after I had left public office, Rosalynn and I returned to Israel. In Jerusalem, we paid our third visit to the Yad Vashem memorial and participated in a simple but moving service to the Jews who were victims of the Holocaust. As we entered and left the shrine, we heard many expressions of pleasure and gratitude that the reciprocal visits by President Sadat and Prime Minister Begin and the negotiations at Camp David had led to peace with Egypt.

A few minutes later I was on my way to Prime Minister Begin's office in the Israeli parliament building; it was almost exactly four years since my previous call on him to hammer out the remaining obstacles to the peace treaty. I was not unprepared for the polite but cool official welcome that awaited me. It was no secret that he and I had strong private and public disagreements concerning the interpretation of the Camp David accords, the settlements policy in the West Bank and Gaza, and his recent invasion of Lebanon.

Even during the days he and I had worked together most success-fully, we had differed on how the Middle East disputes could best be resolved.

Although his nation and mine shared many beliefs and ultimate political goals, he and I had frequently been at odds across the negotiating table as we tried to deal on an official basis with the sensitivities and subtleties of Arab-Israeli relations. Unfortunately, this had resulted in some personal differences as well.

Now, in March 1983, we were together again and, as had always been my custom, I recapitulated my opinions with complete frankness on the more controversial issues almost immediately after we had exchanged pleasantries. First I congratulated him on the courageous manner in which he had observed the very difficult terms of the peace treaty concerning the withdrawal of Israeli forces and the dismantling of settlements in Egypt's Sinai. Then, while he sat without looking at me, I explained again why we believed he had not honored a commitment made during the peace negotiations to refrain from building new Israeli settlements in the West Bank. I described my disappointment that he had not been willing to grant the Palestinians any appreciable degree of autonomy in the occupied territories, and I urged him to make it plain to the Egyptians and Jordanians that Israel would observe the basic elements of U.N. Resolution 242. Then I paused, expecting him to give his usual strong explanation of Israeli policy. He responded with just a few words in a surprisingly perfunctory manner, either because I had aggravated him more than usual, because he wanted to reserve his arguments for incumbent American officials, or because he was preoccupied with other personal or political matters. Perhaps, and most likely, it was a combination of all three reasons.

We had been sitting in a small and sparsely adorned room on the lower level of the Knesset building. The exchange had been cool, distant, and nonproductive. As I left, I noticed that the adjacent room was large, brightly lighted, attractive, and vacant. It was ironic that the number on the door was 242.

The Israel of 1983 seemed different from the nation we had first known ten years earlier. The sense of unanimity among the Jewish citizens and the carefree confidence of 1973 were gone. Despite their impressive military triumph in Lebanon, many Israelis were deeply concerned that the victory had turned to ashes. Military superiority was crucial for the defense of the nation but obviously not adequate for Israel to impose its will on its neighbors. The domestic political debates were much more vitriolic, and it was increasingly uncertain what kind of government the people preferred. Men in uniform were now seen everywhere, and the tension between different kinds of people was obvious. The former influx of Arab visitors from Jordan had dried to a trickle, and there were only a few visits of Egyptians despite the peace treaty that had established open borders and free trade. Even among the most optimistic, there seemed to be little hope for any permanent agreement that might bring peace and stability.

At best, those in Israel who were most willing to end the military occupation, grant the Palestinians basic rights of citizenship, honor the terms of U.N. Resolution 242 and the Camp David accords, and commence negotiations without patently unacceptable conditions were hard put to detect any reliable signs of encouragement from leaders in the Arab-Palestinian camp. The result of negotiations with Lebanon in 1983 was annulled by Syrian pressure in 1984, and the somewhat costly treaty with Egypt resulted in a grudgingly maintained "cold peace." Syria continued to reject any concept of discussions with Israel except at an international conference under the direct sponsorship of the United Nations and with Soviet participation. In 1983, King Hussein proved to be unwilling to join peace talks after Israel's rejection of the Reagan proposal (Appendix 5), when the ever-evasive endorsement of both the PLO and Saudi Arabia was not forthcoming.

Some leaders in Israel expressed concern that during recent years, America's policy in the Middle East had consisted of a series of apparently illogical flip-flops, with a notable lack of resolve to tackle the more politically sensitive issues that had to be addressed before the next step toward peace could be taken. In fact, with some justification, the Israelis were increasingly skeptical about the policies of *all* foreign governments. They are determined not to become overconfident again. Whenever the assessment of Israel's military superiority becomes too certain, it reminds even the doves of the halcyon days after the Six-Day War of 1967, when a feeling of military invincibility led to the embarrassing surprise of the October 1973 attack.

American leaders understand these facts, but there is growing concern that in the near future the differences between the two nations might become even more acute than in the past. There is already disturbing evidence of this growing disparity, particularly over solutions to Israel's severe economic problems.

Speaking for the Likud coalition, for instance, former Prime Minister and now Foreign Minister Yitzhak Shamir has expressed his belief that the roots of most of the conflict in the Middle East have nothing to do with Israel and that a solution of the Arab-Israeli conflict is not likely to lead to regional stability or to open a new era of progress. He minimizes the importance of the Palestinian problem and considers the Jews the natural majority rulers of western Palestine (Israel, the West Bank, and Gaza) with a right and obligation to populate the area further, while the homeland for Palestinian Arabs is to be found in eastern Palestine (the Kingdom of Jordan). He states that since Israel will never give up any of the West Bank, the pre-1967 borders of Israel are now of no consequence, having ceased to relate at all to the search for regional peace. Most of these views are contrary to those of the American leaders.

But some other Israelis with great influence would go even farther — to extend the eventual boundaries of Israel to include substantial portions of Lebanon and the east bank of the Jordan River, and to make a deliberate attempt to force large numbers of non-Jews out of the occupied territories. Former Defense Minister Ariel Sharon, who now plays a key role in the National Unity cabinet, has called for the overthrow of King Hussein in favor of a Palestinian regime in Jordan, even if it is headed by Yasir Arafat. As late as August 1984, Sharon said that the east bank of the Jordan is "ours but not in our hands, just as East Jerusalem had been until the Six-Day War." Even in a National Unity government headed by a moderate Prime Minister, these beliefs and commitments will be powerful factors in shaping Israeli policy, because even a very few defections by opposition leaders could bring down the government.

Although they have demanded that any peace talks must take place only under the Camp David framework, Shamir and most other members of his Likud party never approved the concessions made by Begin during the tedious negotiations with President Sadat. Both Israel and Egypt have honored the terms of the peace treaty involving the Sinai, but over a period of time the original substance of the accords relating to the other occupied territories has been abandoned or modified in vital ways.

At the same time, the greatly escalated program to take Palestinian land and to develop Israeli settlements in the West Bank has been generally interpreted both in and outside Israel as proof that these areas are being absorbed as rapidly as possible in accordance with the long-standing Likud pledge that "Western 'Eretz Yisrael' will never be divided again." As former Israeli Foreign Minister Abba Eban said after all these attitudes evolved: "Unfortunately, it is clear that Israeli governmental policy is so distant from Camp David that when Likud spokesmen invoke the agreement, they are rather like Casanova invoking the Seventh Commandment."

It is well known that some significant disagreements between the leaders of our two countries have always existed — perhaps been inevitable, in fact — and that most of them did not start in 1977, when Begin and I took office. The simple truth is that one of the most cherished, complicated, frustrating, challenging, and least understood of our nation's relationships is with Israel.

Like most other Americans, I have understood and shared the deep and persistent commitment of the United States to the existence, security, and ultimate peace of this small and often beleaguered democracy. It is a matter of consternation and condemnation among Arab leaders, and even in some of the European nations, that the U.S. government budgets more than $7 million each day for the Israelis in economic and military aid and that this level of financial assistance is seldom seriously questioned when the annual budget is prepared in Washington. The reasons for this sustained commitment to an independent Israel are not easily explained to non-Americans.

There is no question that one of the most powerful political forces in America exists in the well-organized and often sharply focused efforts of politically active citizens whose unshakable support for the current policies of Israel's government, whatever they may be, is much more certain than the support of any single group within Israel itself.

However, this is only part of the story; there is also widespread support for Israel among millions of U.S. citizens who are not Jews and who have no relationship at all with lobbying groups. Americans are repulsed by the highly publicized terrorist acts committed against innocent civilians. Memories of the Holocaust are still alive, and there is sympathy and some guilt because of the incredible silence in Washington during Hitler's persecution of the European Jews. Christians of all denominations feel a closeness to Israel because of our religious ties, and tiny Israel appeals to the fondness of most Americans for the underdog. The voices from Israel are heard often on news broadcasts, usually in a favorable context, but with the notable exception of Anwar Sadat no Arab leader has been effective in presenting the views of his people to the American public. Citizens from the heartland of the United States are satisfied that the common religious, ethical, political, and strategic commitments of the two nations are properly and intimately intertwined.

At the same time, government officials in Washington know that their influence on the policies of Israel in moments of crisis is sometimes embarrassingly slight, and often it seems that the Israeli leaders relish the domestic political popularity that comes from tweaking the superpower's nose. Any public criticism of Prime Minister Begin's policies from the White House or State Department was almost certain to precipitate an announcement of new settlements to be built in the West Bank or perhaps the moving of another Israeli office to East Jerusalem.

In spite of these natural ties that bind the two democracies, the fact is that even under the best of interpretations, the interests of the United States and Israel are not completely compatible. The extent of this divergence has not yet been assessed publicly or addressed definitively by political leaders in either country. Since the founding of Israel, American presidents have been able to pursue a fairly wide range of objectives in the Middle East without having to acknowledge any clear conflict among them or to choose between them. Some of the most important are:

• To prevent an Arab-Israeli war that could lead to a super-power confrontation.

• To protect the existence and security of Israel.

• To promote the prospects of permanent peace as a trusted mediator, especially between Israel and its neighbors, based on Israel's withdrawal from occupied territories and a just solution of the Palestinian problem, including self-determination for the Palestinians.

• To contribute to political, economic, and social progress and to enhance the human rights of all people in the region.

• To retain sound and mutually beneficial relationships with moderate Arabs.

• To ensure an uninterrupted flow of oil supplies to Western democracies.

• To prevent a serious escalation in armaments, particularly nuclear weapons.

• To minimize the influence of the Soviets in the Arab nations and prevent their domination of any part of the area.

Some of these American goals are being jeopardized by Israeli policy as forged by the Likud government and apparently being continued because of the political paralysis of the new National Unity government. Questions concerning the withdrawal from occupied territories and Palestinian rights, as expressed in U.N. Resolution 242 and the Camp David accords, now have entirely different answers in Washington and Jerusalem. Such a foreclosure of options by Israel would directly and adversely affect U.S. interests in the Middle East. In times of greatest danger or crisis, American overtures toward peace have served in the past to alleviate tension, to defuse a potential explosion, and to permit the United States to avoid direct military involvement. But even these few opportunities are being limited further.

During recent years, there have been many parallel efforts in seeking peace, all of them centered on the willingness of Israel to exchange occupied territories for peace. This commitment was officially reconfirmed by Israel in the Camp David accords. However, President Reagan's clear statement of this premise in September 1982 was immediately rejected by Begin, who then proceeded to announce new plans for extending Israeli control even further over the occupied territories. At that time, the United States backed down from this confrontation and shifted public attention to the possibility of King Hussein's willingness to accept the President's already rejected statement as a basis for negotiation.

Under the National Unity government, there is a difference of opinion that will be very difficult if not impossible to resolve. Prime Minister Peres and his Labor Alignment associates have condemned the outright rejection of the Reagan statement as a basis for negotiations but have made it clear that they do not agree with all its elements. The Likud is much more intense in its opposition than Labor is in its tentative support. The outcome of this contention is crucial.

Many Israelis are concerned that with the taking of the West Bank and Gaza, there would be no prospect for further peace negotiations, the Israeli-Egyptian peace treaty would probably be abrogated, and the Israelis would have committed themselves to another generation of conflict with their Arab neighbors again united in their opposition to Israel's existence. All of this involves major strategic interests for the United States, and its more clearly defined differences with Israel will not go away.

It is not at all clear how the United States would react if confronted with the extremely uncomfortable choice of whether or not to continue supporting and helping to finance Israeli policies that directly contravene American purposes in the region. The situation has been obscured or confused, and a clear American response has been deflected by the Lebanon crisis and then by the national elections in both Israel and the United States, but the facts cannot be ignored much longer. To prevent the further isolation of Israel within the international community, there will have to be some clearer understanding with Washington as to mutual goals and areas of agreement, whereby the interests of both countries can be recognized and honored.

Some Israeli leaders complain to me that Americans are too interested in the negotiating process and in an unproductive search for agreement among those who have inherent and irreconcilable differences. What they would prefer is unconditional financing and political support without the constant diplomatic pressure from Washington that has caused much of the past friction between Israel and the United States. My response has always been that peace agreements are best for both our countries and that sustained support for Israel must to some degree depend on a good faith effort by the Israelis to live in harmony with their Arab neighbors, to negotiate for peace in accordance with existing commitments, and to respect the human rights of all those they rule.

It is not too late for progress, although some people believe that the fate of the West Bank and Gaza has already been decided and that it is fruitless to discuss this issue anymore. An Israeli government has yet to demonstrate how it might evolve a peaceful and just coexistence of the Palestinians and the Jews. No one knows from experience, therefore, the potential results of such an effort.

Barring a purge of Christian and Moslem Arabs from the area, it is impossible to envision a majority of Israelis ever living in the West Bank and Gaza. Budgetary restraints late in 1983 slowed down the costly Likud effort to populate the areas, where less than 30,000 Jews constitute only 2 percent of the population. However, even if the high rate of building could have been sustained, the more rapid birth rate among the Palestinian Arabs and their determination not to move out of the area would result in little change in the ratio between Jews and non-Jews during the remainder of this century. In Jerusalem, the rate of Arab growth is actually higher than that of Jewish growth, and in general the Palestinian population has tended to increase more rapidly in the same communities where settlement has been most successful. It is quite likely that with sustained Palestinian opposition in the occupied areas, Jewish settlement will continue at a very slow rate at best, except perhaps in the immediate suburbs of Jerusalem.

Meron Benvenisti, an Israeli and former deputy mayor of Jerusalem, has made a definitive study of the population, territorial, and legal changes in the occupied territories, and he believes that the Likud takeover is unlikely to be reversed and that the question of partition is anachronistic. He concludes: "Now, faced with the prospect of ruling over more than a million Arabs who will not have full democratic rights, both sides must offer realistic answers to a different question: Is Israel to be a Jewish state or a democratic one?" These kinds of questions are not easy to answer.

Many people were hoping that the 1984 elections would bring some clear answers and a substantive change in Israeli policy, but the indeterminate results led to weeks of negotiating, and the new government was formed with both the major parties weakened and required to share almost equal power. Only the threat of an economic crisis finally brought them together. Leaders from both parties did endorse a withdrawal of Israeli troops from southern Lebanon — when and if the northern border of Israel could be secured against attacks from the north. With all this, the future of the West Bank and Gaza appeared to be a low priority on the agenda of the hybrid government.

Even with new leaders, Israelis still see their financial situation deteriorating and their nation being forced to abandon the goal of self-sufficiency as it becomes increasingly dependent on aid from the United States for economic survival. Concern about this dependency is not shared by all, however, as explained in the summer of 1984 by the publisher of Israel's leading newspaper, *Ha'aretz:* "Israelis tend to regard American economic aid, which has grown substantially over the last decade, as part of their natural wealth. Dependence on outside help does not cause misgiving. Indeed, Likud politicians have repeatedly said that American aid is not large enough in view of the great benefits to American interests from the very existence and functioning of Israel. As long as no dire need is perceived for basic change in economic policy, basic change is unlikely to come about."

As 1984 progressed, it became increasingly evident that dire need did exist and the fear of some outspoken Israeli economists was that aid from the United States would be *too* generous. Their concern was that the Israeli leaders might once again postpone the difficult decisions required to bring under control a runaway annual inflation rate that moved beyond 500 percent, an equally alarming drain on the nation's financial reserves, and the highest per capita foreign debt in the world. For the first time in its history, Israel became more concerned about the economic crisis than with any military threat.

But economic pressures are not unrelated to the search for peace. The tremendous costs to Israel in continuing the occupation of Arab territory, ministering to the needs of many homeless refugees, expanding an already formidable military capability, and in building settlements in the West Bank and Gaza are becoming much more apparent, and they are already having an effect on some of the government's policies. Settlement construction was virtually ended in the late fall of 1983, and one of the prime incentives for withdrawing from southern Lebanon is the daily expense of this occupation.

Some proposals have even been considered for reducing the previously sacrosanct military budget, but nothing will be done that could possibly weaken Israel's defenses. The resilient Arabs have proven that they can lose wars and each time recover to fight again. There are severe limits to the punishment that Israel can deliver to a defeated enemy. For the Israelis, a demonstration of serious weakness or a major defeat could mean the loss of their lives and their nation. They cannot afford to lose.

Unless there is a massive Arab-Israeli war, the key to the future of Israel will not be found outside the country but within. Neither the United States nor any combination of Arab powers can force its preferences on Israel concerning the West Bank and Gaza, Palestinian rights, or the occupied territories of Syria and Lebanon. The judgments concerning what is best for Israel will be made in Jerusalem, through democratic processes involving all Israelis who can express their views or elect their leaders. The crucial issues are being debated much more vehemently there than anywhere in the outside world, and a final decision has not been made. The outcome of this debate will shape the future of Israel; it may also determine the prospects for peace in the Middle East — and perhaps the world.

# Syria

ABRAHAM'S WANDERINGS would have taken him through the ancient lands of Syria, and he would almost certainly have paused for a while in Damascus. This city, the modern capital of Syria, is considered the oldest city in the world in continuous existence. Located in a vast natural bowl on the edge of an oasis, Damascus had already been settled for more than 3000 years before Abraham, Sarah, and Lot passed by on the way to Canaan.

This area, part of the Fertile Crescent, was one of the four earliest centers of human civilization (the others being similar city-state developments in what is now India, China, and Egypt). There was constant strife between the relatively prosperous indigenous people of the region and the barbarian invaders from the less fertile areas to the north and west. It was here that the ancient Egyptians first confronted the people of the great Euphrates Basin in their ambitious forays northward. In this region national boundaries were constantly changing; nevertheless, the Syria of old is usually defined as encompassing modern Syria, Lebanon, Israel, and Jordan. Now, when some ambitious Arab leaders refer to Greater Syria, they still envision the same territory.

The three great monotheistic religions, Judaism, Christianity, and Islam, all flourished in this Syrian region of the Fertile Crescent. Each group of religious believers is convinced that its own religious covenants and the geographical location of their revelation were ordained by God. Although the Creator's reason for choosing these particular earthly spots has not been revealed, secular historians have surmised that the exceptionally active intercourse resulting from the confluence of trade routes from the Mediterranean, southeastern Europe, the Nile Basin, Arabia, and the Iranian plateau in the Tigris-Euphrates Basin served to disseminate the various religious beliefs.

Not surprisingly, the region has continued to be a center of conflict during the more recent centuries of recorded history, involving many conquerors, including the Babylonians, Amorites, Egyptians, Hittites, Assyrians, Israelites, Persians, Greeks, and Romans. Then came the Moslem Arabs from the southeast, later the Crusaders from Western Europe, the Turks, the Mongols, and the Egyptians again. Finally, beginning in the early sixteenth century, Syria became part of the Ottoman Empire for almost four hundred years.

During and after World War I, the Turks were expelled, and the French struggled with the Arab leader Faisal I for control of Syria. When the French prevailed, they partitioned off the western part, along the coast of the Mediterranean, and established the independent state of Lebanon with a predominantly Christian population. The eastern part of Lebanon had for centuries been the home of Moslems, and they protested their separation from the rest of Syria. Although the French in 1925 promised the Syrians independence and a parliamentary form of government was formed before World War II, it was not until 1946 that, with British help, Syria forced the departure of the last French troops.

The Arabs' failure to prevail in their fight against the new State of Israel resulted in strong criticism of the civilian government in Syria and a military takeover in 1949, but after five years of rule by different military leaders free elections were held, introducing to Syria universal suffrage for women. A wide range of political groups was represented in the parliament, and a radical leftist shift was prevented in 1958 by Syria's joining Egypt to form the United Arab Republic. After three and a half years it became obvious that Egypt's Nasser was dominating the new nation, and dissatisfied Syrian leaders dissolved the union. When a period of instability followed, a radical government was formed in 1966 with President Saleh Jadid as its leader and General Hafez al-Assad as minister of defense. Four years later Assad became Syria's leader.

In order to understand Syria today, it is well to have an outline of its official positions regarding circumstances in the Middle East, because the perspective from Damascus is startlingly different from the views usually espoused in Israel, Europe, and the United States. Following my long talks with President Assad in 1977 and 1983, meetings with other Syrian political and academic leaders, and a study of their official statements published in the Arab world, the pattern of their grievances and beliefs became clearer. Their views on most points concerning Israel are quite compatible with those of many other Arabs.

The Syrians complain that the Israelis consider it the right of every Jew in the world, needy or not, to settle in the Arab territories that they control by force — the West Bank, Gaza, the Golan Heights, and parts of Israel itself — but that they refuse to allow the homeless and suffering Arabs driven out of their country to return to the dwellings and lands to which they still maintain legal deeds. They argue that while Israel claimed the right to its statehood in Palestine in 1948 because it was only re-creating a nation demolished in ancient times, it rejects the recognition of a Palestinian state in the same area — the very place that the Palestinians and their ancestors have inhabited continuously for thousands of years. Furthermore, no other nation on earth recognizes Israel's present claims for lands it has confiscated since 1948. Syrians say that Israelis claim the Jews of the world constitute one people, regardless of obvious differences in their identities, languages, customs, and citizenship, but deny that the Palestinians constitute a coherent people even though they have one national identity, one language, one culture, and one history. Syrians consider these distinctions to be a form of racism by which Israel regards Palestinians as inferior people who are not worthy of national self-determination. They scoff at Israel's claim to be a true democracy, maintaining that political and social equality are only for Jews.

Concerning the search for peace, the Syrians argue that to ensure security for itself, Israel creates excuses to expand, to occupy new lands, and to build permanent military outposts that are developed into civilian settlements, then creates circumstances to defend the new settlements by further expansion, strengthened military forces, and the displacement of the Arab inhabitants. The Syrians believe that the loss of Arab life is considered to be relatively insignificant by the Israelis and their American backers, who associate all Palestinians with terrorism in an attempt to justify this racist attitude. The explanation for such a joint policy is a U.S.-Israeli ambition to dominate the Middle East at the expense of its native people, who want only freedom and the right to live peaceably in their own homes.

By refusing to discuss peace with the Palestinians, the United States and Israel block negotiations, except when they can single out one Arab group at a time and induce it by threats or blandishments to work with Israel and the United States alone. When Sadat agreed to negotiate unilaterally with the United States and Israel and received his payment of the occupied Sinai, Assad claims, he gave the Israelis a blank check for further aggression against Iraq, Syria, Lebanon, and the Palestinians.

Assad maintains that Syria has proven its willingness to work for peace in the following ways:

• By honoring all U.N. resolutions concerning the Arab-Israeli conflict. Neither Israel nor the United States will do so.

• By supporting the overwhelming international decision that the Palestinian people have, like others on earth, a right to self-determination. Neither Israel nor the United States will do so.

• By observing international law, which prohibits the occupation and annexation of land belonging to another sovereign state. Israel will not, and the United States finances this illegal act.

• By defining its own borders and honoring the internationally recognized borders of others. Israel will do neither.

• By offering to withdraw Syria's forces from Lebanon when requested to do so by the Lebanese government. At least until recently, Israel would not make the same commitment.

Syria's standing peace proposal includes the following:

• An international conference to be convened under U.N. auspices to which all parties concerned would be invited, including the Soviet Union.

- The Palestinian people to be represented by their own chosen representative, the PLO.
- The principles of international law and U.N. resolutions to be the basis for any solution.
- The Security Council to guarantee peace among all states of the region, including one formed through Palestinian self-determination.

Although most of these Syrian views are shared by other Arab nations, some countries are willing to accept or ignore existing circumstances long enough to negotiate for incremental progress, as Sadat did. But Hafez al-Assad says that he stands firmly against such "divisive manipulation."

My first meeting with President Assad was in May 1977, when he and I traveled to Geneva, Switzerland, to seek some common ground on which progress toward a Middle East peace might be pursued. I had invited him to visit me in Washington, but he sent word that he had never been to the United States and would be unable to come anytime in the foreseeable future. Little was known about his personal or family life, but Henry Kissinger and others who knew Assad had described him to me as intelligent and willing to discuss even the most sensitive issues with complete frankness.

Hafez al-Assad is four years younger than I, born in 1928. He was graduated from the Syrian military academy and rose rapidly through the ranks to become a general, commander in chief of the air force, and then, in 1966, minister of defense. He successfully placed on others the blame for Syria's humiliating defeat by the Israelis in 1967 and retained effective control of the military. In 1970, he refused to obey President Saleh Jadid's orders to use Syria's air forces in support of the Palestinian militants who were fighting in Jordan against King Hussein. When condemned for this action by party and government leaders, he defied them and used key military units to take power with a successful bloodless coup.

He had a reputation among the other Arab leaders for ruthlessness and brutality toward those Syrians who resisted his authority, and he was well known for his singleness of purpose in protecting his region from outside interference and in expanding

Syria's role as a dominant force in Middle East affairs. Assad considered Lebanon an integral part of his own community and thought it only natural that Syrian forces should have been dispatched in 1976 to stop the Lebanese civil war. He resented any challenge to his own Arab leadership — from Egypt, Jordan, the PLO, or any other source — and was willing to face serious political and military confrontations rather than yield on this principle.

President Assad publicly and consistently condemned Israeli policies concerning the occupied territories and Palestinian rights, but his disagreements were not limited to Israel. His relations with the leaders of Egypt, Jordan, and Iraq had been recently strained, and he was having to shift the role of his 30,000 troops in Lebanon away from exclusive support of the Christian forces and toward a more popular neutrality to accommodate criticism from his Moslem subjects.

During my detailed security briefings, I had been told that Syria was relatively isolated from other nations, that Assad himself usually stood aloof from his fellow Arab leaders, and that now he was almost completely absorbed by the political situation at home. I would not have been surprised to find him unfriendly, ill tempered, or restrained in his conversations with me.

We met in a large Swiss hotel, one frequently used by professional diplomats in dealing on neutral ground with the multitude of issues that preoccupy the enormous and relatively unknown and unseen international bureaucracy. I was led through the lobby by a phalanx of hotel managers, Swiss and Syrian officials, and American security agents and advance staff. We went through a labyrinth of halls and passageways and up an elevator, and finally arrived at the private suite of the Syrian President.

Assad seemed somewhat haughty during our first few minutes together, and with his extremely erect military stance he appeared taller than he was. He maintained a slight smiling expression on his face, as though he was simultaneously amused, friendly, and a little skeptical about what he was hearing. However, I soon found him to be quite gracious, completely relaxed, humorous in his remarks, and extremely interested in my efforts to arrange peace negotiations. We began to enjoy the discussion, parrying back and forth and attempting to outdo each other in precipitating laughter in our audience of aides and advisers around the table. Woven into the next two or three hours of delightful conversation, we were to hear a coldly pragmatic description of Syria's hard-line position.

Assad was obviously doubtful about the success of my efforts to bring disputing parties together around a negotiating table, but he was willing to consider a broad range of options on how we might reconvene the so-called Geneva conference under U.N. Resolution 338, which was the only forum and basis then being considered for comprehensive peace talks. Assad had refused to participate when the United States and the Soviet Union staged the only brief and inconclusive meeting following the disengagement agreements at the end of the 1973 war, but he said that he would always be willing to meet for any serious talks that might be arranged under this framework. However, he objected strongly to bilateral discussions between Israel and any one of its Arab neighbors to the exclusion of the others, and he also opposed the U.S. sponsorship of peace talks without the equal participation of the Soviet Union.

Syria had long had a close relationship with the Soviet Union, nurtured by consistent Soviet support of the Arabs' position in their altercations with the Israelis and usually of the Syrians when they disagreed with other Arabs. As early as 1954, the Soviet bloc had been willing to supply Syria with arms after the French refused to continue their weapon sales, and during the next two decades, the Syrians benefited from high levels of Soviet economic and military aid. Furthermore, when Syria was threatened by the military forces of Turkey and Israel, there were dependable warnings and even large troop movements to prove that the Soviets would intercede directly to protect their Arab friend. One of Assad's first acts as the new President in 1970 was to visit Moscow to reconfirm the close ties between the two nations.

Nevertheless, the Syrians had not been reluctant to displease the Kremlin when it suited their purposes. In spite of Soviet opposition, they had joined Egypt to form the United Arab Republic in 1958. Assad himself had rejected Soviet requests that Syria attend the 1973 Geneva conference on Middle East peace. Three years later, he had moved 30,000 troops into Lebanon and was still keeping them there even though President Leonid Brezhnev objected strongly and publicly to Syria's intervention against the PLO and leftist forces whom the Soviets were also supporting. Although Assad depended heavily on Soviet aid and shared many goals with the Kremlin, he was not a subservient puppet, and I was hoping that he might demonstrate his independence by working with me to overcome some of the obstacles we faced on the road to peace. Furthermore, my own general desire to reconvene peace talks was not incompatible with what the Soviet Union had urged Assad to do, provided the Soviets were not excluded from the forum.

Assad stressed to me that the origin of many problems was the arbitrary subdivision of the region by the colonial powers, Great Britain and France, without regard to natural boundaries, ethnic identity, or tribal unity. Since then, Israel's actions were even worse. He maintained that Israel was admitted to the United Nations in 1949 with the clear proviso that, though Palestine had been partitioned between Jews and Arabs, Palestinian refugees would be allowed to return to their homeland or be fully compensated for their lost property. Prior to 1967, he said, Israel steadily forced Arab inhabitants from their land in violation of U.N. agreements that the Israelis had sworn to honor, and they initiated the 1967 war in order to take even more Arab land. Then the Israeli leaders announced that this was just an intermediate step toward an ultimate "greater Israel," and every action since that time had proven their expansionist commitments.

Assad was convinced that the Israelis did not want peace and would always frustrate negotiations while acquiring more territory. As a matter of conviction and principle, he added, no Arab leader could ever agree to give up any territory no matter how great his desire for peace.

I tried to convince Assad that the Israelis were ready for peace if any Arab leader was ready to negotiate with them directly and in good faith. I emphasized the overwhelming commitment of the Israelis to the security of their relatively tiny nation and their need to be accepted as a permanent entity in the region.

Assad then ridiculed the concept of "secure borders" in the face of modern missiles, airplanes, and other weapons, and said,

"It is strange to insist on secure borders on other people's territory. Israel would take some from Syria, Syria would take some from Turkey, Canada might take some from the United States, and so on. The whole world would become a jungle. The Israelis claim that they took the Golan to protect their settlements, but then they built new settlements on the Golan, some of them only three hundred meters from our territory! Why should secure borders be fifty kilometers from Damascus but three hundred and fifty kilometers from Tel Aviv? To talk of secure borders does not rest on anything real."

Assad suggested that the solution to these border disputes lay in honoring United Nations recommendations and in "demilitarized zones and perhaps international forces in those zones and an ending of the state of belligerency. Forces should be under the overall umbrella of the United Nations, but not to include countries like South Africa, Rhodesia, or Israel. A Security Council guarantee would not be a necessity, but a useful luxury."

Assad claimed that the Christians and Jews in Syria were treated just like any other citizens and with fairness, "but we want them to be citizens of their own country. Syrian Jews should be Syrian citizens, and British Jews should be British citizens, loyal to their own country."

We then discussed the Palestinian refugees from the West Bank and Gaza, and Assad insisted that the U.N. resolutions giving the refugees the right of return or compensation be honored. He emphasized that there could be no alternative to this international commitment, but neither he nor Foreign Minister Abd al-Halim Khaddam, who was at his side, were able to answer my questions about the number of people or the size of the monetary claims that might be involved. I asked if Arafat could speak for the Palestinians, and Assad replied, "He needs some help from all of us. We all must help him. There are some disagreements and problems among the Palestinians, but they are not insurmountable." (In retrospect, this was a signal that Assad might want to influence Palestinian policy and even wrest leadership from Arafat, which he sought to do six years later, in 1983.)

Assad was equivocal about whether there should be an independent Palestinian state in the West Bank and Gaza or, rather, some kind of confederation with Jordan, and he seemed willing to honor the preferences of King Hussein on the subject — which I knew to be the latter choice. I had expected him to demand that the Palestinians have their own nation. Assad's position was consistent with his belief that Arab unity of purpose (as defined in Damascus) was more important than Palestinian nationalism.

Toward the end of our discussion, I asked the Syrian leader to outline the first steps we should take toward a real and permanent peace. He replied, "The most important thing is to prevent a new round of war. If we can end the state of belligerency, then this would lead automatically into a state of peace. Security-linked measures such as demilitarized zones would help buy us time, and we also need economic development and reconstruction to give people confidence that the new situation is good and permanent. These measures would create psychological composure and help to create a new era in the area."

I asked him about the Arab boycott of Israel, and he responded that with the Israelis' present attitudes, there could be no changes concerning trade between them and their Arab neighbors. He added, almost as an afterthought, "We are all the time talking about religion. If Jerusalem is taken from us, we would be soulless. It is inconceivable that we should be clamoring for a return to the 1967 borders and exclude only Jerusalem."

I asked, "Would it make it any easier if we made other exclusions as well?"

He laughed along with our advisers around the conference table and said, "If the Israelis insist on keeping Jerusalem, this shows that they do not want peace, because we are as attached to it as they are."

I replied that I was also attached to Jerusalem, and hoped that all believers would have unimpeded access to the holy shrines and the right to worship there without restraint. Before we adjourned our meeting, Assad promised to make some positive statements about the peace effort, adding that a year or two earlier it would have meant political suicide in Syria to talk about peace with the Israelis.

In Assad, I observed a man who spoke simply for himself and

his country, without self-doubt and with little consideration for how his views might conflict with those of anyone else. Many other Arab leaders seemed to follow almost a party line, but some of Assad's views sounded original, thought out from his own private contemplation. He never deferred to the other Syrian leaders with him, nor did he seem interested in their reaction to his comments. Although Assad gave no indication of being willing to abandon any of his long-term objectives, I came away from our first meeting convinced that he would be powerful and flexible enough to modify his political tactics to changing times and circumstances. Even in his bitterness toward Israel, he retained a certain wry humor about their conflicting views, and he seemed to derive great patience from his obvious sense of history. He professed not to speak for other Arabs, but seemed confident that his influence would be felt in seeking any permanent resolution of differences.

A few months later, Assad kept this promise by stating in an interview that following successful negotiations, he would be prepared to sign a peace agreement with Israel but not exchange ambassadors. He said, "There's no third choice; it's either peace or war." When I heard these remarks I felt more hopeful about the prospects for peace, but in light of subsequent events, my early optimism in dealing with Assad and the entire Middle East question was unjustified. Without my overconfidence, however, I would probably not have been willing to explore the opportunities that did exist.

The main obstacle in 1977 to the planned peace talks was how to include the Palestinians or, more specifically, the PLO. The Israelis would not give diplomatic recognition to the Palestinians and preferred to minimize their role in the discussions. Most Arab leaders and the Soviets insisted that a PLO delegation be treated on an equal basis with those of the national governments. Assad and I had considered several options on how to include them — as members of individual Arab delegations, by having all Arabs form one negotiating group, or by encouraging the Palestinians to designate other trusted Arab leaders to speak for them. That same summer Assad made a constructive proposal that would accommodate Israeli demands — that other Arabs could speak for the PLO — but all such efforts were aborted when President Sadat announced his intention to deal directly with the Israelis by going to Jerusalem. Although Sadat and I were still intending to use his historic move as a major step toward the comprehensive Geneva settlement that Assad had espoused, Syrian cooperation was effectively ended.

Assad was furious when Sadat told him of his planned visit to Jerusalem, and he never forgave the Egyptian leader for his "betrayal" of the Arab cause. He and other Arab leaders saw Sadat as seduced by Israel into a unilateral act that would give him back his own lands at the expense of the Palestinians and other Arabs. The Syrians did everything possible to prevent these direct talks between Israel and just one of its neighbors, then led the effort among other Arabs to isolate and boycott Egypt. Even in death Sadat was not forgiven. The streets of Damascus were filled with cheering throngs when the assassination of Anwar Sadat was announced.

After Sadat's visit to Israel, Assad's condemnation was so intense that many considered him just an obstructionist who would oppose *any* peace initiative and who therefore would be relatively insignificant in resolving Middle East conflicts through negotiations. In effect, his response to the Egyptian-Israeli peace treaty was relatively quiescent: an attempt to avoid a confrontation with Israeli troops and to acquire more Soviet arms to maintain some strategic military balance between Israel and Syria. Assad was biding his time, waiting for an opportunity to reassert Syria's role as a leader among the nations of the Middle East.

His opportunity was to come, perhaps sooner than he expected, in Lebanon. Over a period of years, the Israelis had become more and more aligned with the Maronite Christians, who shared with them a desire to control the Palestinian militants. Meanwhile, in a subtle but complete reversal of allegiance, Assad's forces, which had first entered Lebanon in 1976 to protect the interests of the Maronites (strangely, with American and Israeli approval and over Soviet opposition), had by now become the protectors and supporters of their opponents, a strong majority made up of Moslems, Druzes, and other Christian factions. Their new alignment was generally supported by the Soviets, the Syrian population, and other Arab leaders.

It served Assad's purposes to prevent Israeli retaliatory strikes into Lebanon, so he even cooperated with the Israelis after a fashion by using his considerable influence over the PLO in southern Lebanon to restrict guerrilla action by the Palestinians against Israeli settlements near the border. In effect, Syria helped to arrange a cease-fire agreement between the PLO and Israel that lasted for a year or more. Then, in June 1982, Israeli forces launched a lightning strike deep into Lebanon, toward Beirut, and almost immediately confronted Syrian air and ground forces. Except in the Bekaa Valley, where Syrian troops were firmly entrenched, Israel's tanks and planes prevailed dramatically, and with the embarrassing failure of his armed forces, it seemed likely that Assad was to remain permanently on the sidelines when Middle East decisions were made in the future.

Two months later, Israeli military forces were bivouacked in Lebanon, and American and European forces were supervising the evacuation of PLO troops from Beirut. It then seemed certain that the pro-Israeli President-elect, Bashir Gemayel, would be leading a Lebanon that was quite friendly to Israel. Considering major parts of their mission accomplished, the Israeli forces withdrew to the south to reduce their own casualties and to permit Gemayel's Maronite Christian forces to consolidate control of the country. Then came the dramatic events of September described earlier, and Assad was faced with American and European forces back in Beirut and even further polarization of religious and political factions. The civil war erupted anew. In spite of the presence of the foreign troops, the Druze and Christian militias were locked in combat in the mountains overlooking the city, and American troops and their Lebanese friends were being shelled from the surrounding villages, some of which were under the control of the Syrians.

Assad's patience had paid off, almost solely because of the misjudgments of his American and Israeli adversaries. During these months of relative inactivity by the Syrians, Assad was able to obtain massive shipments of modern Soviet armaments to replace the equipment he had lost during the Israeli invasion. Also, as the

American and Israeli forces and their Lebanese allies began to suffer losses and were placed on the defensive, the military and political position of Assad's Lebanese confederates became stronger.

It was at this time, in March 1983, that I visited Lebanon and Syria at the end of a month-long trip through the Middle East. Contrary to the situations in Egypt, Jordan, and Saudi Arabia, the press in Damascus had soundly condemned me before my arrival and, among other things, called me a betrayer of the Arab cause as the author of the notorious Camp David agreement. I reviewed these news summaries from our embassies with some concern. Syria and the United States were aligned against each other in Lebanon, and the newspaper articles and radio broadcasts in the state-controlled media had to mirror Assad's feelings. It was likely that the people were being deliberately stirred up against us. I wanted to have some constructive talks with the Syrian President, and Rosalynn and I were hoping to see the ancient city and visit some of its holy sites.

There was no need to worry. We received a hospitable welcome from the people and the Syrian leaders. As soon as we arrived at the Damascus airport, I was asked to go directly to the President's office, and Assad and I spent several hours reviewing the events of the last six years, since he and I had met in Switzerland. I had reread the verbatim transcript of that first conversation and had made a mental note to continue our discussion of some of the same subjects. This never happened. In the corner of a large conference room with the chairs and sofas all pushed tightly back against the wall in the Arab fashion, we began a heated debate about more current issues. Assad's interpreter was there to help us but had difficulty keeping up with the President. For the first time, I realized that he was quite familiar with English. He would often reply immediately in Arabic without waiting for my own remarks to be translated, and every now and then he would use a few English words himself.

The Syrian leader was obviously pleased with the latest developments in Lebanon and expressed complete confidence in an expanded role for his country in the future of the Middle East. He smiled as he observed that the struggle was now viewed by the world as being between little Syria and the mighty American superpower, so that the more vigorous our military action was, the stronger and braver Syria appeared as a challenger. Although he did not mention it, I realized that the United States forces were in Assad's back yard, an arena that he could control and manipulate through his proxies in Lebanon. Assad saw the maximum pressure being on Israel and the United States to change the status quo in Lebanon; Syria could afford to sit back and wait for initiatives from both Jerusalem and Washington.

He said that he always knew the Israeli occupation of Lebanon was destined to be a great failure. Assad scoffed at Israel's claims that its action was a response to PLO attacks, pointing out that for more than a year prior to the invasion there had been no Israeli casualties from attacks across the Lebanese border.

I agreed that the war and its resulting occupation had already been very costly in military expenditures, in Israeli lives, and in the worldwide propaganda struggle for sympathy and support.

Assad wanted to talk about the future. He maintained that even if the Israelis retained only a token force in southern Lebanon after the major action was over, their presence would become ever more unpopular even with those few Lebanese who welcomed their initial entry into the country in hopes that they would drive out the PLO.

He said that he and other Syrians monitored news reports from Israel very closely, and he had noted the strong political divisions that had arisen in Israel. He believed that Prime Minister Begin and his government had been deeply embarrassed by Israel's failure to achieve its grandest objectives in Lebanon.

Even in this private conversation, however, Assad would never admit that these political developments might change Israeli policy in any significant way. He took every opportunity to point out the degree of military and economic support from the United States that made possible Israeli aggression against its neighbors and claimed that all Arabs hold Washington responsible for the absence of peace in the area.

I enumerated the many efforts that I and my predecessors in the White House had made to bring peace to the Middle East, and reminded him that Israel was ready and willing to negotiate with him or any other Arab leader in an attempt to resolve the differences between them.

This brought up the sorest subject of all for Assad. He persistently blamed Sadat and the Egyptian peace treaty with Israel for the attack on Lebanon, maintaining that the Israelis would not have taken the risk of concerted Arab retaliation if Egypt had still been free to join forces with the other Arabs. We had a heated exchange. I reminded Assad that Egypt had its land back, and its people were living in peace. I quoted key passages from the Camp David accords to prove that the framework was there for further withdrawal by Israel from occupied territory, for Palestinian self-determination, and for a peaceful resolution of the outstanding differences between Israel and its other Arab neighbors.

He accepted none of this and again accused the United States of financing and helping to plan the invasion of Lebanon. He was convinced that the Israelis did not want peace except on their own terms, that they had no intention of withdrawing from the West Bank, Gaza, or the Golan Heights, and that this fact would preclude any further moves toward peace in the region. Assad expressed surprising confidence and patience concerning Syria's regaining ultimate control of the Golan Heights, and he did not seem at all interested in the active pursuit of this goal in the immediate future.

Assad was certain that Israel's announced goal of destroying the PLO forces would be unsuccessful and that the Palestinians, even after their costly exodus from Lebanon and regardless of who their leaders might be, would manage to retain considerable influence among the Arab leaders and most of the world's people.

I decided to push Assad on some sensitive issues. The other Arab leaders whom I had recently visited were quite concerned about Syria's support of Iran, whose people were not Arabs, in its war with Arab Iraq, so I questioned Assad about this. He was unequivocal about his commitment but somewhat defensive about the decision. He made it clear that his support of the Iranian forces was motivated primarily by his aversion to President Saddam Hussein and other Iraqi leaders, but emphasized that the Ayatollah Khomeini knew without doubt that Syria would join in the defense of Saudi Arabia or any other Arab nation that might be threatened or attacked by Iranian forces.

I then asked him about the peculiar confluence of some Syrian and Israeli interests: both were supporting Iran against Iraq in the current Persian Gulf war; both despised Yasir Arafat, and each had an interest in forcing Arafat and his troops out of Lebanon; both seemed willing to live if necessary with a de facto partition of an unwilling Lebanon, even if it meant accepting the presence of the other in the divided country, with Israelis in the south and Syrians in the east and north; neither wanted an independent Palestinian state in the West Bank; and both respected the strength of the other and carefully honored the disengagement agreement along the Syrian-Israeli border. Assad did not agree with all my premises and even denied that the Israelis favored the Iranians, but he was obviously intrigued with the subject and we enjoyed the discussion.

I pointed out that Israeli pilots with their American-built F-15s had decimated Syria's air defense in their aerial encounters early in the Lebanese war. When I questioned Assad about this, he claimed that the Soviet airplanes he had used in June 1982 were as good as any, but that he had never been able to obtain modern electronic equipment for them. He also asserted that he would not ever make the same mistake again.

Assad did not deny his heavy dependence on the Soviets for weapons and military advisers, and when I asked him about the wisdom of this relationship, he smiled and said, "Will you sell me any arms with which to defend my country, even a pistol?" He denied vehemently that the Soviets had any voice in his decisions, and laughed aloud at a comment that U.S. Secretary of Defense Caspar Weinberger had recently made about Syria's being a puppet of the Soviet Union.

I asked him why Syria had never recognized Lebanon as a separate and independent nation and in many clear and subtle ways considered it part of "Greater Syria." In spite of their close relationships in many areas of political and economic life, neither country has ever had an ambassador in the other's capital and, until recently, they did not exchange visits between heads of state. (It was only after the American withdrawal from Beirut in early

1984 that Assad, in a moment of triumph, received the President of Lebanon in Damascus.)

Assad repeatedly disavowed any designs on his western neighbor, insisting that he and his people recognized Lebanon's independence without equivocation. I suspect that Syria prefers a strong hand in Lebanon's affairs rather than annexation, something like the Soviets' relationship with the more submissive Eastern European countries.

I told him about my examining both ancient and modern maps in Damascus that showed no national border between the two countries and expressed my doubt about his willingness to withdraw Syrian troops as he had promised. He repeated that he preferred a free and independent Lebanon and that he had not changed his commitment to withdraw "when requested to do so by the Arab League and the Lebanese government." A few days later, when I was in Beirut, I asked President Amin Gemayel about this and he said, "That is the way I understand it."

In May 1983, two months after our visit, the United States helped to negotiate a withdrawal agreement between Israel and Lebanon, and I noticed that Assad then added another proviso: "that Israel must not derive any political benefit from its invasion by conditions which encroach on Lebanese sovereignty." In effect, this meant that Israel would have to withdraw its troops from Lebanon before Syria would do so. It was obvious that barring satisfactory settlement terms, the Syrians would do whatever they deemed necessary to assure that any peace agreement or diplomatic recognition between Israel and the existing Lebanese government would not be consummated. Assad would never yield the special relationship between his country and Lebanon that has existed without interruption since the two modern states were created, and he would especially oppose an Israeli advantage in Lebanon.

I reminded Assad that King Hussein and Yasir Arafat were trying to decide under what circumstances Hussein would join in peace talks with Israel, Egypt, and the United States as outlined in the Reagan statement of September 1982, and I tried unsuccessfully to convince Assad not to interfere in the decision. He did not deviate from his position that the only way to deal with Israel was with a unified Arab voice, with full Palestinian participation, and in a U.N.-sponsored forum in which the Soviets as well as the Americans would be involved.

At the end of our first long meeting, we noticed on the wall of Assad's office a large painting that depicted the battle of Hittin in 1187. In that historic engagement, the Moslem leader Saladin defeated the Christian invaders, and the Crusader Kingdom of Jerusalem fell almost immediately thereafter. The Arabs were completely victorious over the West. As Assad stood in front of the brilliant scene and discussed the history of the Crusades and the other ancient struggles for the Holy Land, he took particular pride in retelling the tales of Arab successes, past and present. He seemed to speak like a modern Saladin, feeling that it was his dual obligation to rid the region of all foreign presence while preserving Damascus as the only focal point for Arab unity today. He had no way to know how quickly his hopes for an Arab victory would be realized in Lebanon.

Even before U.S. troops were withdrawn from Beirut early in 1984, most of Assad's predictions had come true and the status of Syria had been dramatically improved. The Syrian President had become generally recognized as a key player in shaping the future of Lebanon and in affecting the course of efforts to achieve stability and peace in the entire Middle East. Now armed with new and sophisticated Soviet weapons, Assad was confident that the Syrians could defend themselves more effectively, but he must have had unpleasant memories of the abysmal record of his forces in earlier engagements with the Israelis.

With the American debacle in Lebanon, the relative strength of the two superpowers underwent a significant change in the region. The Soviets through their close association with Syria achieved a position of influence in this part of the Middle East that they had never before enjoyed. At the same time, U.S.-Syrian relations reached a low point. In August 1984, Assad emphasized this fact by saying, "The United States does not have an independent opinion or an American policy in this region. The United States implements the policy that is decided by Israel." He went on to declare, "Our principal enemy is the United States, and not Israel."

Overall in the Middle East, these developments were quite significant. Syrian-backed Palestinians were able to force Arafat and his followers out of northern Lebanon in December 1983, and Assad was then in a position to speak at least for the Palestinians in his region. Except for the Israelis in southern Lebanon, all other foreign troops were now out of the country, and the Syrians were able to orchestrate a new coalition of Lebanese political factions, which took faltering steps toward reconciling their long and bloody confrontations. In March 1984, Assad demonstrated his power in the region by forcing the Lebanese to abrogate the withdrawal agreement they had signed with Israel the previous year.

As the preeminent Arab power in the region, Syria had long seemed willing to accept a tacit military and political balance or standoff with Israel, but now Assad could consider this just a temporary arrangement as far as Lebanon was concerned. He knew how unpopular the Israeli occupation of Lebanon had become in Israel, and he had the power to expedite the withdrawal of the Israelis by encouraging the relatively moderate elements, like the Shia religious leaders, to take a more militant stance toward the occupying forces still in southern Lebanon.

It is likely that Syria would also remove its troops following an unconditional Israeli withdrawal from Lebanon. Assad would no longer be required to protect Syria's interests with soldiers if there was a reasonably compliant government in Beirut. He would still have a dominant role in Lebanon and could, at the same time, be in substantial control of future efforts to forge peace terms between Israel and its other neighbors. A major goal will be to prevent any negotiations among Israel, Jordan, Egypt, and the United States under the umbrella of the Camp David accords or the Reagan statement of 1982. There is no doubt that Assad has already used both promises and threats in Jordan and within the PLO to bring about the rejection of any such talks.

Yet even with his enhanced position, Assad cannot afford to go too far. Given his stubborn stance against every peace proposal and his severed ties with the large PLO remnant headed by Arafat, Assad could again be ignored and lose the commanding presence he gained during the war in Lebanon. His overt attempts to dominate the Palestinian movement by controlling or destroying

Arafat have not been successful and have aroused wide condemnation among other Arabs. Most Palestinians oppose a Syrian-dominated organization, and those in the West Bank and Gaza particularly condemn Assad for contributing to Palestinian fratricide by driving Arafat and his supporters out of northern Lebanon late in 1983.

Assad is likely to prevail in Lebanon, but even there he faces potential problems. The struggle for political power will continue between the Maronite Christians and their opponents among the other religious communities. The leaders of all the factions who have fought so long for additional power in Lebanon will become less reliant on Assad, their political patron, and he will have to walk a fine line to retain his influence without precipitating another outbreak of violence. Furthermore, Assad must be cautious about the Lebanese Shias becoming too infused with the zeal of Khomeini's Shias in Iran, a religious fervor that could eventually turn against Assad's own regime, which is highly secular in its orientation.

Additionally, he faces potential problems among his neighbors and others who will play a significant role in the Middle East:

- His differences with Saddam Hussein in a potentially formidable Iraq seem irreconcilable.
- His support of Iran has caused deep concern among other Arab states in the Arabian Peninsula and is looked upon as a divisive factor in the frustrated search for pan-Arab unity.
- His direct support of the bloody PLO revolution has made his motives suspect among most Palestinians.
- His relationships with leaders in Jordan and Egypt are shaky at best, and his moves against the PLO have removed at least one obstacle to more independent action by King Hussein and Arafat and encouraged the reentry of Egypt into the Arab fold.
- In America he is considered an enemy of peace and a possible instigator of the attacks against the U.S. Marines in Beirut.
- His growing dependence on the Soviet Union may come to haunt him in the years ahead as the Soviets demand repayment or accommodation to their views.

Although Assad has now led Syria for fourteen years (as long as Franklin D. Roosevelt was President of the United States), his natural political base is not strong. His Alawite religious sect represents only about 10 percent of the Syrian population, and he has had to exert extreme measures when opposing political forces challenged his authority, as was demonstrated as recently as March 1984. This embryonic rebellion was generated when Assad seemed to be seriously ill, an obvious indication of his potential vulnerability.

My impression is that Assad is a very ambitious man, but that he can be patient and flexible in seeking his ultimate goals. His actions and influence over the PLO, Lebanon, and even Jordan in the last several years have proven that he is determined to restrain their respective independent actions in the peace process. Although he has so far demonstrated only a negative influence, under circumstances to his liking, Assad could even be a prime catalyst in achieving an overall peace agreement in the Middle East. He would not want to be isolated and excluded from any peace process that had a chance of making progress, but under any circumstances he would certainly insist on the protection of Syria's interests and on his role in the negotiating process being recognized.

Such a peace could fit within the general framework of the common interpretation of U.N. Resolution 242. Even then, however, it is unlikely that Assad would abandon his ultimate dream of a unified Arab nation, extending along the southern and eastern shores of the Mediterranean Sea and eastward to the Persian Gulf — perhaps with Hafez al-Assad as its leader.

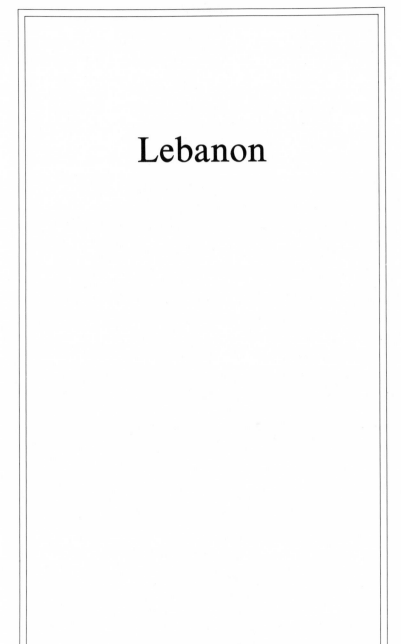

# Lebanon

FROM DAMASCUS TO BEIRUT is only about fifty miles, but our BAC 111 airplane had been flying more than four times that distance since we left the Syrian capital. Now we peered eagerly through the windows from 12,000 feet and exclaimed over the beauty of the Mediterranean seashore and the glistening white buildings as we descended toward the war-torn capital of Lebanon. It looked strangely peaceful even as we circled close to land, and there seemed to be no logical reason that we should have had to take such a circuitous route far north, then west over the sea, and finally southeast toward the airport, where American forces were deployed as part of an international peacekeeping force. In fact, our roundabout journey was designed to avoid flying over any Lebanese land area. This was March 1983, and we were approaching a battleground — the most ravaged, the most shattered, country on the face of the globe.

A few minutes later we were on the ground, surrounded by heavily armed U.S. Marines. As had been the case throughout this month-long visit to seven nations in the Middle East, the American ambassador greeted us and briefed me on the political situation. The military commander reported that spirits were low among his men because of restraints he had placed on them. In order to prevent an international incident, the sailors and marines were being asked not to respond to the taunts and abuse they encountered on the streets of Beirut, even from some of our allies, but to ignore them and concentrate exclusively on the duty of keeping the peace.

We ducked into an armored limousine and were soon careening through the streets, surrounded by escort vehicles filled with armed men. In the cars and on the sidewalks, machine guns pointed carelessly in every direction, including at us. There was an almost total indifference to potential danger from the weapons, and no one seemed to notice the occasional bursts of far-off gunfire. At close range, the devastation of war was almost sickening, much worse than anything I had anticipated from the first impressions from the distant sky. There were enormous piles of rubble everywhere, and the buildings that still stood were hollow shells, each pockmarked with hundreds of projectile or shrapnel holes. It was amazing to see little children playing around the feet of the soldiers on the refuse of recent battles and people still living in some of the devastated homes.

At breakneck speed, with sirens screaming, we traveled on a roundabout route through the city eastward into the hills toward the President's palace. It seemed that every few hundred yards a different emblem, uniform color, and flag were displayed. We recognized the French and Italian uniforms, and the driver said there were also British and at least two kinds of Lebanese militia. The different troops epitomized Lebanon's recent political history: the presence of external powers and the absence of internal cohesion. After a twenty-minute trip, we were welcomed by the handsome young leader and his advisers.

Amin Gemayel had become President of Lebanon only five months earlier, immediately following the assassination of his brother Bashir and the massacre of Palestinians and Lebanese Moslems in the Sabra and Shatila refugee camps. At the time of the Israeli invasion in June 1982, Elias Sarkis was the President of the country. When he resigned in August, Bashir Gemayel was elected by the parliament. There was great concern about this selection because the young Maronite Christian, a leader of the Phalangist militia forces, was known for his eagerness to resort to violence against members of other sectarian groups in order to achieve his political ends and for his love of revenge when his own family or clan was injured by others. It was also known that he was closely allied with the Israelis and that he despised the Palestinian militants. But before he could assume his new duties, Bashir Gemayel, at age thirty-four, was killed by a bomb explosion in Phalangist headquarters. One week later, on September 21, his brother Amin was elected President at the age of forty.

The two men were quite different in temperament and attitude. Amin was known to be a dove and a conciliator, not as politically shrewd as his brother. He had fought bravely in the Phalangist forces but abhorred violence. He was friendly toward the Palestinians in Lebanon, and even during the Israeli siege of Beirut he had met with PLO leaders in an attempt to protect their interests and to resolve the differences that divided his people. He was a lawyer, a very successful businessman, and the editor of a rightist newspaper. Also, although Amin Gemayel would work with whichever of his neighbors was dominant at the time, he was thought to prefer the Syrians to the Israelis.

The President's beautiful palace was on a hilltop overlooking Beirut, and we met the Lebanese leader in one end of a large and pleasant room. I sympathized with him, because it was well known that he was attempting to rule a country that was deeply divided among religious and ethnic groups, each with its own militia. Their loyalty was not to any central government, and it was doubtful that Gemayel had firm control over any part of his own country other than a few of the communities around Beirut.

When we arrived at his office, President Gemayel soon asked about my most recent meetings with other leaders in Israel and the Arab countries, and I gave him as much information as I could without violating confidences. When we discussed my conversations with President Assad of Syria, I asked him about Assad's statement that he would withdraw Syrian troops if so requested after Israel's forces were out of Lebanon. After thinking for a moment, Gemayel said quietly, "That is the way I understand it." I asked what he would do if all foreign troops abruptly left his country. Somewhat brashly, he voiced total confidence that he could deal successfully with the Druze, Sunni and Shia Moslems, and other Christian factions, restore order, and alleviate the terrible problems that the Lebanese would have to face together.

It was obvious to me that he and his troops were not strong enough to control all the disputed areas or to meld Lebanon's factions into any degree of unity. I asked a few questions about this, and he finally said that he would need six more months to be ready for this move, which I presumed meant that foreign troops should stay awhile longer. Since the Syrians and Israelis were showing no indication of leaving anyhow, I did not feel inclined to pursue the subject further. He had enough problems without my casting more doubt on his country's political future, which, after the recent terrible suffering, was still very much in doubt.

Lebanon has long lived with political divisions. The region contained Christian communities from the first century and remained predominantly Christian even after Syria became Moslem. The Maronites broke with the Pope in the seventh century over doctrinal issues but returned to the Roman flock five centuries later. By this time, the Druzes, Moslems, and other Christian groups were established in the Lebanon area. The terrain permitted the different religious communities to live in relative isolation and to preserve their identity and autonomy through the centuries, even while this area was part of the Ottoman Empire for four hundred years, from 1516 until World War I.

Because of the presence of Christian missionaries during the seventeenth and eighteenth centuries, the Maronites established strong social and religious ties with Catholic France. When their very existence was threatened in a civil war with the fierce Druze mountain fighters in 1861, the French forced the Turkish sultans to protect their Christian friends by establishing a small Christian enclave first known as Mount Lebanon. The governing system was organized to allow for a Maronite Christian governor to rule with a council of twelve: four Maronite Christians, three Druzes, two Greek Orthodox, one Greek Catholic, and one Sunni and one Shia Moslem. Political power was shared according to a numerical formula based on the estimated population of the different religious groups, and this system has been maintained in a surprisingly consistent manner over the generations, being just flexible enough to accommodate known changes in the populace.

After World War I, the French controlled Lebanon and Syria. They somewhat arbitrarily amalgamated different religious and ethnic groups into a Greater Lebanon by adding to Maronite Mount Lebanon the Moslem cities of Beirut and Tripoli, the Shia Moslem area of southern Lebanon, and the fertile Bekaa Valley to the east, occupied by Moslems and Greek Orthodox Christians (who considered themselves more Syrian then Lebanese). Instead of being a majority, the Maronites now became the largest minority group, but the French were careful to assure that the total Christian population exceeded that of the Moslems and Druzes. With Lebanon composed of religious and political minorities, a kind of social contract among these groups had to be contrived in order to hold the fragile national community together. Now, with a new governing body of fifteen commissioners, six were Maronites, three Greek Orthodox, one Greek Catholic, two Shias, two Sunnis, and one Druze.

Later, under the French mandate, Lebanon's 1926 Constitution set up a parliament with a membership ratio of six Christians and five Moslems, based on the population of that time. Although no census has been completed since 1932, the ratio has arbitrarily been kept the same. A President is chosen by a two-thirds vote of this National Assembly and by unwritten custom has been a Maronite Christian, with the prime minister a Sunni Moslem and the speaker of the parliament a Shia Moslem. Other government posts come under the traditional purview of other sects; for instance, a Druze holds the Defense ministry, a Greek Orthodox the Foreign ministry, and so on.

Retaining these allotments of political power has been one of the most crucial purposes of the Christian forces in the face of an increasing Moslem population in a nation that is officially self-defined as being Arab in character. Lebanese Christians see no inconsistency with this definition. Except in Lebanon, Christian Arabs make up a relatively small minority in the Middle East, but the six million Christians in Arab countries are proud that their religious heritage predates that of the Moslems. They point out that Christianity was the official Arab religion during the fifth century, and six hundred years later, long after Mohammed's death, a majority of Greater Syria's population was still Christian.

In Lebanon, the relatively equal division between the two monotheistic religions has created a problem in the sharing of power as the groups struggle to protect their political and geographical domains. Loyalty to family and religious group transcends any commitment to national unity. Old political arrangements became outmoded as the Moslem population grew into a majority, and fears of being overwhelmed by another ethnic group have prevented the integration of Lebanon's pluralistic population. Memories of injustices and past conflicts are nurtured by the wronged parties for long periods of time and have precipitated almost constant violent acts of retaliation and revenge.

In order to protect themselves and to prevail on the turbulent national scene, political and religious groups have established independent militias, and the factions have frequently been willing to call upon foreign powers to intercede on their behalf. The Moslem Turks favored the Druzes, the French came in to protect the Maronite Christians, the Russians supported the Russian Orthodox, the Syrians have on different occasions been aligned with various sides, and the Israelis and Maronites have worked closely as military allies. The Americans and Egyptians have also intervened for brief periods when serious disorder threatened the very existence of the nation. Most foreign leaders have been fairly nimble on their political feet, shifting their allegiance to accommodate changing circumstances in Lebanon and always looking for some kind of profit from their involvement, often at the expense of the Lebanese.

It was almost impossible for me to remember the different alignments and factions in Lebanon while I was President, so I finally directed the CIA to include in my daily briefing at least once each week a summary description of the political and religious groups, their current leaders, the size and effectiveness of each militia, any foreign connections, and the latest changes in their status. Only then could I understand the news reports from the troubled country.

Lebanon's leaders have long claimed that their nation's foreign policy was neutral, and they have tried to walk a constantly moving chalk line between East and West and between Israel and Syria. They have not always succeeded, but at least the Lebanese have never been a threat to any of their neighbors. In spite of its good faith effort, however, few other nations in modern times have suffered as much as Lebanon at the hands of such a diversity of foreign powers.

Most Lebanese, while preferring independence, have historically desired close ties to Syria, with many Moslems and some Christians even demanding that the two countries be united. Under the French mandate, which lasted until after World War II, the transportation, communications and electric power systems, the currency, and some administrative functions provided service to Lebanon and Syria as a unit. In 1943, in order to resolve some of the continuing disputes about Lebanon's international orientation, a National Pact was formulated, with the Maronite Christians agreeing to sever their ties with France and to accept Arabic as the official language; the Moslem leaders promised to accept permanent separation from Syria. In 1946, when the last French troops left the area and Syria and Lebanon were independent, however, many of these personal and religious relationships between the two countries remained intact.

In the late 1950s, Egypt's President Gamal Abdel Nasser became a hero in much of the Arab world when he regained control of the Suez Canal by forcibly expelling British troops from his country. This was the beginning of his call for pan-Arab unity. His popularity greatly strengthened the Moslem influence in Lebanon and brought about such strong demands for increased political representation in the government that the carefully contrived political balance was threatened by civil war. At the request of Lebanon's Christian President Camille Chamoun, President Dwight Eisenhower sent American troops into Lebanon in 1958 to preserve order.

For two decades after Lebanon and Israel were born as new republics in the late 1940s, their common border remained relatively peaceful. During the 1967 war between Israel and its other neighbors — Syria, Jordan, and Egypt — Lebanon was careful to remain on the sidelines, but as citizens of an Arab nation, a strong majority of Lebanese condemned the Israelis. These Lebanese also blamed Israel for the influx of more than a hundred thousand Palestinian refugees, who poured into Lebanon after the establishment of Israel.

In 1970, a civil war in Jordan created another wave of refugees who moved into Lebanon, most of them Palestinians who had lived west of the Jordan River before the wars of 1948 and 1967. The newcomers swelled the ranks of Palestinians to nearly half a million, many of whom were forced to live in permanent refugee camps. This multitude of homeless Palestinians precipitated sharp political debates on how the new arrivals should be treated. As might be expected, they found their greatest support and sympathy among the Moslems, but as they became increasingly militant, they came to be resented or feared by Lebanese of all factions.

Unlike Syria, Egypt, and Jordan, Lebanon did not have a strong enough central government or coordinated military force to resist or control the Palestinian militants. Building up what was in effect a state within a state, the Palestine Liberation Organization administered the affairs of all refugees, providing welfare, health, education, judicial, and other services, dealing as equals with many foreign nations, and directing imposing militia forces. The PLO and Lebanese leftists became powerful enough to challenge the sovereignty of the nation's government and to control substantial portions of the country. Furthermore, the presence of the Palestinians and their frequent raids into Israel precipitated strong and immediate retaliatory strikes by the Israelis against the PLO strongholds in Lebanon, even against the heavily populated center of Beirut itself. Much of the resulting animosity was directed at the Palestinians for initiating the attacks.

The situation degenerated rapidly as the Maronite Christian forces and rightist groups attempted to control the Palestinians and their leftist allies. A full-scale civil war erupted early in 1975, which resulted in more than 60,000 Lebanese killed and more than a million displaced from their homes. When the Palestinians and Lebanese leftists gained control of three fourths of the nation, President Hafez al-Assad dispatched large numbers of Syrian troops into the war-torn country in June 1976 to support the Maronite forces and to bring an end to the civil war. This move was obviously designed to protect Syria's military and economic interests, but it was approved by the Lebanese government, Israel, the United States, and later by the Arab League — and strongly opposed by the Soviet Union.

Although the two countries are and will likely remain independent, the leaders of Syria still consider their nation and Lebanon to be inseparable; in the words of President Assad, they are "one country and one people." Most Syrian maps show no national boundary line, few border restrictions have ever been imposed on travel and commerce, and ordinary diplomatic customs are not observed between the two nations.

Despite this, Assad claims both publicly and privately that he will always honor and preserve Lebanon's independence. He resents any implication that his troops are "invaders" or even "foreign forces." The Syrians call them "external" forces, reminding all listeners that they were invited in by the Lebanese leaders and that their presence was approved by the Arab League. Assad insists that neither he nor his troops have ever considered their presence in Lebanon to be anything but temporary.

As long as Israeli forces remain in Lebanon, Assad's claim is not likely to be tested, but it is true that the Syrians have not attempted to establish a permanent civilian presence in the areas they control. One of the Lebanese scholars who attended our Middle East consultation at Emory University late in 1983 lived in the Bekaa Valley region, and I questioned him closely about the Syrian forces stationed there. Although he objected strongly to the Syrians or any other foreigners being in his country and hoped for their early withdrawal, he was positive that the Syrians had never attempted to establish settlements of any kind nor, he said, had they ever interfered with the normal life of the farmers or villagers in the occupied region except when engaged in military action. He estimated that the troops could be completely withdrawn within two days after being ordered out. It remains to be seen whether this command will ever come from Damascus.

Palestinian attacks across Israel's eastern and northern borders were common long before the 1967 war, and preemptive strikes and counterstrikes were regularly launched into and from Jordan,

Syria, and Lebanon. Later, when tight restraints were placed on the Palestinian activists by Jordan and Syria, the only remaining guerrilla bases were in Lebanon. By 1976, when Syrian forces moved into northern and eastern Lebanon, Israel had found some allies among the Maronite Christian forces in the south and had begun to provide armaments and training to the Maronite troops throughout Lebanon. What brought them together at first was a common animosity toward the PLO; later was added a desire by both to see the Syrians expelled and the Maronites in an even more dominant political role. The Israelis also wanted a closer political alignment with a friendly Lebanese government.

Even before Menachem Begin and his Likud government were elected in May 1977, some of the Maronite Christians were already urging the Israelis to move into Lebanon in order to destroy the PLO and dislodge the Syrians. However, this temptation was resisted until March 1978, when, in retaliation for a PLO attack on a busload of its citizens, Israel invaded Lebanon, moved its forces up to the Litani River, and used antipersonnel cluster bombs against Beirut and other urban centers, killing hundreds of civilians.

As President, I considered this major invasion to be an overreaction to the PLO attack, a serious threat to peace in the region, and perhaps part of a design to establish a permanent Israeli presence in southern Lebanon. Also, such use of American weapons including cluster bombs violated the legal agreement between the United States and Israel, which specified that such armaments sold by us could be used only for defensive purposes against an attack on Israel.

In spite of my expressions of concern and the worldwide outcry, Begin seemed determined to keep his forces in Lebanon for an extended period and — in another direct violation of American law — to transfer American weapons, including artillery and armored vehicles, to the Lebanese militia commanded by Major Saad Haddad. These troops had been trained and supported by the Israelis, in order to seal off the southern portion of the country against Palestinian terrorists. In carrying out this assignment, they also prevented Lebanese regular troops and U.N. peacekeeping forces from entering the area.

After consulting with Secretary of State Cyrus Vance and with key supporters of Israel in the Congress, I decided that we could not permit the Israeli occupation of southern Lebanon to continue. In the event that Begin would not accede to our wishes, we prepared to notify Congress, as required by law, that U.S. weapons were being used illegally in Lebanon, which would have automatically cut off all military aid to Israel. Also, I instructed the State Department to prepare a U.N. Security Council resolution condemning Israel's action.

The American consul general in Jerusalem was instructed to deliver a message to Prime Minister Begin that explained these plans and urged that he withdraw his forces. The report came back from Jerusalem that Begin read the message, stood quietly for a few moments, and then said, "It's over."

As the Israeli forces made a staged withdrawal, United Nations troops came in to replace them, and the forces friendly to Israel in the south of Lebanon were strengthened to provide a more effective although not a total barrier to further PLO attacks on Israeli citizens.

Later, in 1981, Begin greatly expanded Israel's political involvement by announcing that it would, in effect, be responsible for the protection of all Christian forces throughout Lebanon. At about the same time, paradoxically, the Syrians helped Israeli government officials to work out a quite effective cease-fire agreement with the PLO — a tacit political recognition of that organization so despised by Israel.

The most recent invasion of Lebanon came in 1982, when a massive array of Israeli military forces entered the country and moved without serious impediment all the way to Beirut. The Israelis explained that they were punishing the PLO because their ambassador in London had been shot. A different group later claimed responsibility for the crime. Earlier that year, American State Department officials had been secretly briefed on a general plan that Israel's Defense Minister Ariel Sharon had in mind if the Israelis moved into Lebanon. After completing their withdrawal from the Sinai, the Israelis considered their obligations to the Egyptians under the peace treaty to be fulfilled. They were now free to make final plans for the operation euphemistically called "Peace for Galilee."

Even as a private citizen I was deeply troubled when Israel in-

vaded Lebanon in June, and I immediately expressed my concern
to some Israeli leaders who had participated in the Camp David
negotiations that the attack was a violation of the accords. Back
came a disturbing reply from Jerusalem: "We have a green light
from Washington."

I called the White House to report what I had heard to President
Reagan's national security adviser, Judge William Clark. He
assured me that the White House had not been involved in any
approval and that there were top-level assurances then being
given to President Reagan by Prime Minister Begin that the pen-
etration of Lebanon would be limited to maximum artillery
range, twenty-five miles. I replied that there were other high officials in Washington outside the White House and that I had
complete confidence in the source of my information from Israel.

That same day the national security adviser sent two of his staff
members down to my home in Georgia to show me the exchange
of messages between Reagan and Begin. These confirmed the
commitment to limit the Israeli advance to twenty-five miles.
However, instead of staying within this limit, the Israeli troops
continued to move north in an uninterrupted drive.

Although the Syrians held their own in land battles in the
Bekaa Valley, the Israelis achieved overwhelming aerial victories
against the Soviet-built Syrian planes above Lebanon, and the
defending Lebanese and Palestinian militia were easily brushed
from their path to the outskirts of Beirut. The Israeli troops en-
circled the city, and sustained bombing of the Lebanese capital
and other cities caused high casualties among the civilian population and aroused intense opposition even in Israel. According to
subsequent analyses, there were several interrelated purposes for
the attack: to remove the threat to the northern border of Israel;
to force the Syrians out of Lebanon; to establish a Lebanese government friendly enough to Israel to sign a permanent peace
agreement; to destroy the Palestinian military forces, capture the
PLO leader Yasir Arafat, and drive any PLO remnants out of
Lebanon; and perhaps to distract attention from the West Bank
and Gaza area and the overall Palestinian question.

It was at this time, a few weeks after the invasion was launched,
that Israel's Maronite Christian friend Bashir Gemayel was
elected President of Lebanon, and negotiations for an Israeli

withdrawal and a peace agreement commenced. Under pressure from Washington, the Israelis made a partial withdrawal to the south and American and European troops were dispatched to Beirut in August to supervise the departure of Arafat and several thousand of his PLO troops, who left the city brandishing their weapons and claiming some kind of victory. Then, in quick succession, the Western peacekeeping forces left Beirut, Bashir Gemayel was assassinated by unknown political adversaries, and Israeli military forces returned to the city and its immediate suburbs. A few days later, several hundred defenseless Palestinians and Lebanese Moslems were slain in the Sabra and Shatila refugee camps and American forces moved back into Beirut, joined by units from Great Britain, France, and Italy.

For several months, Ambassador Philip Habib and other U.S. negotiators attempted to bring about a cease-fire agreement and a withdrawal of Syrian and Israeli forces. In the meantime, American weapons and military advisers were provided to strengthen the Lebanese army, now serving under the newly elected President, Amin Gemayel.

At this point the military and political alignments became more obvious, with the Israelis and Americans giving full support to the Maronite Christian forces and the Syrians aligned with the Shia and Sunni Moslems, the Druzes, and some of the Christian groups that for any reason were opposing the Israeli-Phalangist coalition. The remaining PLO forces were divided, with most of them in northern Lebanon away from the U.S. and Israeli troops.

The slaying of Bashir Gemayel had greatly complicated the tedious withdrawal negotiations between Israel and Lebanon, and it was only after Secretary of State George Shultz interceded personally that an agreement was signed in May 1983 by the Israeli and Lebanese leaders. President Gemayel finally accepted the proposed terms because he believed that Israel and the United States were in a preeminently strong position and would protect Maronite interests after the combat had ceased. Most important, this was seen as a necessary first step in the removal of all foreign troops from Lebanon — Israeli, Syrian, and Palestinian. Although the document called for the withdrawal of both Israeli and Syrian forces, Assad had not been involved in the negotiations, and he refused to see Israel obtain any political victory as a result of the military invasion. He therefore immediately condemned the entire procedure.

The eventual invalidation of the agreement would be of great importance to the Syrians, because it called for an end to the state of war that had existed for thirty-five years between Israel and another Arab country and it gave additional Arab recognition and legitimacy to Israel, as had the Camp David accords and the Egyptian-Israeli peace treaty. Perhaps of more immediate concern, Israel was given the rights of intervention and flights over Lebanese territory while similar privileges were specifically denied to others, including Syria, who might be hostile to Israel. Syria's hegemony over Lebanon was threatened, and the consummation of the agreement would give too much political power to Amin Gemayel and the Maronite Christians at the expense of other groups in Lebanon more closely associated with the Syrians. Once again, the United States was condemned for forging an unfair pact on behalf of Israel while excluding the Syrians and other Arabs from the process.

The failure to acknowledge Syria's vital interests in Lebanon was a public rebuke of Assad, and he considered it an insult that Syria's compliance with the agreement was taken for granted. He also saw it as another step away from dealing with the central causes of the Arab-Israeli conflict: the Palestinian question and the status of the occupied territories. For all these reasons, Assad was determined to force the Lebanese to abrogate the accord. He also saw its potential cancellation as a triumph over the United States, an enemy whom he wanted very much to embarrass.

Supported by the Syrians, the Druze and other Lebanese militia kept the Israeli forces around Beirut under almost constant attack. Casualties were high, and in September 1983 the Israelis withdrew southward, to a line along the Awali River, with only one of their goals accomplished: the PLO troops in Beirut and southern Lebanon had been forced out of the area, leaving Israel's northern border secure.

After the Israelis moved to southern Lebanon, American Marines deployed around the airport on the outskirts of metropolitan Beirut began to come under increasing fire from the Druze and other Moslem militia in the surrounding hills. The United

States responded with airplane flights from navy carriers off-shore, and when its planes were fired on by Syrian antiaircraft batteries, the naval guns responded by bombarding the hills, villages, and gun emplacements with heavy artillery. More and more, it became obvious that the American purpose was to protect Gemayel's Maronite Christians, which effectively created a state of belligerency between the other Lebanese political and military factions and the United States.

In April, a month after my visit to Beirut, sixty-three people were killed by a bomb at the American embassy, and later a deadly explosion took the lives of two hundred and forty-one U.S. Marines in their barracks. These terrorist attacks, combined with the shooting down of American naval planes by militia in the hills surrounding Beirut, aroused strong political opposition to Reagan's policies from the Congress and from the American public. With an election year dawning, there was an abrupt reversal in American policy.

Early in February 1984, President Reagan condemned congressional calls for the withdrawal of the U.S. Marines, stating that he was not prepared to "surrender" and that he did not know of any of the multinational forces that were desirous of leaving. He added that if our troops were to be pulled out, it would leave Beirut under pressure from forces supported by the Soviets and would mean the end of Lebanon as a nation. It turned out that he had already authorized just such a withdrawal, which was officially announced three days later. The European peacekeeping forces left shortly thereafter. This was the first time since the Vietnam War that the Soviet Union and its allies had been able to block a major strategic move by the United States.

When the U.S. and European troops withdrew from Lebanon under pressure, it left Assad "king of the mountain," and the various Lebanese groups, including President Gemayel and the Maronite Christians, had to turn to Syria as the external catalyst that might bring them together. In March 1984, Gemayel was forced to announce that the Israeli-Lebanese withdrawal agreement was canceled, and Assad proclaimed that the Arabs had just won their most important victory over the United States.

For Lebanon, the process of negotiating, signing, and later abrogating the agreement may have been helpful. With internal dissension rampant and the presence of powerful external forces a constant threat, Lebanon was faced with the unsavory choice of disintegration or partition. No matter how favorably disposed the agreement was toward Israeli interests, the harnessing of American involvement had brought Lebanon some much-needed time and financial support. For about a year beginning in the spring of 1983, the Gemayel government had been given a welcome breathing spell from the pressure of its strong Syrian and Israeli neighbors. Also, the internal political discontent in Israel and Assad's effort in northern Lebanon to subvert Arafat's leadership of the PLO helped to divert both countries from more damaging action against their helpless neighbor.

Immediately thereafter, a government of national reconstruction was established, offering some faint hope that the physical and political barriers that divided Lebanon were breaking down. With his acquiescence to Assad's demands that the agreement with Israel be abrogated, Amin Gemayel's status and political influence in Lebanon were greatly strengthened, and Assad capitalized upon this opportunity to expand his relations among the inherently powerful Christian groups. At the same time, Walid Jumblatt and his Druze followers found they had lost strength because of their small numbers (only 6 percent of the population) and the less attractive role of their military prowess.

What do the Syrians want? First of all, stability within Lebanon, with a balanced government representing the different political and religious factions and adequately subservient to Syrian interests. Over time, the role of the Maronite Christians might be reduced and the Arab and Moslem nature of Lebanon enhanced. Assad considers the presence of Israeli troops in southern Lebanon a threat to Syria's security and an unwarranted encroachment on Lebanese sovereignty, and he will undoubtedly attempt to make their stay in Lebanon as costly as possible. If this effort is unsuccessful, then Assad is determined that Syria will be strong enough to hold its own position in Lebanon. He wants to prevent any major confrontation with Israel by the threat of high casualties on both sides and a possible exchange of long-range rocket fire that might include Jerusalem and other Israeli cities.

As far as the Palestinians are concerned, Assad considers himself their primary leader and protector, and now that Arafat and his loyal followers have been expelled from Syria and Lebanon, the Syrians will attempt to speak on behalf of the more militant Palestinians if others seek a separate accommodation with Israel or Jordan. Assad's claiming to be a champion of the Palestinian cause is compatible with his ambition to be at the focal point of the Arab world. Arafat and most other PLO leaders, of course, bitterly resent the Syrian effort to usurp their authority, and most other Arabs support the PLO desire for autonomy. There is no doubt, however, that with the failure of Israeli and American efforts in Lebanon, Syria's influence has been greatly expanded both in and far beyond Lebanon.

Israel has been severely damaged by the Lebanese war. Strong internal opposition was aroused because, for the first time, a major military action by its forces was not considered either a retaliatory strike or defensive in nature. More than six hundred Israeli troops have been killed in the invasion and occupation of southern Lebanon, and this commitment of forces has become more and more unpopular. Although the PLO has been definitely weakened and its attacks across Israel's border have been brought under control, the Shia Moslems who occupy most of southern Lebanon have been aroused against the Israeli occupying forces, and their previous welcome, when the Israelis brought stability to their villages, has turned into open opposition. There has been no general uprising against the strong and well-organized Israelis, but the Shias have been building many small cells of opposition within the area. These are difficult to detect and destroy, and they have been successful in their spasmodic attacks on the Israeli occupying forces. Also, a large number of Druzes who live in Israel and who had maintained a good relationship with the Israeli leaders feel that they have been somewhat betrayed by Israel's actions in Lebanon on behalf of the Maronites and against their fellow Druzes. However, this is not likely to be a serious or permanent problem for Israel.

The war and resulting occupation have been and are incurring heavy financial costs, and Israel now has the additional responsibility of ruling over more than a half million Arabs who live within the occupied area south of the Awali River in Lebanon.

Prime Ministers Begin and Shamir swore not to withdraw from
Lebanon until Syria agreed to do the same. Prime Minister Peres
has promised to remove the occupation forces as soon as Israel's
northern border can be secured from attack, and Israeli-Lebanese
troop withdrawal talks began again in November 1984. However,
preventing harassment across the border from Lebanon will be
difficult to guarantee without full support from the Syrians, and
Assad will not be in any hurry to give his assistance. He is satisfied to keep his own troops in the central and northern portions of
the country, and he can probably afford to sit back and wait for
political pressures in Jerusalem to bring about the withdrawal of
Israeli troops by the new National Unity government without his
having to contribute much to the process. At the same time, as in
the pre-invasion period, Assad will probably do what he can to
constrain any Lebanese or Palestinian attacks across Israel's border. He would undoubtedly prefer the complete absence of Israel's forces from Lebanon, because if a Syrian-Israeli war comes,
this advanced placement of enemy troops at the Awali River
would not be attractive.

Israel appears to be in a no-win situation. The Shia in the south
dislike any external occupying forces in their ancestral homeland,
but would probably not be able to prevent reinfiltration of the
PLO if the Israelis withdraw without adequate security arrangements. This would open up the possibility of renewed harassment
of communities in the northern part of Israel and set the stage for
another Israeli invasion. Ultimately, previous invasions will have
accomplished little or nothing. The answer to this dilemma lies in
the Palestinian question by making progress in the West Bank,
thereby defusing Palestinian opposition to Israel as a reality.

Lebanon has proven to be remarkably resilient in the past,
even in the most difficult circumstances. Lebanese spokesmen
ask, "How many other countries could survive with nine years of
war, more than a hundred thousand dead, a million displaced
and homeless, and three fourths of its soil occupied by three powerful external forces?" They profess satisfaction with their basic
system of government and see no reasonable alternative other
than some fine tuning. It does not have to be based on a "one
man, one vote" principle; the smallest unit is not the individual

but the community, and the Lebanese feel that the religious and ethnic communities must be preserved. No one accepts the notion of partition, which is sometimes contemplated by their powerful neighbors, Syria and Israel, or by others more distant who simply cannot believe that Lebanon can continue to survive as one political entity.

What does Lebanon want? Although the Lebanese have not been able to defend themselves because of their weak and fragmented military structure, at the same time they have never been feared as potential aggressors. Some dream of their country as a Holland or Switzerland in the Middle East, neither involved in conflict nor a staging area for other combatants and benefiting from good relations with all other nations. They want undisputed sovereignty over their own land, security, stability and justice based on internal consensus, and prosperity, which they are sure will follow. They realize that their own country must be unified before its sovereignty can be respected and that the more secure Israel and Syria are, the more secure Lebanon will be. Of course, the Lebanese want both nations to withdraw from their soil, but there is a difference. The Israeli occupation is looked upon as part of the overall dispute between the Arabs and the Jews, whereas the Syrian presence is considered purely an Arab question, to be resolved after other forces are out. On one point the Lebanese are agreed: they do not want the Palestinians to return to their country.

The world has learned some lessons, and future events might be shaped by what has recently occurred in Lebanon. The weakness and fragmentation of the Arab world was vividly demonstrated when Israel's advance into Beirut was relatively unopposed. Accordingly, the need for Egypt's return to the Arab fold was recognized even by some of those Arab leaders who had been most abusive following Sadat's move toward peace with Israel. The military might of Israel still seems unquestioned, but the effective use of this powerful force to shape events in the Middle East has been proven quite doubtful. American influence in the region plummeted with its ill-fated military adventure in Lebanon, while the Soviets ultimately strengthened themselves in Syria and were exploring every opportunity to fill the vacuum in

American relationships with other Arab nations. The military strength of the PLO was destroyed and its forces were scattered throughout many nations, but Arafat somehow landed on his political feet with another of his nine lives, ready to restore his influence and use it in some new and unpredictable fashion. The Begin-Shamir-Sharon political hold on Israel has been weakened, but perhaps only temporarily, and new opportunities for peace might now be explored with a new Israeli government.

To the relief of many, Lebanon is no longer on center stage, and the light of world attention can now be focused on another spot — probably still in the Middle East. Most of the players will still be performing in the same drama, but it has yet to be determined whether the next act will bring tranquillity or more bloodshed.

# The Palestinians

THE BORDERS OF PALESTINE, also called the Land of Canaan or the Holy Land, have never been clearly defined. The name Palestine is an ancient one, derived from the Philistines who lived there. Known as People of the Sea, they inhabited lands primarily on the seacoast of what is now southern Israel and the Gaza Strip. The Bible does not give a very attractive picture of these people, because they did not worship God and because they competed with the authors of the scriptures for control over Canaan. When the Israelites had a Samson or a King David to lead them, the Philistines were sometimes defeated, but against most other leaders they were able to triumph and to enlarge their territories.

The Roman conquerors, wanting to obliterate both the capital and the name of the Israelites after they smashed the final Jewish revolt, chose to call the southern part of their new Syrian province Palaestina. The name was generally accepted, even though the borders of the region fluctuated through the centuries.

At the conclusion of World War I, the League of Nations assigned to Great Britain the supervision of the Mandate of Palestine, which encompassed the lands of modern Israel, the West Bank, Gaza, and Jordan. In 1922, Jordan was separated from the Mandate, and the remaining territory between the Jordan River and the Mediterranean Sea now constitutes what is known as Palestine.

Logically, therefore, "Palestinian" would mean all those who live or have citizenship in the area. However, not much is logical in dealing with the Holy Land. Before the creation of the State of Israel, the Jews of Palestine were called Palestinian Jews, but afterward they became Israelis. Those Palestinian Arabs who did not choose to accept the new state and live in it as citizens continue to call themselves Palestinians. Our definition will include only Arabs and their descendants, both Moslem and Christian, who have lived in the area and who still claim Palestine as their home.

Of the four million Palestinians scattered throughout many nations, more than half now live under Israeli administration — either in Israel as citizens (about 650,000) or in the West Bank and Gaza under the occupation (approximately 1,370,000). The Arab population in Palestine is growing at a rate of about 2½ percent annually. An additional large number is in the area occupied by Israeli forces in the southern part of Lebanon.

When Britain conducted a census in Palestine in 1922, there were about 84,000 Jews and 670,000 Arabs, of whom 71,000 were Christians. By the time the area was partitioned by the United Nations in 1947, these numbers had grown to about 600,000 Jews and 1,300,000 Arabs, 10 percent of whom were Christians. Duing the 1948 war, when Israel affirmed its status as an independent state, about 60 percent of the Palestinians in the territory that became Israel were expelled or fled from their homes.

The United Nations estimated that when the 1967 war began, there were 1.3 million of these refugees, with one fourth in Jordan, about 150,000 each in Lebanon and Syria, and most of the others in the West Bank and Gaza refugee camps. As a result of that war, 320,000 more Syrians, Egyptians, Jordanians, and Palestinians had been forced to leave the additional areas then occupied by Israel. Most of them were unemployable, knowing only how to farm and tend herds, and more than half were in refugee camps. A number of U.N. resolutions were passed (some with U.S. sponsorship and even Israeli support), urging that the more needy and deserving refugees be repatriated, but only a few were ever permitted to return to their homes.

The Palestinians and individual Arab leaders expressed their concern about the increasing Israeli encroachment on the lands and rights of the Arabs. However, it was not until the announcement of Israel's plans to divert water from the Sea of Galilee and the Jordan River to irrigate western Israel and the Negev desert that the first summit meeting of Arab leaders took place early in 1964, called by President Nasser of Egypt. Nasser knew that military action could not prevent the diversion of the water, but the more militant Arab leaders demanded that something be done. In June 1964, the Palestine Liberation Organization was formally organized, with its own military force, to represent the Palestinian people.

After the 1967 war, the PLO was greatly strengthened by a surge of nationalist sentiment among those whose lands had been taken by the Israelis. In order to provide a more unified and common front, Arab leaders and some competing groups of Palestinians quickly acknowledged the preeminence of the PLO. The Palestine National Council became the equivalent of its parliament, later creating a Central Committee and an Executive Committee whose members could act as a cabinet in dealing with matters like welfare, education, information, health, and the military.

In 1969 the PLO found a strong leader in Yasir Arafat, a well-educated Palestinian who was the founder and head of al-Fatah, a guerrilla organization that was orchestrating attacks on Israel from Syria. After he was chosen as chairman of the Central Committee and the PLO, Arafat was able to constrain some of the more radical terrorist groups among the Palestinians, and he turned much of his attention to raising funds for the care and support of the refugees and arousing worldwide support for the Palestinian cause. With this more effective voice, the Palestinians were quickly successful in these efforts. The PLO has been able to establish diplomatic missions in more than a hundred countries and has used its observer status in the United Nations to become one of the most powerful voices in international councils.

The next exodus of Palestinians was not from Israel but from Jordan in 1970, a result of the civil war between Palestinian militants and the Jordanian regular forces. When King Hussein's troops prevailed, the new flood of refugees had only one place to

go: Lebanon. There the Palestinians had a host country that, unlike Egypt and Syria, was not strong enough to reject them and
where the PLO was able to evolve a governmental organization
and even an independent militia. Its forces were free to strike
across the border against Israel, and in much of Lebanon they
were soon powerful enough to challenge the sovereignty of the
Lebanese government.

Lebanon has been most adversely affected by the presence of
large numbers of Palestinians. Each of the guerrilla raids on Israel brought swift retaliation, and much of the punishment from
bombing attacks fell on the Lebanese civilian population, which
increasingly resented their troublesome guests. By forming alli-
ances with the Sunni Moslems and some of the more radical
groups in Lebanon, the Palestinians and their allies gained increasing control over the country, and there were repeated skirmishes as the struggle for authority and power continued. In
response, the Maronite Christians built up their militia to meet
the challenge but proved unequal to the task. The country became ever more weakened and divided within itself, and in 1975 a
destructive civil war erupted. The next year, in June 1976, Syrian
forces moved in to restore order. Eventually the Syrians helped
work out an agreement to limit the PLO militia to prescribed locations and to restrict guerrilla attacks against Israel.

In dealing with conflict and the prospects for peace in the Middle
East, there is no way to escape the realization of how intimately
intertwined are the history, the aspirations, and the fate of two
long-suffering peoples, the Jews and the Palestinian Arabs.

In simplest terms, the Arab-Israeli conflict is a struggle between
two national identities for control of territory, but there are also
historic, religious, strategic, political, and psychological issues
that color the confrontation and retard its amicable solution.
What each wants is no less than recognition, acceptance, independence, sovereignty, and territorial identity. Neither officially
recognizes the other's existence, so any testing of intentions must
be done through uncertain intermediaries. Both seek worldwide
approval and financial, moral, and logistical support from external allies and from one of the superpowers. Each side fears total
destruction or complete denial by the other, this worry being fed

by a history of violence and hatred, during which each tried to delegitimize the other while propounding vigorously the unique and exclusive merits of its own cause.

From A.D. 135, when the Roman Emperor Hadrian completed the suppression of the Jewish revolt in Palestine, slaughtering and scattering the population, the pain of the Diaspora compounded by intense racial persecution has been an ever-present motivation for the Jews to return to their biblical home and to create the State of Israel as a refuge. For Jews, Israel has been the fulfillment of biblical prophecy and the culmination of a dream to establish and live under a government of their own choice.

The Palestinians are suffering from similar circumstances of homelessness, scattered as they are throughout many nations, and their desire for self-determination and their own national homeland has also aroused strong worldwide support. The Palestinians, like the Jews, claim to be driven by religious conviction based on the promises of God, and they consider themselves to have comprised the admixture of all peoples including the ancient Hebrews who dwelt in Palestine, their homeland, since earliest biblical times.

Over the years, both Moslem and Christian Palestinians have suffered from isolation and neglect at the hands of their own Arab brethren and now insist that, through no fault of their own, they are being forced to give up more and more of their ancestral land to make way for the expanding Jewish sanctuary of Israel. While maintaining the legal and moral claim on their homeland, those who remain in Palestine — specifically in the West Bank and Gaza — have had to choose between moving into exile or continuing to live under military rule. Their sense of frustration and despair is increased by their relative impotence in redressing these grievances. They are obsessed with the dream of someday living under a government of their own choice.

Despite — or perhaps because of — these vivid similarities of ancient and recent history, Israelis and Palestinians generally scorn and despise each other and usually deny that there is any parallel between their circumstances. It is as though to recognize in any way the legitimacy of their adversary's case would mean the weakening of their own.

However, each group has taken a starkly different approach to redressing its grievances, and the results have no similarity. Without ever abandoning their most ambitious goals of a uniquely Jewish nation, with boundaries similar to those in the time of King David and surrounded by acquiescent and peaceful neighbors, the Jews have been willing to pursue them in incremental steps, even compromising for a while when necessary, and have made great progress. The Palestinians, on the other hand, have habitually refused to compromise and have remained bound by the consensus position of "all or nothing." In balance, they have achieved little except sympathy and limited support in world councils and from other Arabs. Their only tangible accomplishment is the formation of the PLO, a form of government in exile. This helps to explain the almost unanimous public support among Palestinians for the PLO and its goals and purposes.

There are three basic views about a possible reconciliation between the Jews and the Palestinians. One is that the Palestinian question is the core of Arab-Israeli hostility, and with some form of parity and self-determination for the Palestinians, the conflict will begin to evaporate as the Arab world accepts Israel's political reality. Another view is that following a solution to the broader Arab-Israeli dispute, including the unequivocal acceptance of Israel's existence by a major portion of the Arab world, the Palestinian element of the conflict will be more easily solved. The gloomiest, most pessimistic view is expressed by those who say that no permanent peace can come to the Middle East so long as a Jewish state exists in the heartland of an Arab world or, on the other hand, that granting any element of self-determination to the Palestinians will inevitably be the first step toward the destruction of Israel.

It is simply impossible for others to comprehend fully the intensity of feeling and commitment among these two peoples about their present and past suffering and their determination to end it or avoid its recurrence in the future. We can only explore every possibility for a better understanding among the people who now live in all of Palestine and those who nurture them from outside because of shared experiences or commitments. Partially and with some ambiguity, we tried to address these basic questions at Camp David, but no Palestinians were willing to negotiate on our terms and the promises in the agreement concerning Palestinian rights were never pursued by the Israeli leaders.

On my first visit to the Middle East after leaving the White House, in 1983, I was well acquainted with most of the national leaders. However, I also wanted to know more about the Palestinian people — how they were living, their foremost concerns, how they reacted to existence under a prolonged military occupation, and what they might propose as a peaceful solution. In Cairo, Amman, Riyadh, and Damascus I listened mostly to Palestinian leaders explain their varied perspectives on the Middle East conflict as it related to them and the refugees for whom they claimed responsibility.

The first morning we were in Jerusalem, I had a taste of what I would learn in the occupied territories. As usual, I got up quite early. As I was about to jog around the old city, accompanied by one of the American Secret Service agents, two young Israeli soldiers joined us and said they would lead the way. We proceeded from the King David Hotel to the Jaffa Gate, then turned north around the outside of the ancient walls. As we were running east alongside the Jericho road, I saw a group of elderly Arab men sitting by the curb, reading their newspapers. The sidewalk was almost empty and wide enough for us to pass easily, but one of the soldiers cut to the right and knocked all of the newspapers back into the faces of the startled readers as he ran by. Some of the papers fluttered to the ground. I stopped to apologize to the men, but they could not understand me. Then I told the soldiers either to let me run alone or not to touch anyone else in a belligerent manner. They reluctantly agreed, but added that one could never tell what was being hidden behind newspapers.

In the West Bank and Gaza, I spent some time with Palestinians in all walks of life in both large and small communities and in the rural areas. Again, most were leaders: one was the incumbent Christian mayor of Bethlehem, one a deposed municipal elder living in Gaza and still the undisputed spokesman among his own people. A few were lawyers who were active in defending the rights of their neighbors in the Israeli military tribunals, two or three had been elected to public office in 1976 and were now living in forced exile in Jordan, some were professors in major universities, and quite a number were farmers or villagers who wanted to describe their circumscribed life in the occupied territories.

Most of the Palestinians were Moslems but a surprising number were Christians, and I talked with several priests and pastors about their ministry. They claimed they were increasingly disturbed by the violence around them, and one priest said he and his parishioners had recently been frightened by a "Jewish terrorist group" who had planted a bomb in their chapel. It had been discovered before it could explode. One of the most interesting was a young Christian who was attempting to convince his fellow Palestinians of the advantages of nonviolent resistance, believing that the tactics of Mahatma Gandhi and Martin Luther King, Jr., would be best for his people. He said he had been holding training sessions in some West Bank villages, closely monitored by the Israeli authorities, and he gave me an English-language version of his well-written text.

On the way from Jerusalem to Gaza, I learned about another facet of life among the Palestinians when I was asked by the Israeli authorities to stop at a model Palestinian community to observe the progress being made in the area. Here I was offered a chance to meet with the mayor and the city council so I could ask about how the town was governed. At the beginning I was somewhat confused about who was in charge, but I soon realized that the most outspoken man in the council chambers was the Israeli representative in the "village league." It was obvious that this Palestinian had substantial authority but was something of a pariah in the group, and it was only after some heated exchanges among the assembled village leaders that I began to understand the situation.

It was explained to me that Moshe Dayan, the Israeli defense minister who established policies of governance in the occupied areas after the 1967 war, had decreed that the Arabs must rule themselves as much as possible and that there should be no imposition of an Israeli administration. Most Palestinian affairs were then handled by moderate and respected non-PLO mayors who had been chosen under Jordanian rule or in the 1972 municipal elections. In 1976, free elections were again permitted by the Israelis; PLO candidates decided to participate, and they were elected in a number of municipalities.

In 1980–1981, the Israeli military assumed almost complete control, cracked down on the elected officials, and later set up a civilian administration of its own. An attempt was made to establish a new political elite among the Palestinians by granting special authority and patronage to those amenable to Israeli direction, but these anointed representatives in the village leagues seemed to be scorned by most of their Arab neighbors as quislings.

With the exception of those Arabs who were selected by the authorities to handle some of the bureaucratic duties and dispense political patronage, the Palestinians with whom I met were either members or strong supporters of the PLO, and they deeply resented what they considered severe repression by the military authorities. Most addressed the issue with determination and an element of hope, but some seemed depressed and resigned to their fate. Only rarely did anyone directly criticize the PLO, but one Palestinian attorney did complain that "Arafat and other PLO leaders are more concerned with struggles for political power and the raising and spending of money than with the plight of Palestinians living under the military occupation."

However, the primary condemnation by these people — like that of many Arabs outside the occupied territories — was directed almost equally at Israel and the United States. They denounced our country for financing the Israeli settlements in the occupied territories and for supporting military actions against the Arab countries; they were particularly bitter about our refusal to recognize the Palestinian people or to provide a forum for the resolution of their problems. The pledge our country had made to Israel not to recognize or negotiate with the PLO until it recognized the right of Israel to exist was ridiculed as an illogical and counterproductive political mistake.

Our meetings in the West Bank and Gaza were in various places: private homes, municipal offices, hospitals, vacant classrooms, the backs of shops or stores, and churches and monasteries. In almost every case, those who had agreed to meet with me had arranged to have a few family members or friends present.

At first there would be considerable reticence about broaching any subject that was sharply focused or controversial. We would sip black coffee, tea, or Coke and nibble on sugary candy or cookies, talking about the weather or my general impressions of the area. Slowly the constraints would be dropped and a more lively discussion would develop, often with all the bystanders participating. The Palestinians would often argue with each other, and sometimes even the children would join in. In the larger meetings, usually several people could speak both English and Arabic, and they would sometimes compete with one another in translating for the others.

We also invited a few groups to the American consulate in Jerusalem. These sessions were more formal but no less revealing. The participants presented their views as lawyers would write a brief: carefully, constructively, conclusively — sometimes even with documents to prove their case.

In all the meetings, I tried to present my own views about the need for an end to violence, better communication between the Palestinians and the Israelis and the people of the United States, and support for the peace effort, which had run into an apparent dead end. My description of the Camp David agreements and the Reagan statement as they related to the Palestinians seemed to be news to many of them, and it was obvious that their acceptance of any of these proposals would depend heavily on the PLO's interpretation. I outlined the specific potential benefits for them if such efforts could succeed and urged their support of King Hussein in his then-pending decision about joining the peace talks on behalf of Jordan and the Palestinians. They expressed some hope that Arafat would approve.

These kinds of general issues made up a minor portion of the discussions; what the Palestinians wanted was to catalogue their specific grievances against Israel. Accompanied by American diplomatic officials, who had arranged many of the meetings, most of the time I sat quietly and listened to their complaints.

The Palestinian leaders emphasized that for a generation their people had been deprived of basic human rights. They could not vote, assemble peacefully, choose their own leaders, travel without restrictions, or own property without fear of its being confiscated by a multitude of inexplicable legal ruses. As a people, they were branded by Israeli officials as terrorists, and even minor demonstrations of their displeasure brought the most severe punishment from the military authorities. They claimed that they were arrested and held without trial for extended periods of time, that some of their people were tortured in attempts to force confessions, that their trials were often held with their accusers acting as judges, that their own lawyers were not permitted to defend them in the Israeli courts, and that any appeals were costly, long delayed, and fruitless.

On one occasion I argued with them about their refusal to take the strongest test cases to the Israeli Supreme Court, and I tried to assure the group that they would get a fair hearing and perhaps set a precedent that would be beneficial in many similar cases.

The religious leaders and municipal officials only shrugged hopelessly, but one of the attorneys spoke strongly: "At great expense we have tried this. It just does not work. It is not like the American system, where one ruling in the top courts is followed closely by all the subordinate courts. Here there is one system under civil judges and another under the military. Most of our cases, no matter what the subject might be, fall under the military. They are our accusers, judges, and juries, and they all seem the same to us. When a rare decision is made in our favor, to protect a small parcel of our land, for instance, it is not looked on as a precedent. By administrative decision or decree, a new procedure is born to accomplish the same Israeli goals in a different fashion. Besides," he added, "we cannot take our client's case out of the West Bank into an Israeli court. We are not permitted to practice there."

I asked, "Then why don't you employ an Israeli lawyer?"

He responded, "Sometimes we do, but few of them will take our cases. Those who will are heavily overworked with their own Arab clients who live in Israel. One or two members of the Knesset have tried to be helpful — mostly the communist members."

The Palestinians were convinced that some of the Israeli political leaders were trying through subtle harassment to force another exodus of Moslems and Christians from the occupied territories. They claimed that oranges and other perishable farm products were not permitted to be sold in Israel if they competed with Israeli produce, and so they had to be given away, dumped, or exported to Jordan. The oranges and vegetables of one of the more activist families were sometimes held at the Allenby Bridge, they said, until they spoiled. In some areas the farmers were not permitted to replace the fruit trees that died in their orchards.

Their schools and universities were frequently closed down; educators were arrested, bookstores padlocked, library books censored, and the students, their children, left on the streets or at home for extended periods of time without jobs. They said that any serious altercation between these idle and angry young people and the military authorities could result in the sending of bull-dozers into the community to destroy the family home. Predictably, the Palestinians professed to deplore all acts of terrorism and claimed that Israeli settlers were as guilty as any Arabs in initiating violence but were seldom if ever arrested or punished.

Their most bitter complaint was that foreign aid from Arab countries and even funds sent by the American government for benevolent purposes were intercepted by the authorities and used for the benefit of the Israelis, including the construction of settlements for Jews in Palestinian communities. They claimed that the government had seized U.S. AID funds intended for a center for retarded children in Gaza and that Jordanian and other Arab money intended for education and the development of a poultry industry in some of the poorer communities in the West Bank was being withheld.

I was deeply disturbed by these reports. I wanted to determine if they were accurate and, if so, to hear an explanation from the authorities. Before leaving Israel, I met at length with our own diplomatic officials in the U.S. consulate in Jerusalem and with Israelis who specialized in the occupied territories. I also spent time with a member of the Israeli Supreme Court discussing the legal aspect of these allegations. No one denied that most of the reports were true, but the Israelis maintained that many of them were exaggerated and that there were justifications for others.

From the Israeli point of view, life under a military occupation was inevitably going to be different from that in a free democracy, and severe restrictions were considered necessary to prevent the breeding of a revolution and to minimize acts of violence. Old laws left over from the British occupation formed the basis for holding prisoners without official accusation or trial. The Israeli officials added that there were not many of these cases and that a repeal of such laws was being considered by the Knesset.

As far as the harassment of activists was concerned, I was told that there were often extended delays at the Allenby Bridge, on the border of Jordan, but these were not designed to punish anyone; this was just the inevitable result of bureaucratic confusion in travel between two countries that did not have normal trade or diplomatic relations. It was true that Israeli farm products had first priority in the markets of Tel Aviv and Jerusalem.

Although the American officials had heard the same complaints of militant attacks on Moslem and Christian Arabs, the Israelis insisted that Jewish acts of terrorism were unknown; the Palestinians were undoubtedly speaking of brief clashes between Arabs and Jewish settlers near some of the rural communities. They said that the destruction of an Arab home with dynamite or bulldozers was a rare, deliberate, and highly publicized event, designed to serve as an effective deterrent to adults who might permit or encourage illegal acts by children in the Palestinian families.

Most of the Israeli responses were frank, and we had extensive discussions about each of the Palestinian complaints. The one exception was the interception of foreign aid money by the Israelis. The claim was made that some confiscated funds might have been earmarked to finance acts of Arab terrorism and that the Israelis' control over the Arab communities must be sufficient to prevent abuses that might threaten the peace. There was also some comment about surplus agricultural goods being produced in the West Bank and Gaza that might damage the entire Israeli farm economy. It did not make sense for foreign money to be used to increase the production of some goods, like chickens or oranges. I was told that some AID funds appropriated by the U.S. Congress were kept by the Israeli government when necessary to prevent abuse, but the Israelis claimed that the withheld money was not used to build Israeli settlements in the occupied territory.

The Israelis told me that in every instance there was a legal basis for the taking of land — or it was needed for security purposes. In some key cases, "administrative definitions" had served to circumvent or modify legal decisions. Later, I received a detailed briefing from Meron Benvenisti, an Israeli who had served as deputy mayor of Jerusalem and who was devoting his full time to a definitive analysis of Israel's policies in the occupied territories.

With maps and charts, he explained that the Israelis acquired Palestinian lands in a number of different ways: by direct purchase; through seizure "for security purposes for the duration of the occupation"; by claiming state control of areas formerly held by the Jordanian government; by "taking" under some carefully selected Arabic customs or ancient laws; and by claiming as state land all that was not cultivated or specifically registered as owned by a Palestinian family. Since cultivation or use for farming is one of the criteria for claiming state land, it became official policy in 1983 to prohibit, under penalty of imprisonment, any grazing or the planting of trees or crops in these areas by Palestinians. This was apparently the source of some of the complaints I had heard.

No legal cases concerning these land matters were permitted in the Palestinian courts; they now had to be decided by the Israeli civil governor. Since 1977, when the Likud party gained control of the government, the efforts to take Arab land had been greatly accelerated, and the building of Jewish settlements in the West Bank had become one of Israel's top priorities. Benvenisti added that in spite of all these efforts, there were still only 27,000 Israeli settlers in the West Bank, but that the policies established and the present trends meant that the annexation of the occupied areas was probably a foregone conclusion.

It was true that the Palestinian lawyers were not permitted to practice in the Israeli courts, where most of the land issues were resolved, but I was assured that Israeli lawyers were available to represent the Palestinians. Most frequently, one of the more radical members of the Knesset was cited as an example.

I asked an Israeli Supreme Court justice if he considered the treatment of the Palestinians fair; he said that he dealt fairly with every case brought before him in the high court, but he did not have the power to initiate legal action. I then requested his own personal assessment of the situation in the West Bank and Gaza. He replied that he had not been in the area for more than four years and had no plans to visit there. I told him that if he was to make decisions that affected the lives of people in the occupied areas, he should know more about how they lived. He said with a smile, "I am a judge, not an investigator."

Even the more quiescent Palestinians believed that militants would inevitably become more active on both sides, and during the months since my visit the level of violence has been steadily increasing in the occupied territories, as settlements have expanded and Jews and Arabs have come into closer contact. Israeli officials have discovered and moved forcefully against Jewish terrorist organizations in the area, arresting a number of people and making public some of the evidence and the names of the accused persons.

When I visited with Palestinian leaders outside Israel and the occupied territories — in Egypt, Jordan, Syria, Saudi Arabia, and the United States — I found a completely different community of people. Their attitudes and commitments had been shaped by earlier events, and nowadays they had little if any contact with either the Jews or Arabs who still lived in Palestine. Many of these spokesmen had been driven quite early, in 1948, from what they still consider to be their homes, and they publicly claim the right to use any means at their disposal, including armed struggle, to regain their lost rights.

They spoke more freely and in even more vituperative terms about Israeli policies and concentrated on the long-range goals of the PLO. They rarely mentioned the plight of their brothers in the West Bank and Gaza. Their statements were cast more in the form of academic or political debates and made it clear why the Israelis consider them mortal enemies and why the differences between Israel and the PLO spokesmen seem irreconcilable.

The PLO leaders were just as interested in the "liberation" of communities in Israel proper as of those in the West Bank and Gaza. As one of them said publicly, "We were not established in 1964 in order to liberate Hebron, Nablus, and Gaza, for these were already liberated, but rather we were established to liberate Jaffa, Haifa, Ramla, and the Negev." George Habash, the leader of the Popular Front for the Liberation of Palestine, said in a news interview, "We will accept part of Palestine in the beginning, but under no circumstances will we agree to stop there. We will fight until we take every last corner of it." These militant spokesmen consider it a moral obligation of the Arab world and all who believe in the justice of the Palestinian cause and the rights of the Palestinian people to deny at every step Israel's attempt at acceptance and recognition by the world community.

Yasir Arafat has generally taken a more moderate line, claiming: "The PLO has never advocated the annihilation of Israel. The Zionists started the 'drive the Jews into the sea' slogan and attributed it to the PLO. In 1969 we said we want to establish a democratic state where Jews, Christians, and Muslims can live all together. The Zionists said they do not choose to live with any people other than Jews. . . . We said to the Zionist Jews, all right, if you do not want a secular, democratic state for all of us, then we will take another route. In 1974 I said we are ready to establish our independent state in any part from which Israel will withdraw." There are obviously many differences among the voices coming from the PLO, and listeners interpret the words to suit their own ends.

Those still in Palestine had quite different goals and attitudes. They were seeking the basic human rights of freedom of expression, equal treatment under the law, an end to military rule, ownership of property without its being taken, and the right of self-determination. They wanted to choose their own community leaders and to control their own affairs. Seldom did they mention a Palestinian state in their conversations with me and never the end of Israel's existence as a nation. Quite practical, they favored negotiations with the Israelis as a way to redress their grievances. Most were willing for either the Jordanians or the PLO to negotiate on their behalf, but they would accept the PLO decision as the binding answer to this question. The Palestinians in the occupied territories are still a potential bridge between the Israelis with whom they live and their brethren in Arab countries.

Few PLO leaders show an inclination to relinquish to King

Hussein any portion of their influence or control over Palestinians in Israel or the occupied territories. They consider the PLO the unquestioned instrument to attain the usurped national rights of Palestinian people everywhere and do not even bother to defend the legitimacy of their organization or its actions.

When I inquired about the purposes of the PLO, they seemed somewhat taken aback that I needed to ask such a question, then gave me a pamphlet that stated: "The Palestine Liberation Organization (PLO) is the national liberation movement of the Palestinian people. It is the institutional expression of Palestinian nationhood.... The PLO is to the Palestinian people what other national liberation movements have been to other nations. It is their means to reassert and reaffirm a denied national identity, to recover a suppressed history, to safeguard a popular heritage, to rebuild demolished institutions, to maintain national unity threatened by physical dispersion, and to struggle for usurped homeland and denied national rights. In brief, the PLO is the Palestinian people's quest to resurrect their national existence." It is interesting how many times "national" appears in this short statement.

The PLO is a loosely associated umbrella organization bound together by common goals, but it comprises many groups eager to use diverse means to reach these goals. One of its main goals, with which it has had notable success, has been to gain allies and support from other governments. Each of the many U.N. resolutions supporting Palestinians is cherished as another element of the proof of their effectiveness and of the rightness of their cause. They refuse to forgo violence as a means to their ends and will agree to curtail it completely only to enhance their international reputation *after* a satisfactory agreement with Israel has been reached. Most PLO members have no intention of recognizing Israel's right to exist unless it is willing to grant equal rights to the Palestinians, and they insist that all U.N. resolutions dealing with the Middle East, many of which are highly favorable to the Palestinian cause, must be accepted by the Israelis if the Palestinians are to embrace Resolutions 242 and 338.

The Palestinian leaders are convinced that all the Arab-Israeli wars have boiled up out of the Palestinian problem — in 1948,

1956, 1967, 1973, and the Lebanese invasions of 1978 and 1982 — and, of course, the civil wars of 1970 in Jordan and 1975 in Lebanon. They see the major toehold of the Soviets among the Arabs as directly attributable to the Arabs' reaction against American attitudes on the Palestinian issue. They also predict that if the Israeli-Egyptian peace agreement breaks down or if a confrontation evolves between the superpowers, the same issue will be the cause. With a single-mindedness amounting to tunnel vision, they see the restoration of Palestinian rights as the key to regional and, under some circumstances, even world peace.

Yet even taking all these sobering facts into consideration, there have been some encouraging trends in recent years. There is less rigidity on both sides than there was a decade ago, with a growing recognition in the Arab world that Israel is a reality and an awareness among more Israelis that a solution to the Palestinian question is critical if there is ever to be a comprehensive settlement of the conflict. Furthermore, there are proposals evolving from U.N. Resolution 242 that have some common elements and that also more clearly delineate the differences that still remain.

Palestinians and other Arabs maintain that the Fez statement of 1982 (Appendix 6) is a public acknowledgment of Israel's right to exist and shows a willingness to work out through a transitional period some of the differences that have so far not been addressed directly. The Delphic wording of this statement was deliberate, in Arabic as well as in Hebrew and English. Although its deeper meaning is almost indecipherable by most Western analysts, the Arabs defend it by saying it is there to be explored by the Israelis and others and that, in any case, it is more positive and clear than anything now coming from Tel Aviv or Jerusalem.

Among Americans, however, there is still an unresolved quandary for those who are searching for solutions through negotiation. The realities are:

• The Palestinian issue is a basic cause of the continuing Middle East conflict, and it must be addressed successfully if there is ever to be peace in the region.

• The PLO, with Yasir Arafat as its elected leader, is the entity responsible for the political future of the Palestinians and for negotiations to secure their rights; no one else can assume these functions without specific authorization from the PLO.

- In order to find peace with justice in the Middle East, the United States must play a major role, but, in honoring a commitment made to Israel in 1975, American officials are pledged not to recognize or negotiate with the PLO until it recognizes Israel's right to exist and acknowledges the applicability of U.N. Resolution 242 in resolving the differences in the Middle East.

- The PLO sees U.N. Resolution 242 as seriously defective because its only passing reference to the Palestinians is the word "refugees," while many other resolutions of the U.N. cover the issue much more definitively and are not supported by Israel. Furthermore, to recognize Israel in a unilateral and unreciprocated act would be playing a major political card that would be needed in future negotiations to bargain for their own fate.

It is obvious that in seeking understanding, the Palestinians' greatest failure is in Israel and the United States, among the very people who may well hold the key to their future. Their willingness to resort to terrorist acts, their refusal to make any clear acknowledgment of Israel's right to exist in harmony with its neighbors, their reluctance to permit King Hussein or other representatives to explore opportunities for peace and the assuaging of grievances, and their uncompromising demands that are patently unacceptable to Israel and its supporters have all served to prevent the official recognition of their leaders and the marshaling of further backing for their cause.

During the Israeli invasion of Lebanon in 1982, Arab support for the Palestinians proved to be almost nonexistent or tenuous at best, and a perpetuation of the present stalemate might well make the Arab leaders lose interest in the cause. Another problem is that the scattering and forced relocation of the Palestinians from Lebanon has created a greater physical distance between them and their homeland. The PLO is no longer operating effectively in any area contiguous to Israel. The West Bank and the Gaza Strip, the Golan Heights, and southern Lebanon are under Israeli control, and Jordan and Syria have refused free use of their territory against Israel.

However, in a strange way, the political prestige of the PLO sometimes seems to increase in inverse proportion to its military defeats. After losing its effort to use Jordan as a base of operations against Israel in 1970–71, the PLO rebounded as the exclusive leader of the Palestinian people, with a strong base of operations in Lebanon. After Camp David and the Israeli-Egyptian peace treaty removed Egypt as a major supporter, the PLO seemed to gain new life as other irate Arabs renewed their commitment to the cause. The crushing blows of the Israeli military force in Lebanon in 1982 resulted in the exodus of PLO troops from Beirut, but the PLO again emerged as the sole remaining political symbol for Palestinian self-determination. A little more than a year later, in December 1983, Syrian-supported defectors forced a second evacuation of the PLO militia from northern Lebanon, but again Arafat and his forces were able to survive and to begin rebuilding their political strength. Almost immediately, for instance, the resilient Palestinian leader went to Egypt to repair damaged relations with President Hosni Mubarak. Most recently, in November 1984, the Palestine National Council met in Amman (the same Arab capital that was the scene of Jordanian-Palestinian bloodshed fourteen years earlier). Both events were considered highly significant in the reconciliation of Jordan, Egypt, and the PLO.

The PLO now seems to be pursuing these basic goals:

• Independent authority free from domination by any single Arab power.

• Cohesion within the organization.

• Acceptance as the sole representative of the Palestinian people.

• The maintenance of an uncompromising commitment to liberate as much of Palestine as possible.

• No clear recognition of Israel's right to exist.

• The reestablishment of Arab unity, which involves bringing Egypt back into the Arab fold.

• Increasing support from other peoples for the PLO and its members.

But a large and unresolved question is whether the Palestinians can for very much longer continue their policy of complete rejection of Israel and their demand for total restoration of their homeland with any hope of eventual success. It is much more likely that the PLO is going down a dead end, that the world and even its Arab supporters will tire of actively supporting the Palestinian cause and slowly let it fade into the background. Martin Luther King, Jr., once said that nothing would hurt the black cause in America more than for whites simply to grow bored with it. Nor is the willingness to resort to violence or the threat of violence likely to be any more fruitful in the future than in the past. It must be remembered that by following its present policies of confrontation and inflexibility, the PLO has not gained one inch of territory or any other advantage for the Palestinians. The PLO leaders continue to act against the interests of those whom they represent while refusing to accept any responsibility for the lack of progress.

A genuine move toward peace might bring rich dividends by arousing support in the United States and other nations. There are many Israelis who believe that the Palestinians deserve a homeland and that their basic rights, including the right of self-determination, should be honored. The fate of four million Palestinians depends on whether the PLO chooses to pursue its goals by peaceful means or by continued bloodshed.

# Jordan

H ARDLY WIDE ENOUGH for a jeep, the narrow gorge with vertical sandstone sides reaching hundreds of feet toward the sky seemed always to be converging ahead to a dead end. Instead, our Jordanian guides said, it was leading us ever closer to the Valley of Moses, where the perishing Israelites had miraculously received water from a new spring when God told their leader to strike a rock with his staff. Even in those days, the area enclosed by these precipitous mountain walls had already been inhabited for thousands of years, because it was naturally defensible from enemy attack and it was near the convergence of ancient trade routes — from the Arabian Peninsula to the Mediterranean Sea and from Syria and the great Euphrates Valley to the Red Sea and Egypt.

A thousand years after Moses passed this way, the Nabataeans established a fortress city here, known in biblical times as Sela and now as Petra, and before the time of Christ the dominion of their King Aretas III had been extended north beyond Damascus and west below Jerusalem to the Mediterranean Sea. When Herod fled Jerusalem in 40 B.C., he came to this seemingly isolated spot for assistance and from here continued his journey to Rome. There, with the support of Mark Antony and Octavian, he was quickly crowned King of the Jews and sent back to Palestine where he ruled until after the birth of Christ. Petra continued to be the provincial capital of the Nabataeans for another hundred and fifty years, until the Roman conquerors established the new province of Arabia, with its political center farther north.

As our guides gave us history lessons, they also pointed out the small aqueducts carved out of the solid rock on each side of the winding path, which had brought water to the ancient city. If the legend was accurate, this was the same stream of water that had sustained the Jews during their exodus from Egypt. We moved carefully on our way, slowing often to squeeze past the other visitors who were walking or riding on horseback through the rough and rocky gap. Every now and then there were small stone carvings on the eroded cliffs, apparently with some kind of religious meanings.

After a mile or so our jeep stopped and we climbed out to continue our journey on foot. Suddenly there were gasps of astonishment as the beautiful façade of a Grecian temple appeared through the crevice ahead. It was an enormous carving out of the sandstone cliff, perfectly proportioned, and glowing in a strange way with the multiple reds, purples, and yellows of the indigenous rock.

We examined a few of the man-made caves, some of them tombs and others storerooms, where the Nabataean treasures had been kept secure. We could imagine these deserted edifices bustling with international commerce, wih desert chieftains and royalty exchanging goods and negotiating political deals, and with Bedouin brigands plotting attacks on passing caravans that refused to pay tribute for protection. Afterward, we rode farther through the valley, stopping along the way to climb the cliff walls to visit a few of the still-inhabited cave dwellings. It seemed that many eons and thousands of miles separated us from the current problems of the Middle East.

But at a small village we sat down under a tent to talk to one of the tribal chieftains, and his first comment brought me back to reality. He said with a combination of anger and sorrow that the worst affliction on his people was Israel's taking of the West Bank and the closing of the bridge over the Jordan River near Jericho. The people of Petra and Jordan depended heavily on selling their goods and services to visitors who wanted to see the biblical sites, and the circuitous tourist route through Israel, the West Bank, Jordan, and Egypt had now been closed for seven years.

When Rosalynn and I first set eyes on Jordan in the spring of 1973, we did not enter the country, but gazed from the West Bank through the barbed wire at the green fields across the river. We were privileged tourists, traveling as guests of Prime Minister Golda Meir of Israel. At the Allenby Bridge, we were pleasantly surprised by the large and uninterrupted stream of people going back and forth between the two countries. Border inspections were perfunctory, and there was almost a carnival air about the busy scene.

Now, ten years later, we were back at the same bridge. The situation was completely different. Israeli uniforms were everywhere, and only a trickle of people were crossing the border. The waiting lines extended for hundreds of yards, an uneven row of vehicles and campsites, as though some of the people had been waiting for several days. There was no sense of anticipation on the faces of those going in either direction.

This time we were ready to cross the River Jordan on the way from Jerusalem to Amman, following a great deal of skirmishing by my staff with the diplomatic officials of both countries. The U.S. State Department had advised us to get special passports to make the crossing, because if the documents were stamped first by the Israelis, they would not be honored subsequently by the Arabs. It had become customary for travelers to have duplicate passports just for this purpose, but as a matter of principle I had refused. When we arrived with our single passports, arrangements had already been made so that there would be no altercation about the papers, but it was made clear to us that our continued use of the same documents was a special arrangement for me as former President and a departure from normal procedure.

We left our automobiles and, escorted by Israeli officials, walked onto the bridge with our luggage. We proceeded solemnly to the exact center of the span, thanked our Israeli hosts, and then turned to be welcomed by a committee of Jordanians. There was no exchange of pleasantries between the officials of the two countries.

The surprisingly tropical vegetation of the lush valley on both sides of the river was similar to that of the productive land much closer to the Equator. We were near the lowest point on earth, just a few miles from the Dead Sea, and the combination of the low altitude, high temperature, and river water for irrigation created an especially benevolent environment.

I had read about Raboth-bene-Ammon, the ancient city of the Ammonites, in the biblical accounts of King David's conquests and knew its name had been changed to Philadelphia before the time of Christ. When it was conquered by the Arabs in A.D. 635, its name became Amman. We proceeded to the ancient city, now the modern capital of Jordan. Amman had recently doubled and quadrupled in population as hundreds of thousands of Palestinian refugees and large numbers of Bedouins from the semi-arid plains and deserts continued to move into this major urban center.

Rosalynn and I were driven around the outskirts of Amman by smartly dressed members of King Hussein's Bedouin guards and then taken into the royal compound, on a hill near the old city. From our guest house we could look across a deep ravine at the bustling streets of a residential area, where homes had been built in recent years. Some of the Jordanians in our escort said that it did not seem like many years since King Hussein's grandfather, King Abdullah, had enjoyed placing targets on the unoccupied hill across the valley so that he and the British officers of the Arab Legion could practice their long-range marksmanship.

A Hashemite emir and a direct descendant of the Prophet Mohammed, Abdullah ibn-Hussein had fought well against the Turks in World War I, and the British needed to reward him in some appropriate way. At first he was considered for the crown of Iraq, as recommended by other Arab leaders, but the British decided to give that honor to his brother Faisal. Another throne was needed, so an emirate called Transjordan was created out of some remote desert regions of the Palestine mandate. Abdullah had his crown, but under the mandate the British retained almost full authority. It was not until 1946 that Transjordan became a kingdom and was given any real independence. Even then, the British ambassador retained control over foreign policy and most financial and military matters.

Following the Arab-Israeli war of 1948, Abdullah claimed the land on the West Bank not controlled by the Israelis, including the old walled city of East Jerusalem, with its numerous holy shrines. A congress of selected leaders of the Palestinians in the West Bank voted in favor of being annexed, probably their only alternative at the time of their dispersion. This action was confirmed by a 1949 armistice between King Abdullah and the Israelis, as Transjordan became the Hashemite Kingdom of Jordan and struggled to absorb almost 400,000 refugees who had lost their homes as well as the 400,000 Arabs who still occupied their dwellings on the West Bank. Only 6 percent of Jordan's land was west of the river, but nearly two thirds of the population and a large portion of its natural and financial resources were now Palestinian.

About a third of the refugees were in camps; the others lived wherever they could find temporary shelter — in churches, mosques, tents, caves, shacks, and public buildings. They refused to accept permanent housing, claiming that their only permanent home was in Palestine, a large portion of which had now been declared the State of Israel. Many of the displaced persons remained unemployed and subsisted on food allocations from United Nations relief agencies. Even so, life in the West Bank had been relatively prosperous, so the average Palestinian was better educated, better fed, and more active politically than his East Bank neighbor. When the official merger of the West Bank with Jordan was approved by the Jordanian parliament in April 1950, all Palestinians were offered citizenship in the new country. Many participated in Jordan's political affairs, but they still retained their identity as Palestinians.

Although no serious proposal was to evolve for the establishment of a Palestinian state on the West Bank prior to 1967, there were strong objections among the Arabs to any acceptance of the State of Israel. It was reported that Abdullah was meeting secretly with the Israelis, and he was assassinated in July 1951 by an Islamic militant on the Temple Mount in Jerusalem in the presence of his grandson Hussein ibn-Talal. A little more than two years later, this young man ascended the Hashemite throne when he reached the age of eighteen. By this time, the Palestinians had been allotted half the parliamentary seats and the same portion of top positions in the government. The King continued to press for complete Jordanian independence, and in 1956 he ordered the British officials and military personnel to leave Jordan within a few hours. When they complied with this ultimatum, all dependency on those who had created his kingdom and had financed and nurtured it since its birth was peacefully terminated. It was to be the most popular decision of his reign.

King Hussein's greatest political tragedy came in 1967, when Jordan joined Syria and Eygpt in confronting Israel. Within three days after the war began, Israeli troops had occupied East Jerusalem and the entire West Bank, where they have remained to this day. Jordan lost almost half its population, a major source of tourist income from the holy sites of Jerusalem and Bethlehem, and large areas of productive land. At the same time, almost 250,000 refugees fled from the West Bank and settled in Jordan on the east bank of the river.

Despite Hussein's efforts to control them, the increasingly powerful and militant Palestinians used some of the refugee camps as commando bases for their almost constant attacks on Israel. Many of these militants were perfectly willing to accept the retaliatory raids on Jordan because they weakened Hussein's political power by making him unpopular. One of the objectives of the militant Palestinians was to replace Jordan's monarchy with a republic like that of Nasser's Egypt.

These threats became increasingly severe, and by September 1970 a full-scale civil war was raging in Jordan between Hussein's forces and the guerrilla bands. Syria moved its ground troops across the border to support the Palestinian rebels, but Syrian Defense Minister Hafez al-Assad refused to attack the Jordanians and, with the threat of Israeli intervention backed by the United States, Jordan's regular forces prevailed. The Syrians withdrew, many Palestinians fled to Lebanon, and order was adequately restored. Although he sent some small units to Syria during the October 1973 attack on Israel and to Iraq in its war with Iran,

Hussein has been successful in avoiding any major military engagements involving Jordanian forces since the conclusion of the civil war.

From the river into Amman had been less than an hour's drive, and it was just a short walk from our guest house in the royal compound to King Hussein's palace. Very soon after our arrival, we were enjoying a visit with him and his beautiful American-born wife, Queen Noor. We already knew His Majesty quite well, having met with him on his state visits to Washington and also on the first day of 1978, after he and I had attended a New Year's party as guests of the Shah in Tehran.

After Hussein's rejection of the Camp David accords, his denunciations of the peace effort had brought about strained relations between Jordan and the United States and Egypt. In the fall of 1979, I asked Secretary of State Cyrus Vance to explore with King Hussein at a United Nations session whether or not a visit to Washington would be fruitful. The report to me was that no good purpose would be served by an official meeting between me and Jordan's monarch. But in June 1980, Hussein and Queen Noor made a state visit to the White House, so the tension had eased and there was no remaining estrangement as we met in Amman.

Although now happy with his family, Hussein was obviously a troubled monarch. Since ascending the throne in 1953, he had successfully walked a political tightrope throughout the Middle East turmoil and had become the senior national ruler on earth, now serving in the thirtieth year of his reign. Personally courageous and dedicated to his nation's best interests, he had become very cautious in his political and military decisions, partially because the last time he acted with great boldness was in 1967, when he led his Hashemite Kingdom to a devastating defeat by Israel.

Since that time, military adventurism has not been a temptation for Jordan, and in diplomacy Hussein does not take many big chances. His actions have indicated that without clear backing from both the moderate Arab nations and the PLO and a relatively assured chance of success, he will not embark on an isolated effort to bring peace to the region. However, the growing threats to his kingdom from further Palestinian encroachment did prompt him to renew diplomatic relations with Egypt in September 1984 and to welcome the Palestine National Council to Amman two months later. Both these moves were loudly condemned by Syria and other rejectionist nations.

Of all the countries in the Middle East, only Lebanon shares with Jordan such a deep concern about present circumstances, and Hussein probably worries more than any other leader about how his nation's own interests might be adversely affected by changes yet to come. In contrast, Israel and its other neighbors, Egypt and Syria, are relatively satisfied with the status quo or with a continuation of the present trends in the struggle for power, land, and influence.

As we prepared to meet King Hussein and his family, I thought about how the weak and fragile country had teetered on the edge of destruction or dissolution several times since its birth as Transjordan in 1922. It had been created at the expense of other Arabs, opposed by those Zionists who wanted all of Palestine, both east and west of the Jordan River, ridiculed in its early nationhood by those who considered it a puppet of Great Britain, defeated twice by the Israelis, forced to form a union with Iraq in 1958 for protection against the threats of Syria and Egypt during the days of the United Arab Republic, protected by British paratroops when the Iraqi monarchy was overthrown the same year, saved by a strange combination of domestic and foreign forces during the civil war of 1970, and forced to live in an almost perpetual state of fragile relations with Syria. Also, with extremely limited resources, Jordan had been able to absorb hundreds of thousands of Palestinian refugees and to create a way for them to participate in the nation's political affairs.

When we arrived at the small and comfortable palace for our first visit, Queen Noor brought the youngest members of the royal family to meet us, and she and Rosalynn began to discuss her interesting life as a young American woman in the Hashemite Kingdom. Hussein and I moved into an adjacent room where we talked easily about the latest events in Lebanon, in the West Bank, in the Israeli government, and among the PLO after their forced departure from Beirut. Hussein is a man of small stature, gentle and somewhat solemn in his demeanor, almost deferential at times to his visitors. At the same time he is known as a shrewd political and military leader. He is a good listener and seems to absorb every bit of information or advice available. He is not inclined to be critical of others. My impression is that his fellow world leaders respect his opinions because they are carefully considered before being expressed. Hussein has much more personal strength than his weak kingdom permits him to exhibit.

In his quiet, sometimes almost inaudible voice, King Hussein made it clear that he considered the present unrest, instability, and tension in the region to be as serious as any he had ever experienced. He always listened with special attention to the more extreme statements coming from his fellow Arabs in Syria and from his Israeli neighbors. Of particular concern to him was the repeated threat that the Palestinian question would be solved by turning Jordan into the Palestinian state. He was fearful that new waves of refugees might pour into Jordan as Palestinians were forced out of Lebanon and other Arab countries and because of the Israeli effort to incorporate the West Bank and Gaza into Israel proper. The festering inability of the Palestinians to find a satisfactory means for expressing their legitimate rights is for the Jordanians, even more than for other Middle Eastern nations, considered the basic cause of most political ills that plague the area.

Jordan's leaders see their country caught between two regional military powers, Israel and Syria, each backed by one of the superpowers and each through its actions and words having demonstrated strong expansionist tendencies — potentially at the expense of Jordan. Both of these threatening neighbors are now involved in a massive arms buildup while Hussein's more recent efforts to improve his military capability have been largely frustrated.

Like other countries in the Middle East, Jordan spends a large portion of its human and financial resources on maintaining and improving its armed forces, but Hussein has managed his country's economic affairs with caution, and his external debt is comparatively modest. However, he depends on foreign aid and remittances for about half his annual budget. Also, Jordan's economy has been suffering from the oil glut, which has reduced remittances from its citizens working in the oil-producing nations, and at the same time the reduced income of the richer Arab governments has made it more difficult for them to continue their previous generous grants. Only Kuwait and Saudi Arabia still provide Jordan with funds "to combat Israeli annexationism," as promised at the 1978 Arab summit in Baghdad.

The failure of Iraq to resolve its protracted conflict with Iran has also been a great disappointment to King Hussein, because Jordan's early and enthusiastic investment in an Iraqi victory is unlikely to pay any early dividends of peace in the region or financial aid from Baghdad. Furthermore, King Hussein is troubled by the winds of change emanating from the Ayatollah Khomeini's religious fervor. From Jordan's perspective, the prospect for peace and prosperity in the region seems dim.

Despite Jordan's reluctance to take bold and independent action, there is no doubt that Hussein is a constant force for stability and peace. He takes pride in having supported almost every major international proposal that might end the conflict in the region, including U.N. Resolution 242, the Sinai and Golan Heights disengagement agreements of 1973, the Geneva Conference of December 1973, the US.-Soviet joint statement of October 1977, the Venice declaration of the European powers in 1980, key elements of the Camp David accords, and the Reagan statement and Fez proposal of 1982.

Quite vulnerable to the threats of more militant or powerful Arabs and dependent on support from other equally cautious moderates, he has usually been on the periphery of action. In his recent public statements, Hussein has been quite critical of Syria's attempts to dominate the PLO, of President Reagan's failure to pursue his own proposals for a comprehensive settlement, and of the timidity and indecision of Arafat and other Palestinian leaders. Hussein believes that the need for unanimity or an absolute consensus in Arab conferences is a futile concept that usually produces the worst common denominator and it needs to be changed immediately. Further, he professes to see little chance for ultimate success in peace talks without cooperation from the Soviet

Union, perhaps by reconvening the Geneva conference under U.N. Resolution 338 or by consultation of some kind with the Soviets. Hussein has never been clear on this point.

In my own discussions with a broad range of government and professional leaders in Amman, I have found that the Palestinian problem is of constant, direct, and vital interest in Jordan, the primary subject of almost every conversation about peace in the region.

Hussein made it clear to me how frustrated he was by the shifting of world attention almost exclusively to the crisis in Lebanon, which he considered just an unfortunate distraction from the roots of the continuing warfare: the deprivation of Palestinian rights and the expanding Israeli domination of the occupied territories. Also, the problems in Lebanon are seen as caused directly by the failure of the powers involved even to address with sincerity these central issues.

The Jordanians and most other Arabs persistently equate the plight of the Palestinians with that of the Jews following World War II — without national or individual rights, forced from their homeland, still suffering from the oppression of a military power after more than a generation. In carefully orchestrated presentations to visitors, the Jordanians claim that the present policy of Israel is to tighten its military hold on the West Bank and Gaza, to compete with the Palestinians for the choice locations, and to make life for them as onerous as possible in order to evict the Arab population from the occupied territories. The Jordanians repeatedly emphasize that about 12,000 Palestinians a year are being induced or forced to leave their ancestral homes and move east, either into Jordan or to join the many wandering refugees in other countries.

They quote the latest Israeli figures on how much Palestinian family land is being confiscated by the Israeli military authorities and claim that the basis for the societal structure of non-Jews is methodically being changed from family farming and free enterprise into day labor, with Palestinians becoming increasingly dependent on menial household jobs and other work for Israelis without the right to organize or join trade unions. They quote cases to prove that water resources from the upper Jordan River valley are being channeled almost exclusively to Israelis and that Arabs are even prohibited from digging a new well or deepening an old one dried up by adjacent wells recently dug by Jewish settlers. They condemn Israel's policy of forbidding the delivery of foreign aid through Amman to the West Bank and Gaza for such projects as education, housing, and agriculture.

We had already heard most of these complaints from those living in the West Bank and Gaza. Now, however, we were presented with color photographs, bar graphs, pages of statistics, and documents. It was clear that Jordan's royal family was making the same presentation to other visitors and to audiences in international forums. These highly developed and widely publicized expressions of concern were designed to rally support for the Palestinian cause, to maintain tension in the occupied territories and among Israel's neighbors, and perhaps to remind Palestinians of the reasons for their struggle to regain a homeland.

Political leaders in Amman are convinced that Israel's present move "to colonize and eventually to annex" the occupied territories will not only change the basic character of Israel but will jeopardize the peace treaty with Egypt. This would end all viable attempts to reach a peaceful settlement of Arab-Israeli differences and lead eventually to another, broader and more deadly, holy war, with Moslem forces committed through their religious beliefs to restore the rights of their Arab brothers who live west of the Jordan River or who claim the right to live there. King Hussein never fails to emphasize that this conflict will almost certainly involve a serious confrontation between the two superpowers, with the United States pledged to support Israel and the Soviet Union allied with at least some of the Arab forces.

Even without this cataclysmic war, many Jordanians feel that a failure to resolve the Palestinian issue through peaceful negotiations might also ultimately lead to the destruction of their own nation, and they listen with anger and concern to the threat frequently voiced by some of the more extreme Israeli spokesmen, who extend the ultimate borders of their country beyond the Jordan River and who, when referring to a home for the non-Jews in Palestine, say, "Jordan is Palestine." This threat is real and vital to Jordan's leaders. Referring to a third Palestinian exodus from the West Bank and Gaza, which might be orchestrated by Israel, Jordan's Crown Prince Hassan said recently, "The influx of disgruntled and politically alienated people into Jordan would serve only one purpose: the radicalization of its politics and the destabilization of its society."

In the occupied territories, many Palestinians themselves look to King Hussein for leadership and protection at the same time that they express disappointment and frustration at his Hamlet-like inability to make a decision on Jordan's role. Even while professing publicly that their only legitimate leader is Yasir Arafat and the PLO, they deplore the preoccupation of the PLO leaders with organizational struggles, international propaganda exercises, and maneuvers to obtain financing, and both they and Hussein are convinced that their ultimate salvation might have to depend on representation at the negotiating table from within Jordan. Neither the Palestinians nor the Jordanian leaders have any ready answers to the present problem, but they search ceaselessly for other allies who will keep the blame focused on Israel.

The quandary of who should be the spokesman for the inhabitants of the West Bank and Gaza is mirrored among the Jordanians. Despite his eagerness to protect Palestinian rights and work out an acceptable agreement on the occupied territories, Hussein is bound by the Arabs' Rabat declaration of 1974 that the Palestinians are to be represented exclusively by the PLO, and he considers it inappropriate and perhaps dangerous to be too aggressive in capitalizing on weaknesses and rebellion within the PLO by claiming Palestinian leadership for himself. Feeling so restricted, King Hussein has thus far been unwilling to participate in negotiations to alleviate the increasingly threatening circumstances he sees on the other side of the river.

There is no doubt in my mind that the Camp David accords provided the best opportunity to date for resolving the Palestinian issue and for determining the final status of the West Bank and Gaza, but these goals were frustrated by Prime Minister Begin's obvious moves to control the entire area and by King Hussein's refusal to join the peace talks as Sadat, Begin, and I had envisioned at Camp David.

Although Hussein's participation in those original negotiations was never seriously discussed by either him or me, President Sadat told me at Camp David that he was reviewing the progress of the talks with the Jordanian monarch and was scheduled to meet with him in Morocco on his way home to give him a detailed report. However, Hussein canceled this meeting at the last minute and returned to Amman. As soon as possible after we concluded the Camp David agreement, both Secretary of State Cyrus Vance and I explained the provisions in detail to King Hussein, but it was too late. The great outcry from his Arab brothers convinced him that he should join the rejectionist Arabs in condemning the entire Camp David effort and in attempting to punish Sadat for his participation.

Later acknowledging that the Camp David accords gave a fresh momentum to the peace process, the Jordanians maintain that the potential advantages of these agreements were offset by the neutralization of Egypt, the ejection of Egypt from Arab councils, Israel's increasingly domineering role in the occupied territories, and by new feuds and polarization among the Arab nations. Also, the Camp David agreements did not acknowledge either Jordanian or Israeli sovereignty over the West Bank, but left this ultimate decision to be made at the negotiating table. More recently, Hussein has attempted to heal the Arab breach caused by Sadat's peace initiative and to induce other members of the Islamic community to readmit Egypt to full membership.

The Jordanians were encouraged when, in September 1982, President Reagan announced his interpretation of the terms of the Camp David accords by proposing that, as an acceptable possibility for the future, the West Bank and Gaza under Arab sovereignty be confederated with Jordan (Appendix 5). Almost immediately, in a meeting at Fez, Morocco, the Arab leaders passed a resolution that in carefully crafted circumlocutions supported the Reagan statement and, according to their own private interpretations, recognized for the first time Israel's right to exist (Appendix 6).

In spite of Prime Minister Begin's immediate rejection of this Reagan initiative, King Hussein sought at least tacit approval from moderate Arabs and a clear endorsement by PLO leader Yasir Arafat for Jordan and some designated Palestinians to join the peace talks with Israel, Egypt, and the United States. President Reagan gave the Jordanian leaders direct and unequivocal assurances that Israeli settlement activity would be frozen as a condition of the commencement of the expanded peace talks. Most government-financed construction in the West Bank was stopped late in 1983, primarily because of budget limitations. The Israelis deny any political decision to cease settlement activity.

In February 1983, shortly before I last visited with King Hussein in Amman, the Palestine National Council, acting as a parliament in exile for the Palestinians, passed a resolution approving the concept of confederation between the occupied Arab territories and Jordan. The PLO insisted upon a state first and then perhaps some movement toward confederation; it is clear that Hussein wants confederation, with the Palestinians' being offered a token option for an independent state in the future. With the substance of the two Arab statements regarded as an adequate expression of the Palestinians' right of self-determination and with President Reagan's written commitment to freeze Israeli settlement activity in the occupied territories, Hussein was quite confident that he would be able to join the peace talks.

I urged him to do so, pointing out that at the negotiating table with Egypt, Israel, the United States, and Palestinian representatives, he would find that his stand on many of the controversial issues would be compatible with the positions already expressed in the Camp David accords and in the Reagan statement. It was Hussein's intention to negotiate under the framework of the U.S. proposal that there be a Palestinian entity in the West Bank and Gaza associated with Jordan, but he professed that his long-range objective was to incorporate some elements of the Fez plan, calling for broader Palestinian rights including the option of an independent state. Although it was not the preference of Jordan (and with the knowledge that Israel would never accept it), Hussein felt that as one of his negotiating positions he could not foreclose the possibility of this goal of many Palestinians.

Despite King Hussein's best efforts, a combination of factors finally converged in April 1983 to prevent Jordan's participation in the negotiations: Begin's vehement rejection of the Reagan proposal; Arafat's yielding to extremist pressure and making last-minute demands that Hussein considered to be unacceptable; the lack of clear support from other Arab leaders; and a relative U.S. quiescence in the face of Israel's continued occupation of Lebanon, which made it doubtful that President Reagan would deliver on his promise to freeze the settlement activity. Hussein later said publicly that the last factor was the most significant. Furthermore, during this critical time for Hussein, there were disturbing deviations within the Reagan administration from the long-standing U.S. position on the Israeli settlements: that they were both illegal and obstacles to peace. If the United States now considered Israelis to be free to settle the West Bank at the expense of the Palestinians, asked the Jordanians, what would be the purpose of the peace negotiations?

Another cause for concern was the lack of any coherent approach by the United States to resolving the crisis in Lebanon or even of involving Syrian leaders in an overall peace effort. This point was driven home with the bilateral withdrawal agreement concluded in May 1983 between Israel and Lebanon, after minimal consultation with Syria concerning its own interests in the region. The Jordanians fear that the absence of a general withdrawal agreement would create a permanent stalemate leading to the partition of Lebanon, with Israeli forces remaining in the southern region and eventually absorbing it into Israel after the pattern established in the Golan Heights, the West Bank, and Gaza. This would set another precedent that might be applied to Jordan in the future, and in any case it would drive more Arabs from their homes and create another wave of refugees. This last fear has been alleviated recently as Israel has prepared to withdraw its forces from Lebanon.

The continuing Israeli occupation of Lebanon is seen to be a political and military quagmire, but from Jordan's perspective it has given Israel one of its objectives: until peace talks begin, Israel can use the time to consolidate its hold on the West Bank and Gaza. So far, this has tended to perpetuate Lebanon as the focal point for concern to the exclusion of Jordan's primary interests. Also, realizing that Lebanon was only one element of a broader chain of hot spots in the eastern Mediterranean, the Persian Gulf, and the Red Sea, Jordanians believed correctly that America's focusing its political and military strength almost exclusively on Beirut was a wasteful and counterproductive use of its great resources.

With the announcement in December 1983 of a U.S.-Israeli "strategic alliance," the Arabs felt that the United States was becoming more and more aligned against them and had abandoned its effectiveness in putting firm pressure on all parties to come to the negotiating table. King Hussein's response was uncharacteristically sharp; he felt that under this new alliance "the United States will provide funds to the Israeli settlements, thus flouting the form and substance of the U.S. President's peace proposals."

Of special concern to Hussein was that the hand of the radicals and extremists was being strengthened by the continuing standstill in the peacemaking efforts brought about by the American presidential campaign and the reluctance of the Reagan administration to address the crucial issues of Israeli settlements, the withdrawal of occupation forces, and Palestinian rights. The Jordanians maintain that moderate peacemakers in Israel and in the Arab nations (like King Hussein) will lose hope and be intimidated and that the interests of the United States itself will suffer if it continues to abandon its long-standing role as the broker of peace in the region. The strategic balance between the superpowers will shift even more toward the Soviet Union as Arab people everywhere despair of a balanced and aggressive effort for peace being sustained by American leaders.

King Hussein believes that a strong American role is necessary if any progress is to be made, and in 1983 he called for a bipartisan peace constituency to be headed by U.S. citizens of impeccable reputation whose voices could not be ignored, perhaps former secretaries of state. At the least, this small group would ascertain the facts and submit proposals that could guide an American administration free of undue pressure. When Hussein offered this proposal to top officials in Washington, he argued that this effort would not be politically detrimental to President Reagan but, on the contrary, might permit the advancement of peace and at the same time be politically attractive to most American voters. But there was no discernible response from Washington.

Jordanian officials still maintain that with America committed at the highest level of government to the peace process, Jordan would likely take an active role in order to implement U.N. Resolution 242. They are also convinced that adequate support will be forthcoming from the moderate Arabs and Palestinians to make these peacemaking efforts possible and productive.

They believe that most factors that prevented this action in April 1983 have now become less significant. The fragmentation of the PLO, the reduced Syrian influence on Arafat, and greatly improved relations between the PLO and Jordan have increased the possibility of Jordan's acting with more authority for those in the West Bank and Gaza, and Hussein is seeking some means for assuming this responsibility.

King Hussein was frustrated by the diplomatic inactivity during the 1984 U.S. election year and lashed out verbally at this delay, but through domestic and foreign policy initiatives he has struggled to keep alive the potential for negotiations in 1985. He does not wish to be unduly bound by the political extremism in the Arab world, nor does he wish to deviate from the basic Arab demands for a restoration of Palestinian rights. He would like to chart an almost impossible middle course that ensures a degree of Jordanian independence in decision-making but at the same time does not alienate his moderate Arab brothers. His ongoing discussions with Palestinian leaders, the reconvening of his long-dissolved parliament with half its members Palestinians from the West Bank, and his helping to convene the Palestine National Council in Amman in November 1984 all demonstrated his desire to associate more closely with the Palestinian leadership inside and outside the occupied territories. The normalizing of diplomatic relations between Jordan and Egypt two months earlier also enhanced Hussein's influence as a moderate leader who might make a move toward peace.

Hussein does not want to be the exclusive Palestinian representative; he prefers to establish a workable and mutually nonthreatening relationship with the PLO. One inherent problem with this is that if Hussein depends on their approval, PLO militants who do not want any compromise with Israel can veto Jordan's desire to negotiate for the future of the West Bank and Gaza. One way to escape this quandary would be Jordan's acceptance of a clear request from Palestinian leaders in the occupied territories that Hussein speak for them in concert with the PLO. Also, a restoration of close ties between Jordan and the United States and some firm indication of American responsiveness to Hussein's desire to negotiate could alleviate some of his other financial and military concerns.

To protect their own interests, Jordanians will try to maintain a stabilizing role both in the context of the Arab-Israeli conflict and in inter-Arab disputes. Hussein has been leading his country through this kind of political wilderness since he was eighteen years old, and he is a master at dealing with ever-changing questions and challenges. If there is any answer to Jordan's present quandary, he is the best man to find it.

His brother Crown Prince Hassan bin Talal has repeatedly stressed that the ultimate concept is of Jordan and the occupied territories' being a kind of terra media — a middle ground — between Africa and the oil-producing countries of the Arabian peninsula to the south and the skilled manpower and high technology of Lebanon, Syria, and Iraq of the northern region, with Arabs living in harmony and cooperation with a secure and peaceful Israel.

# Egypt

I T IS ONLY a half-hour flight between Cairo and Tel Aviv — an easy route for the plane but an extremely difficult political road that for years was reserved almost exclusively for Americans conducting "shuttle diplomacy." I had made the trip in *Air Force One* as President, but in the spring of 1983 it was different. I had never seen Mount Sinai, called Jabal Musa by the Arabs, and my last-minute request to the Egyptian officials before leaving their country was that our private plane be cleared to head southeast instead of northeast over the Sinai desert so that we could circle the historic site. This spot is believed to be Mount Horeb, where Moses received the Ten Commandments from God. Even for our gracious hosts this was a difficult request because it was such a departure from the normal flight paths, and our takeoff was delayed for about an hour while the necessary high official was located and induced to grant final approval.

We circled over the 7500-foot peak and got a glimpse of St. Catherine's monastery, which has huddled against the north face of the rugged mountain for more than 1450 years; it is the oldest continuously occupied Christian monastery on earth. This is a holy place to Jew, Christian, and Moslem and was the subject of several discussions among President Anwar Sadat, Prime Minister Menachem Begin, and me at Camp David. Sadat saw this "Mountain of God" as the symbol of peace, but the prospects for realizing his dream of a shrine for all three religions to be built there seemed quite remote now, in 1983, with a war raging in Lebanon and relations between Egypt and Israel strained almost to the breaking point.

Although Anwar Sadat had been dead for seventeen months, we were fulfilling with pleasure a promise that Rosalynn and I had made on one of our official visits to return for a more leisurely and personal journey through his country. After we arrived in Egypt, one of our first excursions was to Sadat's boyhood town northwest of Cairo, not far from the main route to Alexandria. There we met his wife, Jehan, their children and grandchildren, and all the in-laws and close relatives. Strangely, our first topic of conversation was about chickens and eggs, a business venture then being considered by the family. We toured orange groves on the small farm and then sat on the sunny terrace drinking Sadat's favorite mint tea, which I had often shared with him during the Camp David negotiations. Then we walked through the village streets.

Sadat and I had often compared my home in Plains, Georgia, with his early home, and I could almost have recognized it from his enthusiastic descriptions. We enjoyed the excitement of his neighbors as they struggled to direct the human traffic jam that accompanied us through the narrow streets. Although we were running behind schedule, we yielded to their pleas that we visit a few of the homes of which they are especially proud — all paid for with royalty fees from Sadat's autobiography, *In Search of Identity.*

Through the delta area between Cairo and the village, we observed the rich farmlands and the ancient style of irrigating, cultivating, and harvesting. Rosalynn and I discussed Egypt's history, its intriguing blend of changing and unchanging customs, and the profound impact on the Middle East during the last two decades of the two leaders who came to look upon themselves as political descendants of the mighty pharaohs, Anwar Sadat and Gamal Abdel Nasser. During the rest of our trip, we would be learning about this ancient and modern history at first hand.

*

After a thorough tour of the Cairo museum and the pyramids with the Egyptian director of antiquities, we traveled from the lower delta region south, up the Nile River to Luxor; from there we visited Thebes, the Valley of the Kings, Karnak, and other ancient sites. We investigated the more notable tombs of the pharaohs, the ancient cities filled with their beautiful statuary, and spent some time with archaeologists, who were busy photographing and cataloguing the thousands of items and deciphering the hieroglyphics at some of the more remote, less famous places.

One morning as we were approaching the entrance to the tomb of Tutankhamen, a group of Israelis saw me and immediately began to sing "Hayveynu Shalom Aleichem" — "Peace Be with You." We stopped to listen; I noticed that my eyes were not the only ones that glistened. It was a beautiful moment. I went over to talk to them, and they thanked me "for giving us the opportunity to visit our new friends in Egypt." Like these and other groups of Israeli tourists, the Egyptians we met in their homes and marketplaces were pleased and thankful for the end of war, and many expressed their gratitude almost equally to me, President Sadat, and Prime Minister Begin.

I learned that 33,000 Israeli tourists were coming to Egypt each year and that they were quite pleased by their friendly reception. This number was in addition to the 50,000 Palestinians from the occupied territories who cross the border into Egypt without incident, almost all of them from Gaza. Limited by both political and economic constraints, however, only about 2000 Egyptians visit Israel annually, few of whom are tourists.

We spent several days on a comfortable ship, moving slowly up the Nile and observing through binoculars and at close hand the people of Egypt performing their daily tasks, working the rich soil by hand and with oxen, camels, or water buffaloes much as they had when the early kings ruled and the boats plying the river were propelled by sails of papyrus or the oars of slaves. On the way we stopped at Esna, Edfu, and Kom Ombo. Our plane met us at Aswan, where we toured the mighty dam before flying farther south to the remarkable statues of Abu Simbel, resting high on the shore of Lake Nasser just a few miles from the Sudanese border.

On the river, the ship tied up at a different landing every night, and each morning I arose before dawn to run for a while. I particularly enjoyed these times of exploration and relative solitude. An Egyptian security agent jogged with me along the dusty roads and trails, sometimes beside the river, at other times directly away from the stream into the relatively narrow irrigated region among the small plots of rich land and through the villages. At that time of day the roads and streets were not crowded, but they were already alive with farmers going to the fields or carrying their produce to the larger markets along the riverbank. All of them seemed to know who I was, and it was interesting to stop along the way to talk about crops or animals or family life. The security agent was a native of the Luxor area, and he was kept busy answering many of my questions and serving as interpreter.

One morning we saw an exceptionally large camel and stopped to admire it. The proud farmer was on the way to the village where our boat was moored for the night, and he insisted that I take a ride on the huge beast. I quickly changed the subject and we returned to the ship, where I prepared to meet with the mayor and other village elders before we got under way. It was still quite early, shortly after sunrise, and after exchanging greetings with the officials we moved through the narrow streets to observe the town as it came to life. The merchants were opening their shops and the farmers arranged their fruit and other produce in stalls or on benches and tables in a central square.

We noticed a hubbub on a nearby corner, the sounds of shouts and laughter, and we walked over to see what was causing the commotion. Too late, I recognized my farmer friend with his great camel. Several of the crowd ran to greet me, and it was obvious that they were expecting me to go for a ride. I tried every excuse, but soon found that even my own security agent had forgotten his duty to protect me and had joined the chorus. I finally yielded to the unanimous demands that I risk my life or forfeit my manhood.

With much difficulty, the farmer and his friends induced the camel to kneel on the ground, and they spread one of their best blankets over the wooden rack lashed on top of his hump. Everyone gestured for me to climb aboard. It was not easy to reach the designated stirrup, which was just a loop in a rope hanging not far below the apex of the contraption. When I was finally sitting on the hard wooden frame, the farmer stepped back and yanked the animal's halter.

The security agent yelled, "Hang on as tight as possible!" just as the first tremendous lurch came. I weathered this only to be faced with a second and then a most surprising third. The saddle jerked back and forth, each time almost perpendicular to the ground. Holding desperately to the wooden rack, I was thrown from the camel's neck to an embarrassing position heading toward his tail, with the crowd alternately cheering and moaning as I wobbled wildly around but was never near where I was supposed to be. When the camel and I finally reached a fairly even keel I was desperately hanging on, and I was barely able to kick back as the beast repeatedly attempted to bite me. Cheers and laughter rang through the village.

I rode for about two blocks — not too badly, I thought — and finally dismounted with a number of deep bruises but no broken bones. The happy farmer congratulated me, saying that I was the only one other than him who had ever ridden his camel. Drenched with perspiration, half hot and half cold, I thanked the owner of the dangerous vehicle for this honor, nodded to my large cheering section, and walked stiffly and with what dignity I could muster to one of the nearby shops. Everyone roared with laughter when the mayor asked, "Did that remind you of the Middle East peace negotiations?" I replied, "Yes, but this morning we made more progress and I got off easier."

At one of the outdoor stalls I found some bamboo walking sticks and shepherd's staffs, which the shopkeeper explained were made by steaming and bending the material. I thought they would be good souvenirs, but left them when the shopkeeper refused to quote a price, saying, "In this village you cannot pay." After the ship had sailed and the town was far behind, the steward delivered to our stateroom a complete collection of the merchant's wares.

In each place along the river I tried to talk to as many of the local officials and other Egyptian people as possible, and I found them quite knowledgeable about the peace agreements with Israel and almost as eager to express their appreciation to Begin as to Sadat and me. In private homes there were often photographs of Nasser, a few of Sadat, and occasionally one of me. On the walls were tourist folders, pictures, flags, and other mementos of nations where the family's sons were working, with Libya being the most frequently remembered.

On Sunday we worshiped in an ancient Coptic church in a village on our route and were reminded of the tenacity of these Christian believers, whose patron was Saint Mark. The priests shared tea with us after the service, noting that the rites had not been changed appreciably during the last sixteen centuries. They were most concerned about the house arrest of their pope, whose activities had been constrained by Sadat and who was still being held in custody by President Mubarak. The Copts had refused to select anyone else to lead them, and I promised to intercede on their behalf with the Egyptian officials. Since then, I have done this several times, and Pope Shenouda was finally released in January 1985.

Unlike the situation among Christians and other believers in the Western nations, there has been no proliferation of new sects or doctrines in the world of Islam since medieval times, and the same pattern of orthodoxy persists among the Christians, who for ages have survived relatively intact as minority groups among the Moslems. Since the Iranian revolution, however, Moslem groups have become more militant, and the leaders of Egypt and other Arab nations have sometimes responded to these religious pressures with the uncharacteristic persecution of non-Moslems. Throughout Islam, one can detect a growing anti-Western feeling. The mistreatment of the Coptic Christian Pope Shenouda is just one example of this disturbing trend.

Egypt first became a unified nation more than 5000 years ago, in 3100 B.C., when a great king named Menes brought upper and lower Egypt together. The invention of hieroglyphics at about the same time enabled the kingdom to record its own glorious history of cultural and political maturity.

Unlike Syria and the other nations of Mesopotamia, Egypt was not a crossroads of trade and commerce or a center of constant war when civilizations were first struggling for dominance. The ferment of contention with outside forces and ideas was missing in the relatively peaceful Nile Valley, so new philosophies and religious beliefs evolved very slowly and the people concentrated on building, craftsmanship, and agriculture. Because of its relative prosperity, Egypt was well known as a reliable source of food even in those earliest times, so it is not surprising that when Abraham finally arrived in the promised land of Canaan only to discover a drought and famine, he continued into the Nile delta — perhaps not far from Sadat's family farm — to purchase supplies for his family and flock. He received a hospitable welcome and the extended visit added to his already great wealth; the story of this visit was certainly known to his immediate descendants.

When another great famine came to Canaan, the family of Abraham's grandson Israel (also known as Jacob) went again to Egypt — perhaps to the same place — to save themselves from starvation. There his descendants remained for four centuries, first in freedom and later as slaves of the pharaohs until Moses led them back to the Promised Land. The Bible records that even after they were free, the hundreds of thousands of wandering Israelites looked back with longing to their lives in Egypt.

From time to time, Egypt extended its authority along the eastern shore of the Mediterranean and into Syria and on several occasions was itself invaded by immediate neighbors in Africa and by enemies from east of the Sinai. In general, however, even when their land was occupied by foreign forces, the Egyptians were able to retain their relative independence and cultural isolation and continued to prosper from international trade and commerce.

During the eighth and seventh centuries B.C., the Jewish kingdoms of Israel and Judah were destroyed in Palestine by the Assyrians and Babylonians, and Egypt was handed crushing defeats by these same great powers from the Tigris-Euphrates Valley. A few decades later Egypt was occupied by the Persians, thus beginning a long period of foreign domination. Alexander the Great vanquished the entire region in 332 B.C. and initiated an era of Greek influence that finally modified the ancient Egyptian culture and still persists. Then came the Romans, a short while before the birth of Christ, and again Egypt was the focus of a biblical drama. The family of Jesus was forced to seek refuge from the vassal King Herod the Great, who had ordered all male babies around Bethlehem to be killed. Joseph, Mary, and their baby escaped into Egypt and stayed there until after the death of Herod. The Romans ruled Egypt for almost seven centuries, during which time Christianity became the national religion and Coptic the language of the people. Then the powerful tide of Islam rose in the seventh century and swept the Romans from the Middle East. For more than a millennium, the political and cultural lives of the Egyptians and others throughout the Middle East have conformed to the teachings of the Prophet Mohammed.

Of all the countries in the region, Egypt has experienced the most prolonged history of Western colonialism, since most of the other Middle Eastern nations remained part of the Ottoman Empire until World War I. At that time Egypt had been dominated by Great Britain for more than a generation. As the Second World War approached, nationalist pressures in Egypt were finally forcing the British to yield some independence to the local people, but Mussolini's invasion of Ethiopia in 1935 convinced most of the Egyptians that maybe London's protection might not be their worst option for a few more years. Even so, hatred of the British caused a serious political division within Egypt, and a group of younger officers were inclined to support the Nazis. Because of these internal pressures it was not until 1945, just a few months before the end of the war, that Britain was successful in convincing Egypt to declare war on Germany.

With British encouragement, Egypt helped to form the Arab League that same year, with Transjordan, Yemen, Saudi Arabia, Iraq, Syria, and Lebanon joining Egypt as original members. Later, the other Arab countries of North Africa and the Arabian Peninsula also joined the organization. The headquarters of the Arab League was established in Cairo and remained there until Sadat signed the Egyptian-Israeli peace treaty in March 1979. Then, to punish Sadat, the other Arab leaders voted to move the League's base of operations to Tunis.

After World War II, the Egyptians continued their struggle for independence, but it was not until after the 1952 revolution that the British influence was substantially decreased. In June 1956, seventy-four years of military occupation by Great Britain finally ended, and a month later Nasser nationalized the Suez Canal. In November, the British managed, with French and Israeli help, to retake the Suez Canal. Nasser's troops performed very poorly, and it was only political pressure from the United States, the Soviet Union, and other members of the United Nations that forced the occupying troops to withdraw.

This long history of colonialism left very unpleasant memories in the minds of the Egyptians and other Arabs. For the last three decades, their leaders have consistently resisted any foreign interference in their internal affairs and have claimed nonalliance with the superpowers. Yet they often found themselves close to either Moscow or Washington when their countries were in need of military or economic aid.

Four years before the Egyptian revolution the State of Israel had been established, and its presence transformed the political life and character of the region. However, during Israel's early days, the Egyptians and practically all the Arabs considered the establishment of a Jewish national home to be a short-lived mistake, an act committed by the British for their own political ends. The extent and depth of the Jewish issue took Egyptian and other Middle East leaders by surprise; they were simply not prepared to face it. They failed to recognize the need for a haven or shelter for the Jewish people, and they underestimated the strength and tenacity of the Zionists in obtaining and keeping their foothold in Palestine. Both sides believed that the situation could be resolved by force. The Jews believed that the inhabitants would either leave the land or share it with them; the Arabs believed that they could prevent large numbers of Jews from coming or staying.

Gamal Abdel Nasser emerged as the dynamic leader of the new republic of Egypt and soon established his country, supported by the Soviet Union, as the driving force of the Arabic world. One of the Arabs' main purposes was to meet the Zionist threat. By the mid-1960s, Nasser and other Arab leaders were preparing for a war that they considered inevitable, and, when it came in 1967, it brought a humiliating Arab defeat, including the loss of Egypt's Sinai.

Following Nasser's death in 1970, Anwar Sadat became President, and he began a slow but steady move away from the Soviets and toward the United States. This decision culminated in his expelling from Egypt thousands of Soviet advisers in July 1972 and the recalling of ambassadors from Moscow and Cairo. This was a dramatic move, but within a few months the ambassadors were back at their posts and the Soviets were again supplying Egypt with advanced weapons at a rapid pace to match those being delivered to Israel by the United States.

Sadat and Syria's President Assad began to plan secretly that the next war (which came in October 1973) would be one of limited objectives, not an all-out effort. Perhaps with the benefit of hindsight, Sadat's followers now claim that the exact objective of the Egyptians was to pave the way for real peace between the Arabs and Israelis. This could only be negotiated if Arab dignity was restored and if there prevailed a basis of equality and mutual respect on potential future battlefields. Sadat felt certain that if these limited goals were reached, his people would support him in a move toward peace.

This time, at least in the early stages of the October war of 1973, the Egyptians used the Soviet weapons with more effectiveness than they had in the 1967 war. However, the Kremlin could not match the large quantities of war materiel airlifted to Israel by the United States. With the Egyptian army in danger of being destroyed, the Soviet prime minister, Alexei Kosygin, flew to Cairo to establish a cease-fire. When the Israelis refused to observe the arrangement, the Soviets warned both President Nixon and the Israelis and made obvious plans to send their forces into Egypt. Under American pressure, the Israelis observed the cease-fire terms, but not until the United States had put its global military forces on a high state of alert, preparing for a serious showdown between the superpowers.

After the indeterminate 1973 war was over and the Arabs had their psychological victory, Sadat was looked upon as a great military hero with the potential of realizing Nasser's unfilled promise. Sadat, who said he had considered possible terms of a settlement with the Israelis as early as 1971, now had the negotiating parity he had sought. In October 1973, Sadat went before the Egyptian parliament and proposed convening an international conference for peace to be composed of the Middle East disputants and chaired jointly by the United States and the Soviet Union. However, when such a conference finally convened (without Syria) in December 1973, the effort immediately proved futile. From Sadat's perspective, the disengagement agreements of 1974 and 1975 in the Sinai and Golan Heights involving Israel, Egypt, and Syria were a poor and limited substitute for what he had in mind.

Egypt had received great assistance from the Soviets, but following the negotiation of the Sinai withdrawal agreements, it became obvious that Sadat was again shifting his nation's interests toward the Western democracies. Sadat told me later that he did not want another influx of Soviet "advisers" in Egypt; he had seen the strong opposition of the Soviets to the withdrawal negotiations with the Israelis and he believed that the United States was more likely to provide an avenue to further peace talks.

Sadat wanted a modern and prosperous Egypt allied with the West, and he was even willing to conclude a separate peace with Israel and so endanger his nation's standing in the Arab community. Sadat felt that for too long Egypt had been a spear point for the Arab world, that its young men had been most frequently sacrificed in the wars against Israel. He saw great benefits for his Arab brothers from an end to war, and he felt that if Egypt could be free from the constant and debilitating confrontations with Israel, he could help in the rejuvenation of Arab political and social life and join in warding off common enemies. It was a profoundly important development in Middle Eastern history when Sadat decided that he would no longer be bound by the Arab League rule of unanimity and could act independently of Syria, Libya, the PLO, and others, who continued to reject any negotiations with Israel.

Shortly after I became President, several border disputes broke out between Egypt and Libya, and the Soviet support of the Libyans further alienated Sadat. He began to sever his military, cultural, and commercial ties with the Soviet Union, and relationships between the two nations were at a low ebb by the time Sadat announced plans to visit Jerusalem in November 1977. The Egyptian people seemed to accept all these rapid policy changes with relative equanimity.

When I first met Sadat in April 1977, his inclination to work with us on peace negotiations was already well developed, but he had not decided on any schedule for his actions. He told me that he was looking for a real, comprehensive, and just peace agreement, backed by both superpowers, which would bring a new balance and equilibrium between Israelis and Arabs and would treat Palestinians with justice. We reviewed some of the basic elements crucial to progress, and he later supported the terms of the joint U.S.-Soviet communiqué of October 1977 (Appendix 3). I considered this to be a necessary prelude to reconvening the Geneva peace talks. Strong objections to the communiqué were raised from Israel and particularly from the American friends of Israel, not concerning the substance of the text so much as the potential consequences of having two superpowers presiding over a meeting of reluctant and incompatible negotiating parties. I was aggravated by the criticisms and could see all the opportunities for progress slipping away.

Three days later Sadat sent me a private and personal letter; the Egyptian foreign minister who delivered it later resigned in protest because of its contents. It urged that I not do anything that would interfere with Sadat's ability to negotiate directly with the Israelis, a portent of Sadat's plan to visit Jerusalem.

Then I met with Israel's foreign minister, Moshe Dayan, to assure him that our previously described policies had not changed and that in our joint communiqué the Soviets had simply decided to agree with the U.S. position. The Israelis were not convinced, and hopes for peace talks were still fading. I sent Sadat a handwritten letter telling him how "extremely important — perhaps vital" it was for him to give me his help at that crucial moment. We discussed various possibilities by telephone, and on November 9 he made his surprising offer to go to Jerusalem. Begin quickly relayed through me his invitation for Sadat to speak to the Israeli Knesset, and shortly thereafter the historic visit was made.

In his speech to the Israeli Knesset, Sadat laid down in no uncertain terms the strong Arab position. It is interesting that after some considerable discussion he had decided not to follow the counsel of his advisers that he make the speech in English for the world audience. Instead, he made it in Arabic for the benefit of his Arab neighbors and expressed the wish that he could also have spoken Hebrew. The symbolism of his presence was so powerful that his words were largely ignored. The reaction in Western nations was overwhelmingly favorable, that of the moderate Arab leaders was cautious at best, and the Israeli public responded with excitement and enthusiasm. Syria broke diplomatic relations with Egypt, and high officials in Damascus, Baghdad, Tripoli, and the PLO called for Sadat's assassination.

In December 1977, Begin came to the White House to discuss a peace proposal for the Sinai and the West Bank, and there was a flurry of meetings between the Egyptians and Israelis that culminated shortly after Christmas in a visit by Begin to Ismailia, near the Suez Canal. Sadat reported to me that the session was totally unsatisfactory, a real setback for the peace initiative. Begin was insisting that Israeli settlements must remain on Egyptian land. It was beginning to appear that the only permanent result of Sadat's bold move was an end to any prospect for a Geneva conference. On a fast New Year's trip, I consulted with the leaders of Jordan, Iran, Saudi Arabia, and Egypt; I found the other Arabs somewhat supportive of Sadat in private but quite critical in their public statements, honoring a pledge of unanimity with their more radical Arab brothers.

During the early part of 1978, the situation went from bad to worse, and Sadat sent me word that he intended to come to the United States and publicly condemn Begin as a betrayer of the peace process. In February, Rosalynn and I invited Anwar and Jehan to Camp David for a personal visit, and after a weekend of intense talks, Sadat was convinced to try again for some kind of agreement. Secretary of State Cy Vance helped with the new efforts, but within a few weeks it became obvious that the Israelis and Egyptians would never agree on any of the key issues.

Finally, in an act of political desperation, I decided to invite both Begin and Sadat to Camp David so that we could be away from routine duties for a few days and, in relative isolation, I could act as mediator between the two national delegations. They accepted without delay, and in September we held our private thirteen-day session.

A result of major compromises, the Camp David accords provided for an end to Israeli military rule, the granting of full autonomy for the Palestinians in the West Bank and Gaza, and a negotiating procedure for determining the permanent status of the other occupied territories, with the Palestinians participating in the determination of their own future. A framework for an Egyptian-Israeli agreement was signed, calling for Israel's withdrawal from the Sinai and the dismantling of settlements on Egyptian land, diplomatic relations between Israel and Egypt, borders open to trade and commerce, Israeli ships guaranteed passage through the Suez Canal, the Sinai demilitarized, and a permanent peace treaty to confirm these agreements (Appendix 4).

On September 17, 1978, we joyously signed the accords at the White House, but the celebration was short-lived. It seemed almost impossible to make any further progress. Six months later, in March 1979, I decided to go to Cairo and Jerusalem to try to resolve the remaining issues, and we were able to conclude the peace treaty, which called for a complete Israeli withdrawal from Egypt's Sinai and normal relations between the two countries. This success was followed by a few months of cooperation and easy communication between Egypt and Israel, but since then the negotiations have stalled completely. No progress has been made. The Israelis have not offered any appreciable autonomy to the Palestinians, and in fact the Begin-Shamir governments tightened their hold further on the occupied territories. Furthermore, neither the Jordanians nor the Palestinians have been willing to join the talks.

Sadat always insisted that the first priority had to be given to self-determination for the Palestinians, and all of us (perhaps excepting Begin) were convinced that these rights had been protected in the final document. All of us (including Begin) were also confident that the final terms of the treaty could be concluded within the three-month target time. The Americans and the

Egyptians knew that if Israel began building new settlements, the Palestinians, Jordanians, and other Arabs could never be convinced that the Camp David commitments would be honored. To them, a promise to grant the Palestinians "full autonomy," with an equal or final voice in determining the ultimate status of the occupied territories, while building large and permanent Israeli settlements would obviously be a mockery.

Perhaps the most serious omission of the Camp David talks was not clarifying in writing Begin's promise concerning the settlement freeze during the subsequent peace talks. The Egyptians believed that their worst error at Camp David was omitting the phrase "self-determination" as it applies to Palestinian rights, but I doubt that Begin would have accepted the possibility of an independent Palestinian state. Sadat and I also failed to keep King Hussein of Jordan adequately informed as the final terms of the accords were evolving, which undoubtedly contributed to his refusal to join the subsequent autonomy talks.

During my many conversations with Sadat, I often expressed apprehension about Egypt's growing isolation from the other Arabs, but he would scoff at my concern. He was certain that his initiative accurately represented the Egyptian people's aspirations for peace, and he was equally convinced that most of Israel's other Arab neighbors had the same ambition — among the people themselves. He strongly condemned the leaders of those nations for their shortsighted timidity when they failed to follow his example.

Sadat proved to be right about the fruitlessness of these attempts to punish Egypt. Try as they may, the other Arabs could not long exclude or ignore Egypt, with its formidable armed forces, its central location, its strong cultural heritage, its heterogeneous population of 47 million, its large external work force, and the willingness of its recent leaders to explore bold, new concepts. A Tel Aviv University professor said recently that the Arabs' attitude toward Egypt during their attempted boycott reminded him of an old headline in the London *Times*, FOG IN CHANNEL. EUROPE ISOLATED.

To the "rejectionists" in the Arab world, who could not bring themselves to abandon their determination to destroy Israel,

Sadat was a traitor; he had betrayed his own Arab brothers for personal glory and for unwarranted advantages for his own country at the expense of others. There were repeated calls for the ostracism of Egypt and the death of Sadat, but the Egyptian leader was not disturbed and calmly proceeded to pursue the goal of peace.

Early in the morning of October 6, 1981, the telephone rang in my home in Plains, Georgia. A reporter asked for my reaction to the attack on Sadat, quickly adding that the attempted assassination had not been successful, that he had only suffered minor injuries. I expressed my condemnation of terrorism, then put in a call to Egypt. I could not reach Sadat but talked to the American ambassador, who assured me that the Egyptian leader was well and that the would-be assassins had been caught. During the day I talked several more times to Cairo and watched on television as the tragic news was revealed. Anwar el-Sadat was dead at the hands of misguided religious fanatics. It was a great personal loss for me and a severe blow to the prospects for peace in the Middle East.

Since then, President Hosni Mubarak has been careful to keep the commitments made by his predecessor. During my more recent meetings with Egyptian leaders, it has been quite obvious that they are searching for a way to reassert Egypt's leadership both within the Arab world and as a major force in the peace process in the Middle East. My impression is that for the time being, the Arab world comes first, while the Egyptian-Israeli peace treaty remains intact. Mubarak, a loyal protégé of Sadat, lacks his boldness and perhaps his strategic concepts but is determined to remain true to his legacy. Mubarak is calm and patient, more interested and involved in the internal political and economic affairs of his country than his predecessor, and he has generally acted under difficult circumstances as he and his closest advisers believe Sadat would have done.

It is most instructive to listen to the Egyptian voices, because this country has provided the major leadership of recent years, both toward pan-Arabism under Nasser and toward an independent peace with Israel under Sadat. Without Egypt, the Arabs have been and are unlikely to initiate either an effective peace or a war with Israel.

The Egyptian leaders have felt most deeply the hopes and disappointments, the triumphs and tragedies, the closeness with and the alienation from their Arab brothers. The ancient land of Egypt still lives as a nation of Africa as well as an integral part of what we define as the Middle East. Within a generation, Egypt has forged a close political liaison with the Soviet Union while rejecting America and then formed an even closer relationship with the United States while excluding the Soviets. Most important, however, Egypt has, in a way, been the experimental laboratory for a peace initiative to resolve the ancient dispute between Arab and Jew, and its present leaders still acknowledge this heavy responsibility.

In any discussion of political circumstances in their region, the Arab leaders emphasize the gnawing centrality of the Palestinian question and point out that Egypt was preoccupied with this "Palestinian problem" long before there was an Israel. Like Sadat, President Mubarak considers the situation in the Middle East part of a global problem, ultimately involving the superpowers and the alignment of their friends and allies.

The Egyptians make it clear that the peace treaty between the two nations is still based on the overall framework that encompassed progress on the West Bank and Gaza and Israel's willingness to grant full autonomy and then self-determination to the Palestinians, and they show a deep concern about Israel's policies in the West Bank and Gaza. They now describe the territories as being filled with "small new ghettos of Israelis armed and looking at the Arabs around them as enemies," and see the growing settlements as aggravating and perpetuating the hatred that Sadat believed had ended with his visit to Jerusalem and the subsequent agreements.

Moderate Egyptian leaders who publicly acknowledge the advisability of accommodation with Israel and who strongly support the treaty have received a series of hard blows during the last four years. They see political restraints in the United States and the Egyptian pledge of peace with Israel as having partially nullified the deterrent effect of these two nations on Israel. They are highly embarrassed by constant reminders from other Arabs that since Egypt withdrew as a military counterforce, the Israelis have invaded Lebanon twice, annexed the Golan Heights, further tightened their hold on Jerusalem, bombed the Iraqi nuclear reactor, and greatly escalated their settlement activity in the occupied territories.

The distress of the Egyptians has been intensified by the reaction from Washington: greater military aid to Israel and the announcement of a "strategic alliance" in spite of what the Egyptians consider a number of unnecessarily belligerent acts by Israel.

Nevertheless, the Egyptians retain some hope that Sadat's dream of peace and their continuing support of his actions will still bear fruit. They have so far been frustrated by the unfulfilled presumption that Jordan would accept the basic premises of the Camp David accords and join the peace process, at least under the Reagan statement of 1982, which they call "a euphemism for Camp David."

Most Egyptians look upon King Hussein as a man of courage, and they are pleased that Jordan's monarch decided to renew diplomatic relations with Cairo in September 1984. It is a hopeful sign that Egypt and Jordan are creating a centrist group of Arab interests, willing to seek self-determination for the Palestinians through negotiations. Although Jordan has disavowed the Camp David accords, Mubarak (and perhaps Hussein) realizes that this agreement is the only official Israeli acknowledgment of Palestinian rights. The Egyptians will encourage Jordan's monarch to take the next step toward peace, but they acknowledge publicly and privately that Hussein cannot move too boldly. He must have assurances from the PLO and moderate Arabs that he will not be abandoned or condemned for his efforts. An Egyptian spokesman explained this patient attitude by saying, "Hussein is not Sadat, and Jordan is not Egypt."

The more optimistic Egyptians see the focus of worldwide interest and even some apparently negative factors giving the situation fluidity and offering potential opportunities for progress. More stability in Lebanon and the strengthened influence of Assad may give the Syrian leader a greater sense of security. Egyptian spokesmen believe that Syria's demands in Lebanon can be met without jeopardizing Lebanese existence or sovereignty, provided other Arab leaders and world opinion are marshaled in favor of protecting Lebanese rights. Also, the fragmentation of the PLO and the breakdown of Syria's influence on Arafat might provide an opportunity for Hussein to speak for or with the Palestinians in peace talks. Even Israel's settlement policy has increased fears in Jordan and encouraged Hussein to prevent a third exodus of West Bank Palestinians to the East Bank, thereby stabilizing the Arab population in the occupied territories. The continued war between Iran and Iraq and the resulting concern in the other Persian Gulf states about the prospect of a spreading conflict illustrates the advantages of peace and stability in the region. The public debate in Israel about the recent events in Lebanon and the occupied territories, as well as the obvious inadequacy of having peace with just one Arab state, strengthens the forces for peace and moderation. The welcoming of Egypt back into the Arab fold will certainly increase Mubarak's influence. And an administration in Washington free of the pressures of an election year may be more bold in its efforts. Some moderate Arabs see an analogy between the second Reagan administration and Dwight Eisenhower's second term, when Israel was forced to withdraw from the Sinai in March 1957. They hope to see some similar efforts from Washington that might encourage Israel to withdraw from other occupied territories.

The Egyptians have watched the peace movement in Israel and have been pleasantly surprised to find some Israelis even more fervent than many Arabs in their support of Palestinian rights. They observed with great interest that 400,000 Israelis took to the streets to protest the murder of the Palestinians in the two refugee camps during the invasion of Lebanon in 1982. Egyptian leaders hope the Israelis who support the Camp David accords and peace treaty share with them the knowledge that peace between the two countries in the Middle East power struggle no longer needs to be a "zero-sum" game, wherein each side can only gain at the expense of the other. It is possible for both Israel and its neighbors to benefit at the same time. Egyptian leaders acknowledge the political paralysis in Israel's hybrid Unity government, which makes Cairo continue to look to Washington for any negotiating initiative.

The Egyptians emphasize the significance of the Arabs' willingness to accept the principle of coexistence with Israel, and maintain that there is adequate proof that they can live in peace with Israel once a formal peace agreement is signed. They use as evidence the withdrawal agreements of 1974 and 1975 involving Israel, Syria, and Egypt and the Egyptian-Israeli peace treaty of 1979 — all of them upheld in spite of Sadat's death, the "annexation" of the Golan Heights, and the invasion of Lebanon.

Through constant and quiet diplomatic efforts, Egypt has attempted to stimulate other Arab states and the PLO to join the peace process. Although it was not present at the Arab summit conference at Fez in September 1982, Egypt supported the Arab plan that emanated from those meetings, which alluded to the acceptance of all states in the region. The Egyptians are convinced that a majority of Arabs are reconciled to the inevitability of making peace with Israel. Most Arabs demand an answer to the "Which Israel?" question before any discussion can begin, but some are increasingly willing to find or shape the answer through negotiation.

The Egyptians look to the United States to reason with the Israeli government, but, like other Arabs, they have been disheartened by inconsistency in Washington. They were astonished and publicly infuriated by the Reagan statement after the Fez summit conference, which showed an impatience with or condemnation for Arab compromises while the reaction to Begin's total and immediate rejection was relatively benign. This unequal treatment damaged the U.S.-Egyptian relationship and Egypt's standing as a moderate among Arabs.

Spokesmen in Cairo call for the following new steps toward a resumption of the comprehensive peace process:

• A real change in attitude among the parties involved, including the willingness of the Palestinians and Jordan to join in peace talks with Israel and of the Israeli leaders to cease settlement activity during the talks.

• Pledges of no violence during negotiations.

• A show of good faith by Israel's withdrawing its forces from Lebanon.

• A conceptual merger of the common features of U.N. Resolution 242, the Camp David accords, the Reagan statement, and the Fez resolutions, including the assumption of a transition period before defining the ultimate status of the West Bank and Gaza.

- Putting the negotiating process in the hands of moderates.
- The use of "constructive ambiguity" to resolve temporarily those extremely sensitive issues such as Jerusalem which require a higher degree of trust and communication than are presently possible.
- The encouragement of West Bank and Gaza Palestinians to negotiate in a direct way, either by a statement from Arafat, the mayors, or other trusted leaders in the occupied territories or from Jordan's reconstituted parliament.
- The full and persistent involvement by the United States as mediator (not advocate) in dealing with the crucial issues of Palestinian rights and the withdrawal of Israeli forces from the other occupied territories.

At some time, the Egyptians, Jordanians, and Palestinians must move together in dealing with the Israelis, and for a *final* settlement to be possible, the Syrians must be included. For all this to happen the Egyptians know they must play an integral role, but they prefer to stay in the background for a while until the intentions of the United States, Israel, and Jordan can be ascertained.

Without making any public concessions, Egypt has been restored to membership in the Islamic Conference and is moving quietly and effectively to establish genuine relationships with individual Arab nations. There is a small minority in Egypt that believes that it can and should remain independent of the turmoil and intrigues of the other Arab nations, but most disagree with this philosophy.

The first significant move in demonstrating Egypt's changed status was the meeting between Arafat and Mubarak in December 1983, shortly after the second forced Palestinian departure from Lebanon. In consulting with the Egyptian president, Arafat was attempting to shore up his reputation among the Arabs as the undisputed leader of the Palestinian cause. In effect, he violated the Baghdad summit recommendations of 1978 and the 1983 Palestine National Council resolution, which prohibited any contact with Egypt until it abrogated the Camp David accords and the Israeli peace treaty. The battered Arafat showed his independence, which helped to give Mubarak a chance to call for the renewal of the Jordan-PLO dialogue with hopes of rejuvenating the peace talks.

Egyptian leaders now consider most of the PLO leadership to be relatively moderate; they prefer that Arafat be protected and supported in his wavering inclination for Jordanian and Palestinian representatives to join the peace talks. When President Mubarak and King Hussein visited President Reagan in February 1984, the Egyptian President was publicly emphatic in his support of Arafat. In November 1984, the Egyptians were pleased to see King Hussein welcome the convening of the Palestine National Council in Amman.

A basic premise for Sadat, and for President Mubarak, has always been that the peace treaty was just one part of the overall Camp David agreement, and Egypt will honor the entire package as long as Israel does. The hope is that the Israelis will not, either in practical ways or through legal means, abrogate the agreements concerning Palestinian rights, their withdrawal of military forces from the West Bank and Gaza, and the specific terms of U.N. Resolution 242. Such a final action, so often threatened by Israeli leaders, would end Sadat's dream for peace and bring Middle Eastern affairs back full circle — to an isolated Israel surrounded by united and implacable Arab foes, waiting patiently as they prepared for another opportunity to strike a fatal blow.

# Saudi Arabia

IT WAS THE EARLY SPRING of 1983, my first opportunity to return to Riyadh as a private citizen, and we had to wait for a few minutes in the airport's private lounge for the Saudi officials to complete their routine examination of our group's documents. Rosalynn and I enjoyed the Arabic coffee, poured dextrously from the curved spout of an ornately carved *finjan* into a tiny cup. We wondered how the waiter could avoid spilling a few drops of the dark, thick liquid on the beautiful carpet and what might happen to him if he marred the woven work of art. When we were ready to leave for the guest palace, we waggled our empty cups from side to side to indicate that we did not want another refill. One or two in our party did not like the strong brew and left some of it in the cups as they were returned to the serving tray. In each case, the waiter casually threw the coffee onto the carpet, then stacked the dishes and left. Later, a diplomatic official explained that a used carpet was considered more precious than a new one, and that it was an indication of hospitality for a host to demonstrate that guests of honor were the prime consideration and that dishes, furniture, and other household goods were relatively insignificant.

To Westerners, Saudi Arabia is a strange country; for a long time its geographical isolation protected it both from colonial domination and from the imposition of European habits and customs. However, with the Saudis' oil riches and growing influence in regional and international affairs, the opinions and decisions of their leaders have become important in determining the future of the Middle East. I knew they were enjoying relative stability in their own country but shared the general concern about potential threats from the new and uncontrollable events in Afghanistan, Yemen, Lebanon, and Iran.

I had wanted to visit King Fahd while in Saudi Arabia and was disappointed to learn that he was meeting with tribal leaders in the desert and was not expected to return to the city for a while. Instead, a full schedule of consultations had been arranged for me with Crown Prince Abdullah, Defense Minister Prince Sultan, Foreign Minister Prince Saud al-Faisal, and other leaders of the Saudi government, most of them members of the royal family. As it happened, late in the evening after we arrived, I was informed that King Fahd wanted us to join him the next day at his desert camp, about 200 kilometers north of the capital.

In the morning we awakened to the startling sound of a heavy downpour. This made helicopter flights impossible, and, as the rain continued, even the streets and roads to the airport became totally impassable. Riyadh had an unbelievable five inches of rain and just a rudimentary drainage system, so there was no place for the water to go; the floodwaters simply filled in the lowest places, many of which were in the streets themselves. There portable pumps were constantly filling dozens of large tank trucks, which hauled the water out of the city and dumped it in the desert. At midmorning the sun came out, and after a few hours some of the streets were passable again. We were driven to the nearest helicopter landing site and were soon on our way.

For mile after mile we flew low over the sand dunes and normally dry streambeds, some near the city now filled to overflowing. There were several irrigated farms, and we were surprised at the profusion of wildflowers in many places. Among the low hills and dunes were any number of black goathair tents, which housed the nomadic families who followed the transitory grass patches with their flocks. As we circled over one or two of these temporary settlements, we noted that in every camp there were ponies and a few camels, which were used for normal transportation, and most often a dusty but expensive Land Rover parked nearby. These, the pilots said, were used for frequent long trips into the distant city.

Finally we ascended to a higher altitude to clear the plateaus that abruptly rose a thousand or more feet above the surrounding desert floor. After another half hour we saw the encampment ahead in the distance, a remarkable desert city of snow white tents arranged in large circles. There seemed to be no permanent road of any kind going to the site, just the tracks of the vehicles that had brought the temporary residents to their meeting with the King. I could discern no reason for the choice of this particular place, but the pilot said it was especially beautiful following the infrequent desert showers. As we circled closer, we noticed that immediately behind each of the main tents was an elaborate mobile home perched on a large Mercedes truck chassis, modern additions to the traditional tent dwellings of the Saudi chieftains. Just beyond the periphery of the camp was a group of portable diesel electric generators and an elaborate array of satellite dish antennas to provide power for the several hundred desert homes, international communications for the nation's ruler, and television entertainment for those at the campsite.

All these modern conveniences were taken for granted, but so was the ancient ritual of his majesty's going into the remote desert to meet with tribal chieftains from throughout the kingdom. They had come, not only to pay homage and to repeat their pledges of loyalty, but also to confer with their leader on domestic and international policy, to report on their tribal affairs, and to request goods and services for their people.

After we had light refreshments in one of the mobile homes, I was asked to join the King while Rosalynn was whisked off to visit the Saudi women, none of whom I ever saw on this or any other trip to the country. They were in a different camp entirely, over the sand dunes and out of sight.

I had known Fahd ibn Abd al-Aziz Al Saud for several years and had consulted with him while President in both Washington and Saudi Arabia. Then he had been a most powerful crown prince, with many international duties assigned to him by his half-brother King Khalid. Both men were members of the royal family of Saud, which had ruled parts of the Arabian Peninsula for most of two and a half centuries.

During much earlier days, before ships sailed around the continent of Africa, Arabia served as one of the prime land routes between India and the West, and its various rulers were both rich and powerful. Historical records are scarce, but we know of the Queen of Sheba, who came from Arabia to visit the even more powerful King Solomon of Israel in about 1000 B.C. Subsequently, some of the Arabians accepted Judaism, and a Jewish kingdom was established in the southwestern corner of the peninsula; in the fourth and fifth centuries A.D. many of the people became Christians. The history of the region was chaotic because the many political and religious conflicts brought about constant changes in leadership and in alignments among the tribes.

Then came the Prophet Mohammed, who sought to unify the tribes of Arabia into a commonwealth of Islam. The caliphs who succeeded him after his death in A.D. 632 expanded the rule of Islam to Damascus in 635, Jerusalem in 638, Alexandria in 642, and Persia in 643. Later, the faith was extended west to Spain and east to India. In the process of this expansion, Damascus and then Baghdad and other cities became the dominant centers and Arabia was relegated to a mere province, its remaining importance being as the site of the two holy cities of Islam, Mecca and Medina. For centuries thereafter, the Arabian Peninsula was forever being rearranged into many rapidly changing tribal principalities.

During the early years of the twentieth century, the father of Khalid and Fahd, Abd al-Aziz Al Saud, was successful in bringing together the different regions of the peninsula under his dominion, and in 1932 he consolidated them into the Kingdom of Saudi Arabia. With a proper blend of force and compromise, religious revival and agricultural reform, as well as a large number of carefully planned marriages, the King was able to overcome the tribal jealousies and conflicts and to emerge as the recognized leader of a wide geographical area. He ruled with great effectiveness until his death in 1953, and was then succeeded by his sons Saud, then Faisal, Khalid, and now Fahd.

Commercial oil production was begun in Saudi Arabia in 1938, later bringing almost unbelievable wealth to all of these heirs and their subjects. With these riches, Saudi Arabia was catapulted into a position of political and economic leadership during the 1970s that put enormous pressure on the royal family. However, they maintained political stability within the kingdom and greatly enhanced their leadership role among the other Arabs by resolving their own internal differences through close and secret consultation, by carefully dispensing part of their oil income, and by capitalizing on their preeminence as custodians of the holy places of Islam. The Saudi rulers were able to preserve an acceptable balance between delivering the material advantages of a modern state and at the same time preserving the proper degree of religious commitment. They also offset their absolute authority with a remarkable closeness to their subjects.

King Khalid told me on my first visit to Saudi Arabia that each day he opened his doors to many dozens of citizens who wished to see him, and offered food and hospitality to his visitors. One evening each week, the women of the royal family were permitted to bring their problems and requests to him. He traveled widely through the desert kingdom with a fleet of tractor-trailers carrying a complete mobile hospital and personally welcomed those who needed medical treatment. When I expressed concern about the time-consuming extent of these administrative chores, he replied that the kingdom could not survive if its leaders ever abandoned this commitment of personal service to its people.

During my earliest visits with members of the royal family, I was originally surprised and somewhat doubtful but later convinced of the paramount importance of the religious beliefs that color their public and private statements and shape their actions and negotiating positions. With their power and prestige, the royal family can enjoy the flexibility of practical decisions, but it is helpful to understand that to a great extent their Islamic faith is the basis for the laws of their land, the legitimacy and authority of the royal family and their rule, and the role of leadership played by the Saudis within the Moslem world.

Late in May 1977, when Crown Prince Fahd made his first official visit to the White House, we had a working supper for our guests, for top administration officials, and for key members of the Congress. One of the Americans, Speaker of the House of Representatives Thomas P. ("Tip") O'Neill, Jr., asked the Saudis how they were able to institute such rapid economic growth in their country with no apparent outbreak of revolutionary forces, as had been observed in other conservative religious nations undergoing rapid change.

The crown prince responded with a most effective explanation concerning the stabilizing influence of religious faith on the people of his nation. He said that the Saudis had long been deprived of some of the necessities of life that were taken for granted by citizens of the Western world, but with their oil wealth they were now able to improve their living conditions, educate their children, and prepare more permanent employment for the time in the distant future when depleted oil reserves could not supply their basic needs. The teachings of the Koran guided them in humble living and in how to assimilate cycles of material prosperity and deprivation without their basic way of life being subverted by outside influences. The paramount duty of the royal family, he said, was to accommodate the pressures of modernization without letting Western culture violate the teachings of Islam. If there were ever an irreconcilable conflict, he prayed that their religious beliefs would always come first. He added that the leaders of Saudi Arabia were human and fallible like others, but they knew that as long as the people were convinced of their religious integrity, the royal family would keep the loyalty of their subjects. All of us were deeply impressed by his somewhat hesitant but eloquent words.

Since then I have noticed that in public statements designed to explain their philosophy, their political principles and priorities, and their positions on current international issues, the Saudis seldom overlook an opportunity to stress the centrality of their special responsibility to guard the holy places of Islam and to provide leadership, financial support, and unity in the Moslem world.

Now, in the desert, I proceeded to the central tent and was welcomed by the King and his nephew, Foreign Minister Prince Saud al-Faisal. The tent floor was covered with Oriental carpets, and there were some long, cylindrical cushions on which to lean back when seated. However, I was asked to go to a nearby cozy and air-conditioned mobile home for our discussions. We were scheduled to meet for an hour or so and then join the tribal chieftains and the rest of my party for the evening meal, but it was more than five hours later that King Fahd and I concluded our wide-ranging talk. He began by complaining about the personal discomfort of having to limit his consumption of sweet tea; he had formerly enjoyed drinking forty or fifty cups a day during almost continuous consultations with his visitors. This was the chief element of a strict diet imposed by his physicians to reduce his weight and to correct other physical problems that he described as minor and relatively inconsequential.

The King was most eager to describe the domestic affairs of his nation: advances in employment, education, housing, women's rights, agriculture, transportation, defense, and the political relationships centered on the royal family. He outlined in some detail programs to develop human services and skills that were included in a series of sequential "five-year plans." Then he emphasized, as the Saudis have been doing most frequently since the Iranian revolution, that this was to "modernize," not "westernize," their society.

He seemed more relaxed when he turned the conversation to the role of religion in the lives of his people, the same subject we had discussed at the White House. He admitted that the high moral standards of the Koran were not fully met on many occasions in either their religious or secular affairs, but he emphasized that they guided his personal relationships with tribal leaders and with the most lowly of his subjects. Furthermore, he said, the Islamic faith provided the common ground on which all Arab nations attempt to reconcile their differences and to act in concert on even the most difficult and divisive issues.

Fahd deplored the negative stereotype of Arabs in the United States and other Western nations and the resulting misconceptions about his nation and its people: that the strength and influence of Saudi Arabia depends solely on wealth and that the oil fields are its most precious possession, that the government of the royal family is unstable or lacks the support of its subjects, that other less fortunate Arabs and particularly the Palestinians could ever be forgotten, and that momentary economic developments or political issues might transcend the unchanging commitments and principles that have for so long guided the rulers in his family. He reiterated that his people had survived for generations without oil and that he and other leaders were routinely preparing for a future when their reserves would be largely depleted.

He especially appreciated my approval of selling the F-15 airplanes to Saudi Arabia in 1978 and our furnishing the AWACS planes with American crews to monitor possible air attacks against his country from across the Persian Gulf. Fahd could not understand how the United States or any of our European allies could object to an adequate Saudi military defense force, which was needed to protect the nation's extensive and relatively vulnerable borders. He emphasized that the Saudis' unchanging orientation is against the atheism of the communist world and that there exists a natural desire among the hundreds of millions of Moslems on earth to be friendly and to work in harmony with the Western democracies.

Both the King and the foreign minister particularly wanted me to know that the protection of the holy cities of Islam was their highest military responsibility, and they urged me to examine a map on which they pointed out the religious sites and the long distances involved in their relatively large nation. Bordering the vital Persian Gulf with the Iran-Iraq war on their doorstep, with communist forces in nearby countries, and separated by only a few miles from Israel, Saudi Arabia saw itself surrounded by uncertain and potentially hostile neighbors.

One of the prime elements in furthering their religious beliefs and in helping to ensure regional peace and stability is the Saudis' commitment to Arab brotherhood, particularly with the Palestinians, whom they consider severely victimized. In 1977, when I was exploring with Middle East leaders every possible degree of flexibility to bring about negotiations, the Saudis had been almost unique in insisting at all times that the Palestinians have the right to an independent state. King Fahd pointed out that the remittance system, which permits workers from poorer countries to send wages home from their labor in richer ones, vividly illustrates the economic interdependence of the Arab nations, and he emphasized the common culture, religion, language, and commercial opportunities that exist among the peoples of the Arab world.

However, there are also many centrifugal forces tending to force the Arab peoples apart. The Saudi leaders always express complete confidence that they themselves can retain their wealth, stability, and status as keepers of the holy places, but they are forced to contend with the splintering of the faithful of other nations into revolutionary religious fragments, often in the bloodiest of conflicts. King Fahd discussed the Iranian revolution, the occupation of the holiest mosque in Mecca by hundreds of religious fanatics in 1979, and the more recent bombings in Kuwait as serious threats to stability unless there could be an alleviation of misguided revolutionary fervor. More and more, Jordan was feeling a threat to its own well-being or even existence from the growing Palestinian crisis in the occupied territories, and a desire for peace and the resolution of this issue was threatening King Hussein's commitment to the rule of Arab consensus, an underlying foundation of Saudi diplomacy.

Because of these challenges to harmony and stability, Saudi diplomats were being uncharacteristically obvious in their attempts to preserve Lebanese independence and to lessen the tension between Beirut and Damascus. In the process they, like others who braved this political morass, had suffered the consequences of terrorist retaliation by some of their diplomats' having been assassinated. However, in the words of Prince Bandar bin Sultan, the Saudi ambassador to the United States and a key negotiator in Lebanon, they consider success in this effort to be "little more than a Band-Aid unless the Arab-Israeli conflict is comprehensively resolved."

In Iran, the Ayatollah Khomeini has defied all efforts to resolve the long and extremely costly war between his country and Iraq, but the greatest potential threat to regional stability is not the possibility of Iran's attacking other Persian Gulf nations but its exporting the Shia religious zeal and political revolution to the more stable and conservative Moslem regimes. This could become a direct challenge to the Riyadh government, headed by the royal family of Sunni Moslems.

Since Syria was supporting Persian Iran in its war against the Arab nation of Iraq, I was surprised to find a relatively friendly attitude toward President Assad among the Saudi leaders. They made it plain to me that there were frequent high-level consultations between Riyadh and Damascus and that a clear understanding existed about the relationship between the two countries — even including Syria's involvement in the Persian Gulf war.

The Saudis acknowledge these serious divisions and wars among their brothers, but in responding to Western criticism, they often mention the conflicts ranging from civil wars to world wars that have been fought among Christians. Acknowledging the difficulty of reaching a consensus among Arab leaders, they emphasize that all of them have to be willing to make major concessions, often interpreted in the West as evidence of weakness or deviousness as each is forced to modify a previously expressed preference or opinion. The Saudis insist that any attempt by the United States or others to fragment the Arabs further or to prevent reconciliation among them is contrary to the best interests of all who desire peace and stability.

There is no doubt that the Saudis want stability in the region and constantly strive to achieve it, and whenever there is an absence or steady erosion of pan-Arab unity, as there has been over the past several years, the Saudis are most concerned. The Egyptians, after being excluded from Arab councils, are just beginning to resume a portion of their previous unifying influence but without surrendering their commitment to peace with Israel or their strong ties to the West. This means that among the Libyans, Syrians, and South Yemenis they are still despised or at least distrusted, but even in this difficult case the Saudis have worked quietly to heal any serious rifts in Arab ranks.

The superpower struggle is also a divisive factor among the Arabs, with the Soviets always eager to expand their influence in the region. Syria is increasingly dependent on the Soviets for arms and military advice; Afghan freedom fighters are struggling valiantly to avoid complete Soviet domination; Ethiopia has welcomed thousands of seemingly permanent Cuban and Soviet "advisers"; South Yemen is considered to be completely within the Soviet fold, and, in October 1984, North Yemen signed a

Friendship and Cooperation treaty with Moscow. At the same time, the United States has most often enjoyed a good relationship with the other Arab governments, but the ill-advised military action in Lebanon and the announcement of a U.S.-Israeli "strategic alliance" late in 1983 have caused deep concern among America's most loyal Arab friends. When such a decision was first rumored, the Saudis called it "highly destructive of sound and permanent relationships between the United States and the Arab world."

In spite of the Soviet presence in Afghanistan, disturbances and threats on their own peninsula from South Yemen, and even the war between Iraq and Iran, the Saudi leaders look upon the Arab-Israeli conflict as being the most serious obstacle to any permanent resolution of differences. They reminded me that all of the nuclear alerts of the last fifteen or twenty years have come about because of developments in the Middle East, and they see their region as by far the most likely place for any superpower military confrontation to occur in the future.

In addition to other challenges to Saudi leadership, the potentially beneficial impact of Arab oil wealth is diminishing. When OPEC money was flowing freely, the major oil-producing states had almost unlimited funds to help the other Arab brothers financially or to influence them to be more cooperative in preserving harmony and avoiding any strife that might endanger this constantly rising income. With the Iranian revolution, the Persian Gulf war, and the sharp reduction in demand and price for Arab oil, the time of almost unlimited funding has ended.

In the past, it has been generally assumed that the United States would play the major role in working among the various parties to bring about further steps toward reconciliation and peace. However, in recent months this presumption has been increasingly challenged by the Arab leaders, who express doubt publicly that the American leaders will be willing to face the domestic political consequences of trying to induce Israel to negotiate, to withdraw from the occupied territories, or to honor the basic commitments in U.N. Resolution 242 or the Camp David accords.

How do the Saudis feel about the Israelis and their presence? They are usually quite circumspect in their public comments, but

there is no doubt that the Saudi leaders share the almost unanimous Arab feelings of resentment and antagonism toward the
encroachment of Israel on land that was previously occupied and
ruled by their Moslem brothers. They consider the Israeli occupation of any portion of Palestine to be parallel to that of the Crusaders, who "were able to maintain a costly, bloody, and
precarious presence of a sort on and off for about a century at that
Eastern edge of the Mediterranean." They consider that to be
"hardly any time at all in history, as the abiding patterns of our
part of the world must be measured." One Saudi spokesman has
referred to Israel as a "transplant, dependent on permanent and
ever-increasing artificial respiration from outside, yet unwilling
or unable to become a part of the area."

The Saudis realize, however, that in Jordan and Egypt and
among many displaced Palestinians, the overwhelming desire is
to move a bit more expeditiously than is implied in the hundred-
year example of the Crusaders, and they have expressed their
support for resolving the ongoing conflict through peaceful negotiations, provided the potential results will not jeopardize the
fundamental rights of the Palestinians as expressed in various
U.N. resolutions.

King Fahd was especially proud of the Fez declaration, which
grew out of the August 1981 "Fahd statement," and looked upon
these Arab proposals as an adequate basis on which further
progress toward peace might be made. Although to Western eyes
the phrases composed at Fez are very general and difficult to de-
cipher, the Saudis see only narrow differences between this declaration and the Reagan statement, which preceded it by only a
week. Prince Sultan said recently in an interview, "I do not believe there is an Arab country which wants to enter into a direct
war with Israel. The Arabs declared their opinion at the Fez
summit. They now want and desire peace based on right and justice. The peace door is still open and work in this direction is
continuing."

In spite of the obvious power of the Saudi leaders, there is no
doubt that Americans and many others expect too much from
them and fail to recognize or acknowledge that, with all their
wealth and prestige, the Saudis do not have unbounded influence

in the Middle East. I know that on several occasions Americans have expected our Saudi friends to "deliver" some of the other Arabs or at least to be bold leaders themselves when issues of importance were at stake. We expected them to moderate the Arab condemnation of Sadat after his peace initiative, to support strongly the Camp David accords, to induce Jordan and the Palestinians to join the peace talks then and again in April 1983, and to induce Syria to accept the terms of the withdrawal agreement between Israel and Lebanon later that same year. We were often disappointed — at times even somewhat angry — when our expectations were not realized.

As one knows the Saudis better, it is easier to understand their caution in dealing with extremely controversial issues and why their influence is limited. The Saudis' attitudes toward diplomacy and their discreet political style have been shaped by the circumstances of their existence. They have a relatively small native population, their military is not a major force, they are surrounded by potentially dangerous neighbors whom they cannot afford to aggravate too much, and their own leadership is predicated on compromise and the forging of a consensus among independent and volatile leaders in a highly divided Arab world. Almost invariably when I was President, I felt that our own basic goals were compatible with those of the Saudi leaders and that they were inclined to be helpful whenever possible. I might add that the Saudis and many others greatly overestimate the influence of the United States, and they never understood why we cannot "deliver" our own friends in the Middle East whenever it suited our purposes.

Without abandoning the essence of their religious faith or the common goals of the Arab world as defined by the most recent expression of consensus, the leaders of Saudi Arabia will be inclined to dampen tendencies toward revolution or anarchy in their region. They prefer stability among existing regimes, compromises when Arab unanimity is at stake, peace in the region, and a political orientation toward the West. Although the Saudis look upon Israel as a disturbing irritant that might ultimately be removed, in the meantime, they would probably give tacit support to a peace arrangement based on U.N. Resolution 242 or the

Fez declaration, which they consider close enough to the Camp David accords or to the Reagan statement to provide a basis for negotiation.

In a cautious way, the leaders of Saudi Arabia can be a crucial and beneficial force in the Middle East when it is clear that their influence can make the difference in bringing peace and stability to the region as an alternative to war and continuing political turmoil.

# The Future

THERE IS NO MAGIC ANSWER to the Middle East puzzle, and it is unrealistic to address the extremely complex issues and conflicting points of view with any marked degree of optimism. Since the Israeli-Egyptian peace treaty was signed, much blood has been shed unnecessarily and hopes for a negotiated peace have faded. At the same time, it is impossible to abandon the search for peace in spite of the almost insurmountable obstacles.

The questions to be considered are almost endless: What possibilities does the future hold? What are the prime requisites for peace? Can there be a relatively stable peace that merely perpetuates the present circumstances and trends? Will those who are aggrieved be content to wait quietly for a doubtful peace settlement in the distant future? Must the situation steadily deteriorate until another crisis causes the interested parties to act? Is there a better prospect for success from a quiet and persistent diplomatic effort or from a bold and public move toward negotiations? What common ground already exists on which the contending parties can build a more secure future? Most chilling of all, could the present differences lead to the use of nuclear weapons or a direct military confrontation between the superpowers?

I have spent a substantial portion of my public life dealing with these questions; more recently, I have spoken to literally hundreds of people in order to get the broadest and most balanced view possible. I have always been sustained in times of greatest discouragement by the conviction that the people in the region — even those Syrians, Israelis, and Palestinians who are most distrusted by their adversaries — want the peace efforts to succeed. The rhetoric and demands from all sides may be harsh, but there are obvious areas of agreement that can provide a basis for progress. Private discussions with the Arab leaders are much more promising than any analysis of their public statements would lead one to believe, and in Israel there is a strong element of moderation that is rarely heard or appreciated in the neighboring states.

The situation in the Middle East continues to be unstable because of two crucial factors. First, the Arabs refuse to give clear and official recognition to the right of Israel to exist in peace within clearly defined and secure borders. Second, the Israelis refuse to withdraw from the occupied territories and to grant the Palestinians their basic human rights, including self-determination.

Other complications are the absence of a clear and authoritative Palestinian voice; the refusal of both sides to join peace talks without onerous conditions; the sustained presence of external forces and continued bloodshed in Lebanon because of the civil strife: Israel's expansive settlements policy in the occupied territories; strains between Israel and Egypt because of the Lebanese invasion; the increasing influence of the Soviets in the region, which enhances their ability to block negotiations; the terribly destructive war between Iran and Iraq; the rise in Islamic fundamentalism; and the lack of any protracted effort by the United States to pursue peace based on the agreements already reached.

An imposing list — but there is more. Opposing forces tend to become further radicalized by the arrogance of victory or the hopelessness of defeat. In any confrontation, the most abusive statements of a few are always remembered and nurtured by those who already despise each other. Insecurity breeds paranoia, and this leads to the ultimate concern among the Israelis and Palestinians that prevents any move toward mutual recognition or alleviation of hatred: the threat of extinction or the loss of identity as a people.

The Middle East is fluid, ever-changing, and it is difficult to predict what might next take place within the PLO and between the Palestinians and other Arabs; among the domestic political factions in Lebanon and between those groups and the external military forces; on the shores of the Persian Gulf; and in Israel concerning its policy in the occupied territories. Economic pressures, particularly on Israel, are bound to increase. These changes can contribute either to peace or to escalating bloodshed.

Even the ultimate horror of mutual destruction is not totally unthinkable. It is widely assumed that Israel has atomic weapons or the capability to deploy them quickly and that the Soviets have pledged to protect their client states from such an attack with any means necessary. What would the United States do? It could not stand aloof if the Middle East burst into flames. This is only a remote possibility, but it is clear that desperation on either side could precipitate a more serious regional confrontation than has been seen before. There must be no further delay if present opportunities are not to be lost forever.

In spite of the obvious need to resolve differences, the peace effort does not have a life of its own; it is not self-sustaining. Israel and most Arab regimes have become increasingly preoccupied with domestic problems, which include resurgent religious identity, rising expectations among more literate constituencies and the emerging middle classes, a fear of further intrusion by external forces including the superpowers, and a drastic reduction in oil revenues. These factors have caused great concern to some Arab states that heretofore had focused more on external matters, including peace with Israel and a just solution to the Palestinian question. Now, Arab leaders are tending to free themselves from their Palestinian burden. Furthermore, a mounting economic crisis has forced the Israeli leaders to concentrate on domestic affairs. The indeterminate 1984 elections left Israel somewhat hamstrung in international diplomacy and perhaps incapable of launching any bold move toward substantive negotiations with the Syrians, Jordanians, or Palestinians.

The situation is obviously not hopeful, but neither is it hopeless if leaders can be persuaded to concentrate on the progress already made and the many areas of agreement that now exist and to explore any possible new avenues toward peace.

In November 1983, President Gerald Ford and I were co-chairmen of a Consultation on the Middle East at Emory University in Atlanta, Georgia. We invited many of the American statesmen who had helped to conduct the negotiations during the past few years as well as key government spokesmen from Egypt, Jordan, Syria, Lebanon, Saudi Arabia, and the Soviet Union. An expert on Palestinian affairs analyzed the views of his people, and a half-dozen Israelis described the many opinions then current in their nation. There were heated discussions, including the public cross-examination of each speaker by friend and foe. Old wounds were reopened, examined from all sides, and sometimes healed. There was some vitriol on a few occasions, but no one walked out of any session in anger.

In an academic environment with the sessions conducted by two former U.S. presidents, it was possible to put aside the ancient restraints and share information and opinions, and during private times between the public debates there was an even more unrestrained and productive exchange of ideas among the participants. It was exciting to see scholars and diplomats from Jerusalem, Tel Aviv, Damascus, Cairo, Amman, and other university and government centers eagerly becoming acquainted with one another. Many of them had devoted their lives to studying the works of each other, but they had never had a chance to meet.

The assembled leaders were particularly impressed by the degree of consensus among the agreements and resolutions already supported by the different nations and factions, and they recognized how valuable this understanding would be as a basis for negotiations in the future. At the end of the consultation, a group of the more senior spokesmen asked President Ford and me to relay what had been learned to the secretary of state, the national security adviser, and Democratic and Republican leaders in both houses of the U.S. Congress. We complied with their request within a week.

As we have seen, several of the pertinent U.N. resolutions have been endorsed by both Israel and the Arab countries. U.N. Resolution 242 still has currency and is the umbrella document, accepted by most governments in the Middle East, under which other proposals have been bred. U.N. Resolution 338, generally accepted, calls for direct negotiations among the disputing parties, an important basis for future progress. Despite its severe criticism from many sources, the Israeli-Egyptian treaty remains as a vivid demonstration of the achievements of diplomacy and the possibilities that still exist.

Although the disparities among them are usually emphasized, the 1978 Camp David accords, the 1980 Venice Declaration of the European powers, the 1981 Fahd plan, and the Reagan statement and the Fez resolution of 1982 all contain significant common elements that could be expanded if pursued in good faith. In all the official agreements and proposals, there is a presumption of the exchange of occupied territory for mutual recognition, security, and real peace. Even with all the inconsistencies, this in itself would provide an adequate foundation for substantive negotiations among the interested parties — provided they sincerely want peace, are willing to forgo unacceptable conditions, and are prepared to honor the documents they themselves have already signed. There must be some element of boldness to break the existing stalemate, an acceptance of peace talks without any assurance of the outcome, and the courage on the part of some Arab leaders to escape from the effective veto of unanimity or consensus.

Tangible progress has already been made:

• Sadat has proven that in real negotiations with Israel, peace and withdrawal from the occupied territories are possible.

• The 1979 peace treaty between Israel and Egypt and the 1974 Israeli-Syrian withdrawal agreement have been meticulously honored. Israel and Lebanon have conducted direct negotiations. There is a long-standing history of cooperation between Jordan and Israel in matters concerning the West Bank and Gaza and the Palestinians who live there. Most of its Arab neighbors have, therefore, accepted the permanent existence of Israel as an indisputable fact and are no longer calling for an end to the State of Israel, though a residue of that feeling does remain.

• Even among those who acknowledge the right of self-determination for Palestinians, there is a growing consensus that some federation or confederation might be an acceptable arrangement between the Jordanians and the Palestinians in the West Bank and Gaza.

• Almost everyone has accepted the principle of a transition period between the present unsatisfactory situation and the ultimate opportunity for people to decide their own destiny in a climate of peace.

It was clear to me early in the spring of 1983 that King Hussein was ready to move toward peace talks under the general umbrella of U.N. Resolution 242 or the Reagan statement, and I am convinced that he is still looking for the opportunity. Some prerequisites must be fulfilled for him to act: a demonstrated willingness by Israel to negotiate in good faith; proof of U.S. determination in reopening the peace process; at least tacit approval from Saudi Arabia and perhaps some other moderate Arabs; and a rational explanation for his speaking on behalf of the Palestinians. In 1983 it was not clear that any of the requirements were met, but he was almost able to proceed without them. There are still opportunities for them all.

Although Begin and his Likud government immediately rejected the ideas proposed by President Reagan, many if not most Israelis have responded positively to the prospect of Jordan's joining the peace talks along with Palestinian representatives under the general principles of U.N. Resolution 242, the Camp David accords, or Reagan's statement. With strong leadership from Washington, this could be possible. Hussein's convening of the Jordanian parliament with half of its members West Bank Palestinians gives some indication that this might be the avenue he seeks for representing the Palestinian position in future peace talks. Hussein could not conclude a final agreement with Israel concerning Jerusalem or even the West Bank and Gaza, but now that Jordan has renewed diplomatic relations with Egypt, he could help take evolutionary steps toward a more comprehensive accord. King Hussein is a slender reed on which to rest the prospects for peace, but he is still a necessary participant in future negotiations. Either increased threats to Jordan's existence or the alleviation of some of his present concerns could induce him to play this vital role.

Assad rejects the concept of bilateral discussions between any individual Arab state and Israel and would do what he could to prevent them, but he has reiterated to me and others his willingness to negotiate with Israel and other interested parties on the basis of U.N. Resolutions 242 and 338. Also, Syria has been very careful to observe the terms of the 1974 withdrawal agreement with Israel. Assad is unpredictable, but he would probably not have the support of his Soviet or Arab benefactors if he threatened to attack Jordan if Hussein went to the negotiating table.

Israel has made substantial commitments to peace as confirmed by the Camp David accords, by the withdrawal of its forces from the Sinai, and by U.N. 242 and other resolutions that they have officially supported. There are some caveats and interpretations with which the Arabs would have to contend, but this is part of any negotiating process. Also, the National Unity government headed by Shimon Peres has made an effort, at least during its first months in office, to improve living conditions for the Palestinians in the West Bank and Gaza. Cairo clearly sees a direct link between progress in the pace of normalization between Israel and Egypt and the removal of administrative and political restraints on the Palestinians in the occupied territories.

The Arabs in conference and through their public statements have, in fact, recognized the need for negotiating with the Israelis in order to reach a peaceful settlement of differences. Although the cautious words are not explicit and do not assuage the concern and resentment of even those Israelis who wait for an opportunity for progress toward peace, the Arab leaders have stated that these ambiguities are what negotiations are designed to resolve.

The initiative for peace talks must come from the United States, barring some crisis so profound that Israel would be forced to turn to the United Nations and an international forum to protect its interests. Even under these unforeseeable conditions, the deep involvement of the United States would be mandatory for negotiations.

However, President Reagan's administration has shown little interest in diplomacy as a means of resolving regional disputes. Contrary to the policies of his Democratic and Republican predecessors, he has tended to prefer the threat or use of American military force instead of negotiation. This preference has been particularly painful and embarrassing in the Middle East, where the shuttle diplomacy of Henry Kissinger under Presidents Nixon and Ford and the Camp David talks under my administration were for a number of years a valuable and productive aspect of the Middle East scene. Under Reagan, the peace process has come to a screeching halt, and the debacle in Lebanon severely damaged or destroyed our influence in that area. Except for one well-crafted speech in September 1982, soon forgotten in Washington, there have been no sustained efforts to bring peace to the region by dealing with the basic causes of animosity and warfare. Some efforts have been made, however, to help arrange a satisfactory withdrawal of Israeli forces from Lebanon.

Not surprisingly, I find that among the people in the Middle East the United States is roundly condemned — for being too active with its guns and troops and not active enough at the negotiating table, for being too subservient to the Israelis and too free with the sale of weapons to all sides, and for giving private assurances to leaders and then forgetting them when the inevitable pressures build. There is widespread criticism of Washington for being impotent as well as for being omnipotent but overly timid.

In spite of this criticism, almost everyone still recognizes that the role of the United States is crucial. After his unsuccessful attempt in 1983 to resolve differences among Lebanon, Israel, and Syria, Ambassador and special negotiator Philip Habib remarked: "In all of the travels that I have made through the area I never found anybody who said to me, 'Go home, Yankee!' The response was 'Stay here, Yankee, but agree with me.' "

For many years, America's leaders were known and expected to exert a maximum influence in an objective, nonbiased way to achieve peace. In order to resume this vital role, the United States must be a trusted mediator, even-handed, consistent, unwavering, enthusiastic, a partner with both sides and not a judge of either. Although it is inevitable that at times there will be a tilt one way or the other, in the long run the role of honest broker can again be played by Washington. As has already been proven, any successful negotiations must have the full and obvious involvement of the President and the secretary of state.

No matter how well qualified, designated negotiators at the ambassadorial level can be little more than messengers and are highly unlikely to secure the kind of suggestions or concessions from the heads of other governments that can lead to substantial achievements.

*

There are certain American principles and ideals that have either historically guided U.S. negotiators or that are now recognized as necessary for a comprehensive peace in the Middle East:

- The security of Israel must be preserved.
- Differences between adversaries should be resolved by peaceful means, certainly without direct Soviet or American military involvement.
- Accommodation must be sought through negotiation with all parties to the dispute, with each having fair representation and the right to participate in free discussions.
- The sovereignty of nations and sanctity of international borders should be honored in order to avoid continuing bloodshed.
- There is no place for terrorism, which tends to subvert peace initiatives and to perpetuate hatred and combat.
- Human rights must be protected, including those generally recognized in the U.S. Constitution and under international law. These would include the right of self-determination, free speech, equal treatment of all persons, freedom from prolonged military domination and imprisonment without trial, the right of families to be reunited, and the right of nonbelligerent people to live in peace.

To address the controversial issues in the Middle East is not an easy task; it is fraught with political danger. The willingness of the United States and other negotiating partners to accept this risk and to face the prospect of failure, rejection, or unpopularity is one of the missing elements in the peace process.

Disputes within Israel and the differences among the Arabs and between them and Israel cannot be resolved without face-to-face discussions to reduce hatred and the threat of continuing or escalating warfare. Indeed, some have avoided the crucial issues by relying too much on collective international efforts as a substitute for direct peace initiatives. U.N. resolutions and unilateral statements are all very well in their place, but they are no substitute for negotiations on the most specific and controversial issues.

No nation needs to abandon its ultimate goals as a prerequisite to negotiations. Anwar Sadat expressed maximum Arab views in his historic speech to the Israeli Knesset (a speech that Syria's President Hafez al-Assad could have made without changing a substantive word). Sadat maintained the same goals until his death, but, in the meantime, he made strides toward peace for his people and justice for the Palestinians by acknowledging the need for incremental progress through negotiation.

The key issue and one of the most controversial, of course, is what to do about the Palestinians, who have lived for more than a generation as refugees or for more than seventeen years under continuous military occupation. There can be no successful negotiations for permanent peace unless the Palestinians are included. American officials acknowledge this fact even as they refuse to recognize or negotiate directly with the PLO. Ambassador Habib said, "In the search for peace in the Middle East, there can be no solution without a solution of the Palestinian question. . . . The Palestinian question, however you want to define it, is at the core." In his confirmation hearings for secretary of state, George Shultz affirmed this belief. However, acknowledging the problem has not led to any persistent attempts to resolve it.

It is to be remembered that the Camp David accords, signed by Sadat and Begin, ratified by the signatory governments, and endorsed in the Reagan statement of 1982, require "full autonomy" for the inhabitants of the occupied territories, the withdrawal of Israeli forces and military and civilian governments, and the recognition of the Palestinian people as a separate political entity. The Palestinians themselves are to participate in further negotiations, and the final status of the West Bank and Gaza is to be submitted "to a vote by the elected representatives of the inhabitants of the West Bank and Gaza." Furthermore, the accords generally recognized that continuing to treat non-Jews in the occupied territories as a substratum of society is contrary to the principles of morality and justice on which democracies are founded. For a while, at least, Begin and Sadat were able to demonstrate that these apparently insurmountable problems concerning Palestinian rights might be overcome.

So far, the peace treaty between Israel and Egypt has survived some strenuous tests: Sadat's death, the Israeli withdrawal from the Sinai, and the Israeli invasion of Lebanon. This legal bond needs to be nurtured for its own sake and as an example of the benefits that can come with peace. Egypt can act as a natural bridge between the would-be peace negotiators and the rest of the Arab world, a role that Cairo would be willing to play and one that the United States should quietly encourage. Nowadays, a "cold peace" prevails between Egypt and Israel, but it is hoped and expected that withdrawing the Israeli forces from Lebanon and resuming the peace talks under the Camp David formula or the Reagan statement will warm up the relationship.

As I remember so vividly from the Camp David discussions, the problem with words is always present, and only through good faith negotiations can this difficulty be overcome. For instance, the concept of "self-determination" for the Palestinians is already assumed both in the Camp David accords, signed by Egypt and Israel, and in the Reagan statement, which was accepted by many Arabs. The phrase is interpreted by some Israelis as defining exclusively an independent Palestinian state in the occupied territories. But some kind of federation between the West Bank and Gaza and Jordan has been envisioned by many Arab leaders. Another problem with semantics has arisen with interpretations of the basic meaning of the Camp David accords and of the compatible Reagan statement. Although many of the current Israeli leaders did not vote for the Camp David accords, they now insist that "Camp David" is the only framework within which they will negotiate; yet for King Hussein the title of "Camp David" would be unacceptable as a basis for possible peace talks.

Another difficult question concerns the effect of the Soviet Union on the prospect of resuming peace talks in the Middle East, and there is no consensus about what Syria will do.

It seems to be the role of the USSR to stay, to avoid, and to spoil — to remain in the region, to avoid any direct confrontation with the United States, and to prevent any successful effort toward a lasting peace settlement from which the Kremlin is excluded. One unfortunate result of the recent Lebanese war has been to enhance substantially the ability of the Soviets to achieve these goals. Capitalizing on the errors of the Reagan government, the Soviets have now reached the greatest level of influence in the Middle East since before they were expelled from Egypt by Sadat. They are firmly established in Syria, which advocates a multinational negotiating format that includes the Soviet Union, as was envisioned under U.N. Resolution 338. Frustrated with the timidity of the American leaders, Jordan and even Egypt have more recently expressed some agreement with this multinational approach. The U.S.-Israeli strategy, on the other hand, has been to exclude the Soviet Union from any negotiations and so far to limit Syria to discussions involving withdrawal from Lebanon. The text of the U.S.-Soviet statement of October 1977 can provide a basis for possible Soviet involvement in the future (Appendix 3).

Before a final and comprehensive peace can be achieved, Syria must be brought into the negotiating process also, being both part of the problem and part of the potential solution. Syrian leaders have real security concerns, but they do not want to become puppets of the Soviet Union. They retain a desire for economic aid and cooperation from the Western world. However, their needs are not likely to be realized without a recognition of Israel's rights to peace and security and the acceptance of a free and independent Lebanon. It is unlikely that President Assad will cooperate anytime soon in an overall peace effort, and his threats to subvert such talks will continue. However, with a strong American commitment to both negotiations and negotiators, it will be possible if necessary to ignore Assad's threats and wait for a later opportunity to bring peace between Syria and Israel.

In the search for a permanent solution to the Middle East disputes, there are some basic requirements and some considerations that may be helpful:

• The Arabs must acknowledge openly and specifically that Israel is a reality and has a right to exist in peace, behind secure and recognized borders. Based on this action, the internal debate within Israel must be resolved in order to define Israel's permanent borders.

• Israel must reconfirm its willingness to withdraw from occupied territories, as required by U.N. Resolution 242 and reconfirmed in the Camp David accords. This could be done in stages that would allow a degree of mutual trust to develop, but completed within a specific time as negotiated.

• Palestinian human rights, including the right of self-determination, must be acknowledged. This would leave open the real possibility of confederation between the Palestinians and Jordan.

• The focus on Lebanon should not be at the expense of a revitalized peace process. There has to be a simultaneous (or two-track) effort: to resolve current crises like Lebanon and to solve the basic causes of the Middle East dispute. They are not mutually exclusive but are inextricably related. No rejectionists should be allowed to prevent movement on Israeli recognition and security or on granting Palestinian self-determination by creating or perpetuating crises.

• Conditions for negotiation should be abolished. Despite denials, they exist: "All Israeli settlements must be dismantled before we will negotiate." "There will be no peace talks until Israel (Syria) gets out of Lebanon." "We will only negotiate under Camp David (U.N. Resolution 242; the Fez resolution; the Reagan proposal)." "The PLO must (must not) be present." "Threats against my country from within Lebanon must first be removed."

• Compromise is necessary from both sides in any negotiation. Each participant must have the freedom to pursue his own objectives and has to have some fair assurance that these views will be considered. Clear distinctions must be made between what their dreams and ideology dictate and what is pragmatically possible. Israel cannot reconstruct the Kingdom of David nor can the Palestinians erase Israel from the map. Neither can predict or impose on others the ultimate outcome of the talks. Each must remember that any final agreement has to be both voluntary and acceptable by the other side.

• Both Syria and Israel have a right to expect that neither will be attacked from Lebanon by the occupation forces of the other.

• Antagonists cannot be expected to take the initiative. In the Middle East, hatred and distrust are too ingrained and pride is too great for any of the disputing parties to make concessions and invitations that they know will almost inevitably be rejected.

• Without American leadership, an international forum under U.N. Resolution 338 is the only logical alternative, and the obstacles in this path to peace are almost insurmountable. The best first step might be for the U.S. secretary of state to explore the options unofficially among the disputing powers to ascertain as broad a base of potential agreement as possible. On this can be initiated semiofficial and then official peace talks, either in a multinational format or as bilateral discussions. Without violating the Kissinger commitment to the Israelis, U.S. officials could determine the PLO's willingness to proceed with peace talks without recognizing or negotiating with the PLO.

In any future peace efforts the United States must, by word and deed, convince both the Arabs and the Israelis that it intends to be fair and unbiased toward all sides.

When a promising negotiation evolves, the United States must be willing to join others (including the Europeans and Japanese) in offering the economic incentives necessary to bolster what will be at first a fragile understanding and be prepared to help the peacemakers fend off the radicals and extremists who will seek to subvert what is being carefully created and nurtured.

In the final analysis, the different peoples of the Middle East have their own viewpoints, their own grievances, their own goals and aspirations. But it is Israel that remains the key, the tiny vortex around which swirl the winds of hatred, intolerance, and bloodshed. The indomitable people of Israel are still attempting to define their young democracy — its basic character now and for the future, its geographical boundaries, the conditions under which the legitimate rights of the Palestinians can be honored and an accommodation can be forged with its neighbors. These internal decisions will have to be made in consultation with Arabs who are basically unfriendly, perhaps as difficult a political prospect as history has ever seen.

Many Israelis, like their neighbors, are eagerly seeking a measure of normalized existence. The Arabs must recognize the reality that is Israel, just as the Israelis must acknowledge Palestinian claims to civic equality and their right to express themselves freely in a portion of their territorial homeland.

The Bible says that when the first blood was shed among His children, God asked Cain, the slayer, "Where is Abel thy brother?" And he said, "I know not. Am I my brother's keeper?" And the Lord said, "What hast thou done? The voice of thy brother's blood crieth unto me from the ground. And now art thou cursed . . ." (Genesis 4:9–11). The blood of Abraham, God's father of the chosen, still flows in the veins of Arab, Jew, and Christian, and too much of it has been spilled in grasping for the inheritance of the revered patriarch in the Middle East. The spilled blood in the Holy Land still cries out to God — an anguished cry for peace.

# Afterword

SINCE THIS BOOK first went to press early in 1985, not much has changed in the region, except that most of the trends observed a year ago have continued and some have accelerated. There are two encouraging notes: Under persistent public pressure because of high casualties among its troops, the Israeli government removed most of its military forces from southern Lebanon, including a "final" withdrawal in June 1985. (Israel retained control of a substantial strip of Lebanese territory, claiming that this southern buffer zone is necessary to protect northern Israeli villages from attack.) Also, King Hussein of Jordan has persevered in his attempts to find a way to the negotiating table, and there have been positive responses from Prime Minister Shimon Peres.

Although the Israeli government has made some progress, it has failed to resolve its serious economic crisis and has turned increasingly to the United States for financial aid to sustain its economy. The inclination of Prime Minister Peres and his Labor coalition toward a peace initiative has been opposed by Foreign Minister Yitzhak Shamir's almost equal role in shaping the nation's foreign policy. The refusal of the Likud to consider any potentially viable effort to carry out the terms of the Camp David agreement or to accept the key elements of the Reagan statement has served to perpetuate the diplomatic stalemate. Under these circumstances, the Likud is scheduled to inherit the office of Prime Minister at midterm, in September 1986. However, Prime Minister Peres has built up a relatively high level of public support, and there is little doubt that the Labor Party leaders are assessing the advisability of deliberately forcing a showdown vote, probably on the peace issue, that would bring down the government and precipitate a new election.

Despite the success of the Israelis in minimizing attacks from across the Lebanese border, skirmishes and terrorist attacks have persisted within the occupied areas of the West Bank and Gaza and even beyond the region. Following each such bloody episode, the attacking party claimed that its action was only a response to terrorist acts by the other side. The most serious exchange occurred in October 1985, when Israel's air force bombed the PLO headquarters in Tunis in response to the deaths of three Israeli citizens who were murdered in their sailboat in Cyprus. Despite Arafat's denial, the Israelis claimed that the PLO was guilty of the crime. It was estimated that sixty people died in the air raid, including a number of Tunisians who happened to be in the vicinity. In initially approving the raid as a proper response to terrorism, President Reagan aroused the fury of Tunisia and the rest of the Arab world. A few days later, the White House announced that such an attack "could not be condoned," and the United States subsequently abstained from vetoing a U.N. Security Council resolution that condemned Israel's action.

The political forces within Israel have become increasingly polarized, with the extreme right strengthened by the nation's economic hardships and the continuing series of bloody altercations between Jews and Arabs. Although the rabid anti-Arab statements of Rabbi Meir Kahane have been condemned by the government, his demands that the political rights of Palestinians be further curtailed and that the government adopt a policy of forcibly removing them from Israel and the occupied territories began to find greater popular acceptance. Kahane's popularity as measured by public opinion polls increased ten-fold from the 1 percent portion of votes he received in the most recent election.

Many Israelis agree that the most significant development in the region during the past year may turn out to be the increasing activism by Palestinians in the West Bank and Gaza. A new generation of young leaders has begun to attack Israeli soldiers and civilians directly, resulting in a growing number of deaths of Jewish men and women. Most of the assaults seem to have been precipitated by local circumstances, without direct instigation from outside, but external factors have, of course, encouraged this unprecedented militancy. The relative success of some Arab forces in 1973 and more recently of Shiite Moslems in Lebanon has tended to dispel the image of Israeli military invincibility that constrained a generation of Palestinians after the 1967 war, and it is clear that the destruction of the PLO military infrastructure in Lebanon did not destroy Palestinian national consciousness. Although its military strength has repeatedly proven to be superior, Israel remains faced with the reality that it cannot achieve its goals of peace and security by the use of force.

More aggressive efforts by Israeli settlers to penetrate the Palestinian communities have sometimes deliberately forced direct confrontations, and the growing influence of Kahane has added to the intensity of feeling on both sides. The release of 1150 Palestinian prisoners in exchange for 3 Israeli soldiers in May 1985 has also affected the situation. About 600 of the prisoners returned to the occupied territories and were welcomed home as Palestinian heroes. Their influence and example plus the pardon for their previous crimes have undoubtedly encouraged more militant activity among their young neighbors.

For Israel, then, the invasion of Lebanon has proven to be quite costly. Not only did almost seven hundred of its troops perish but violence along the northern border and within the occupied territories has continued. Relations with Egypt and other Arab countries have been further strained. Economic problems have been exacerbated, and there has been further polarization among the many domestic political factions, particularly between the various religious groups and those whose motivations are distinctly secular.

The weakened PLO — having lost most of its military forces, being uprooted from its foothold in Lebanon, and being physically dispersed among Tunisia and other Arab nations distant from Israel — has only partially compensated for this loss of

strength and prestige. Arafat has attempted to build upon his reconciliation with Egypt, and to some degree the PLO has found an
ally in King Hussein and a partial haven in Jordan, which has the
only concentration of Palestinians adjacent to Israel and the occupied territories. President Mubarak of Egypt has welcomed this
revived partnership, and it has been tacitly accepted by the
Saudis and most other Arab leaders. But the PLO remains under
sustained physical attack: hostile Lebanese militia forces regularly assault Palestinian settlements and refugee camps in and
around Beirut; a variety of armed groups continue to attack pro-
Arafat forces in the northern Lebanese city of Tripoli; and all
PLO factions have sustained losses from Israeli reprisal raids
against training bases and staging areas of Palestinian militants.
Furthermore, repeated acts of international terrorism publicly
sponsored by the PLO have damaged the Palestinian cause
among many world leaders.

Lebanon is still torn by strife, with many people being killed
each week in pitched battles in the streets of Beirut or Tripoli.
Leaders of the combatants continue to turn to Damascus to ask
that the Syrian forces in Lebanon help restore order. Although
Assad has strengthened his influence in Lebanon, he has been
unable to quell the violence, and his troops are always faced with
the prospect of sinking deeper into the quagmire of civil disorder.

In February 1985 a joint Jordanian-Palestinian statement was
issued that expressed a willingness to negotiate with Israel. The
carefully crafted words were interpreted in a much more liberal
manner by King Hussein than by PLO spokesmen. According to
Hussein, the parties agreed to accept all U.N. resolutions, including 242 and 338, and to consider a form of confederation between
Jordan and Palestinians in the occupied territories in lieu of a
completely independent Palestinian state. Strong objections from
some PLO members threatened a schism in the organization, and
a revised statement was negotiated. Hussein attempted to use the
more attractive elements of this proposal to induce the United
States to begin exploratory talks with a joint Jordanian-Palestinian delegation, to be followed by negotiations with Israel under
the terms of U.N. Resolution 338. Later, in August 1985, Arab
leaders in a summit meeting neither approved nor condemned

this initiative, permitting Hussein to continue his efforts to revive the peace process.

In an October speech to the United Nations General Assembly, Hussein repeated his call for peace talks and stated for the first time that Jordanians and a Palestinian group were prepared to negotiate with Israel "promptly and directly." In the same forum, Prime Minister Peres made a cautious but positive response, which was condemned by Likud spokesmen, particularly Ariel Sharon.

Faced with a reinforced Syrian military force and adamant opposition from President Assad to his peace initiatives, Hussein has requested arms sales from the United States. Although the Jordanian request received approval from the White House, it has been opposed by Israel and by a majority in the U.S. Congress. Most Israelis believe that King Hussein's interest in the opening of direct talks with Israel is linked to the Jordanian request for an arms deal with the United States, a contention that may not be disputed by Hussein. In any case, he has made some progress in reconciling his differences with Assad, strongly disavowing any move toward bilateral negotiations with Israel and insisting upon an international forum within which to conduct any possible peace talks. This would open the way for the Soviets to reinsert themselves into the Middle East peace discussions, a move that would not be acceptable to the Israelis under existing conditions. One means of opening this possibility has been considered by both countries: the reestablishment of diplomatic relations between the Soviet Union and Israel.

President Mubarak has continued, with some success, his quiet efforts to bring Egypt back into the Arab fold. At the same time, he has encouraged the joint effort of Jordan and the Palestinians to keep the peace issue alive and has attempted to honor the words if not the spirit of the Israeli-Egyptian peace treaty. Mubarak's position in the Arab world and his relations with the PLO were considerably complicated with the release by the Egyptian government of four Palestinian hijackers of the Italian cruise liner *Achille Lauro* in October 1985. The terrorists departed from Cairo on an Egyptian airliner, and their subsequent apprehension by U.S. Navy planes gave the appearance that Egypt had acted in collusion with the United States, though both Washington and Cairo denied any such collaboration. Although the purposes of the hijackers of the Italian liner remain unclear, this act of terrorism also resulted in the murder of an American passenger. The hijackers were delivered to Italian authorities for trial.

President Ronald Reagan and Secretary of State George Shultz have expressed interest in the Hussein-Arafat proposals, but neither has chosen to become actively involved in the Middle East peace process. Therefore, there has been no aggressive pursuit of peace based on this most recent initiative, the Camp David accords, or the Reagan statement of September 1982.

The most dramatic involvement of the United States in the Middle East has resulted from a series of attacks on American citizens by radical Palestinians, who have come to look upon Americans as anathemas, associated directly with the Israeli invasion and occupation of Lebanon and considered to be enemies of Christian Arabs and Moslems.

In June 1985 a TWA plane was taken by hijackers. One U.S. Marine was brutally murdered and thirty-nine other passengers were held captive for several days. The militant Shiite kidnapers demanded the release of more than seven hundred Lebanese who were being held captive in Israel. Finally, after a series of obscure political maneuvers, during which all parties refused to admit that they were negotiating with each other, the kidnap victims were released. President Assad was believed to have interceded at the request of the U.S. government. Although Israeli officials denied any relationship between the two events, the Lebanese prisoners were subsequently set free. At the time of the airplane hijacking, five American citizens had already been held captive in Lebanon for more than a year, with their captors demanding the release of a group of their fellow militants imprisoned in Kuwait for bombing attacks on embassies.

The Iran-Iraq war has entered its sixth year with no sign of abatement. It has been enormously costly in lives and financial expenditures. The Arab oil-producing nations have been forced to spend a substantial portion of their dwindling oil revenues on this conflict. At the same time, the thrust of Moslem fundamentalism has continued to create more disunity in the Arab world and, in most countries, has brought about a cautious reexamination of domestic affairs to ensure stability in the face of potential subversion.

In general, then, there have been no major changes in the Middle East during the last year. Both the Arabs and Jews have continued to suffer economically, and the region is torn by dissension — within Israel, between Israel and its neighbors, and among the Arab nations and the Palestinians.

However, diplomatic processes are under way among the Jordanians, Egyptians, Palestinians, and Israelis, and some Middle East leaders are shuttling back and forth to Washington, seeking guidance and support. A few general premises seem to be evolving: to assuage Syrian demands, both Hussein and Mubarak now insist on an international forum in lieu of direct bilateral negotiations; restored diplomatic relations between Israel and the Soviet Union may be a prerequisite for such peace talks; there is a strong possibility that the weakened and divided PLO will play a minor or secondary role at the negotiating table; in Israel, Peres has found that a carefully defined peace initiative is his best opportunity for forcing a sharp political showdown between him and the Likud coalition, and in this process he has proven to be less paralyzed than initially believed as head of the national unity government.

Pending further progress toward an international peace conference, some leaders of Israel and Jordan are exploring ways to proceed toward joint rule of the West Bank and Gaza areas. There are real possibilities for some agreement that might include the following:

• Unilateral steps by the Israeli government to reduce Israeli involvement to a minimum and to grant additional rights to the Palestinians in the occupied territories. This would include increased autonomy, improved employment opportunities, fewer restrictions on foreign aid, a voice in the selection of local officials, an end to restrictions on travel, and reduced censorship of books and newspapers. Palestinians in East Jerusalem would have voting rights in the selection of the "autonomy council."

• Joint rule over the West Bank and Gaza by Israel and Jordan for a period of time not to exceed five years. No new Jewish settlements would be built and those in existence would not be expanded. Israelis living in the area would retain their own citizenship, and Palestinians would have full rights to participate in Jordanian political affairs. There would be an official Jordanian presence within the Moslem holy places in East Jerusalem.

• A strong police force composed of Jordanians and Israelis, with each having primary responsibility for enforcing laws among their own citizens.

These peace efforts are still being thwarted by the same factors described in this book which have for so long been dominant in the region. In spite of strong opposition from powerful and militant groups, there is no doubt that any tangible move toward peace by the Jordanian, Israeli, or Palestinian leaders would be approved by most of their constituents. It still remains to be seen which forces will prevail.

November 20, 1985

# APPENDICES

# INDEX

# Appendix 1

## United Nations Security Council Resolution 242, November 22, 1967

The Security Council,

Expressing its continuing concern with the grave situation in the Middle East,

Emphasizing the inadmissibility of the acquisition of territory by war and the need to work for a just and lasting peace in which every State in the area can live in security,

Emphasizing further that all Member States in their acceptance of the Charter of the United Nations have undertaken a commitment to act in accordance with Article 2 of the Charter,

1. Affirms that the fulfillment of Charter principles requires the establishment of a just and lasting peace in the Middle East which should include the application of both the following principles:

(i) Withdrawal of Israeli armed forces from territories occupied in the recent conflict;

(ii) Termination of all claims or states of belligerency and respect for and acknowledgment of the sovereignty, territorial integrity and political independence of every State in the area and their right to live in peace within secure and recognized boundaries free from threats or acts of force;

2. Affirms further the necessity

(a) For guaranteeing freedom of navigation through international ways in the area;

(b) For achieving a just settlement of the refugee problem;

(c) For guaranteeing the territorial inviolability and political independence of every State in the area, through measures including the establishment of demilitarized zones;

3. Requests the Secretary-General to designate a Special Representative to proceed to the Middle East to establish and maintain contacts with the States concerned in order to promote agreement and assist efforts to achieve a peaceful and accepted settlement in accordance with the provisions and principles of this resolution.

4. Requests the Secretary-General to report to the Security Council on the progress of the efforts of the Special Representative as soon as possible.

# Appendix 2

## United Nations Security Council Resolution 338, October 21–22, 1973

The Security Council

1. Calls upon all parties to the present fighting to cease all firing and terminate all military activity immediately, no later than 12 hours after the moment of the adoption of this decision, in the positions they now occupy;

2. Calls upon the parties concerned to start immediately after the cease-fire the implementation of Security Council Resolution 242 (1967) in all of its parts;

3. Decides that, immediately and concurrently with the cease-fire, negotiations start between the parties concerned under appropriate auspices aimed at establishing a just and durable peace in the Middle East.

# Appendix 3

## Joint U.S.-Soviet Statement on the Middle East, New York, October 1, 1977

Having exchanged views regarding the unsafe situation which remains in the Middle East, U.S. Secretary of State Cyrus Vance and Member of the Politbureau of the Central Committee of the CPSU, Minister for Foreign Affairs of the U.S.S.R. A. A. Gromyko have the following statement to make on behalf of their countries, which are cochairmen of the Geneva Peace Conference on the Middle East:

1. Both governments are convinced that vital interests of the peoples of this area, as well as the interests of strengthening peace and international security in general, urgently dictate the necessity of achieving, as soon as possible, a just and lasting settlement of the Arab-Israeli conflict. This settlement should be comprehensive, incorporating all parties concerned and all questions.

The United States and the Soviet Union believe that, within the framework of a comprehensive settlement of the Middle East problem, all specific questions of the settlement should be resolved, including such key issues as withdrawal of Israeli Armed Forces from territories occupied in the 1967 conflict; the resolution of the Palestinian question, including insuring the legitimate rights of the Palestinian people; termination of the state of war and establishment of normal peaceful relations on the basis of mutual recognition of the principles of sovereignty, territorial integrity, and political independence.

The two governments believe that, in addition to such measures for insuring the security of the borders between Israel and the neighboring Arab states as the establishment of demilitarized zones and the agreed stationing in them of U.N. troops or observers, international guarantees of such borders as well as of the observance of the terms of the settlement can also be established should the contracting parties so desire. The United States and the Soviet Union are ready to participate in these guarantees, subject to their constitutional processes.

2. The United States and the Soviet Union believe that the only right and effective way for achieving a fundamental solution to all aspects of the Middle East problem in its entirety is negotiations within the framework of the Geneva peace conference, specially convened for these purposes, with participation in its work of the representatives of all the parties involved in the conflict including those of the Palestinian people, and legal and contractual formalization of the decisions reached at the conference.

In their capacity as cochairmen of the Geneva conference, the United States and the U.S.S.R. affirm their intention, through joint efforts and in their contacts with the parties concerned, to facilitate in every way the resumption of the work of the conference not later than December 1977. The cochairmen note that there still exist several questions of a procedural and organizational nature which remain to be agreed upon by the participants to the conference.

3. Guided by the goal of achieving a just political settlement in the Middle East and of eliminating the explosive situation in this area of the world, the United States and the U.S.S.R. appeal to all parties in the conflict to understand the necessity for careful consideration of each other's legitimate rights and interests and to demonstrate mutual readiness to act accordingly.

# Appendix 4

## A Framework for Peace in the Middle East Agreed at Camp David

## Documents Agreed To at Camp David, September 17, 1978

Muhammad Anwar al-Sadat, President of the Arab Republic of Egypt, and Menachem Begin, Prime Minister of Israel, met with Jimmy Carter, President of the United States of America, at Camp David from September 5 to September 17, 1978, and have agreed on the following framework for peace in the Middle East. They invite other parties to the Arab-Israeli conflict to adhere to it.

### PREAMBLE

The search for peace in the Middle East must be guided by the following:

— The agreed basis for a peaceful settlement of the conflict between Israel and its neighbors is United Nations Security Council Resolution 242, in all its parts.*

— After four wars during thirty years, despite intensive human efforts, the Middle East, which is the cradle of civilization and the birthplace of three great religions, does not yet enjoy the blessings of peace. The people of the Middle East yearn for peace so that the vast human and natural resources of the region can be turned to the pursuits of peace and so that this area can become a model for coexistence and cooperation among nations.

— The historic initiative of President Sadat in visiting Jerusalem

* The texts of Resolutions 242 and 338 are annexed to this document.

and the reception accorded to him by the Parliament, government and people of Israel, and the reciprocal visit of Prime Minister Begin to Ismailia, the peace proposals made by both leaders, as well as the warm reception of these missions by the peoples of both countries, have created an unprecedented opportunity for peace which must not be lost if this generation and future generations are to be spared the tragedies of war.

— The provisions of the Charter of the United Nations and the other accepted norms of international law and legitimacy now provide accepted standards for the conduct of relations among all states.

— To achieve a relationship of peace, in the spirit of Article 2 of the United Nations Charter, future negotiations between Israel and any neighbor prepared to negotiate peace and security with it, are necessary for the purpose of carrying out all the provisions and principles of Resolutions 242 and 338.

— Peace requires respect for the sovereignty, territorial integrity and political independence of every state in the area and their right to live in peace within secure and recognized boundaries free from threats or acts of force. Progress toward that goal can accelerate movement toward a new era of reconciliation in the Middle East marked by cooperation in promoting economic development, in maintaining stability, and in assuring security.

— Security is enhanced by a relationship of peace and by cooperation between nations which enjoy normal relations. In addition, under the terms of peace treaties, the parties can, on the basis of reciprocity, agree to special security arrangements such as demilitarized zones, limited armaments areas, early warning stations, the presence of international forces, liaison, agreed measures for monitoring, and other arrangements that they agree are useful.

### FRAMEWORK

Taking these factors into account, the parties are determined to reach a just, comprehensive, and durable settlement of the Middle East conflict through the conclusion of peace treaties based on Security Council Resolutions 242 and 338 in all their parts. Their purpose is to achieve peace and good neighborly relations. They recognize that, for peace to endure, it must involve all those who have been most deeply affected by the conflict. They therefore agree that this framework as appropriate is intended by them to constitute a basis for peace not only between Egypt and Israel, but also between Israel and each of its other neighbors which is prepared to negotiate peace with Israel on this basis. With that objective in mind, they have agreed to proceed as follows:

A. West Bank and Gaza

1. Egypt, Israel, Jordan and the representatives of the Palestinian people should participate in negotiations on the resolution of the Palestinian problem in all its aspects. To achieve that objective, negotiations relating to the West Bank and Gaza should proceed in three stages:

(a) Egypt and Israel agree that, in order to ensure a peaceful and orderly transfer of authority, and taking into account the security concerns of all the parties, there should be transitional arrangements for the West Bank and Gaza for a period not exceeding five years. In order to provide full autonomy to the inhabitants, under these arrangements the Israeli military government and its civilian administration will be withdrawn as soon as a self-governing authority has been freely elected by the inhabitants of these areas to replace the existing military government. To negotiate the details of a transitional arrangement, the Government of Jordan will be invited to join the negotiations on the basis of this framework. These new arrangements should give due consideration both to the principle of self-government by the inhabitants of these territories and to the legitimate security concerns of the parties involved.

(b) Egypt, Israel, and Jordan will agree on the modalities for establishing the elected self-governing authority in the West Bank and Gaza. The delegations of Egypt and Jordan may include Palestinians from the West Bank and Gaza or other Palestinians as mutually agreed. The parties will negotiate an agreement which will define the powers and responsibilities of the self-governing authority to be exercised in the West Bank and Gaza. A withdrawal of Israeli armed forces will take place and there will be a redeployment of the remaining Israeli forces into specified security locations. The agreement will also include arrangements for assuring internal and external security and public order. A strong local police force will be established, which may include Jordanian citizens. In addition, Israeli and Jordanian forces will participate in joint patrols and in the manning of control posts to assure the security of the borders.

(c) When the self-governing authority (administrative council) in the West Bank and Gaza is established and inaugurated, the transitional period of five years will begin. As soon as possible, but not later than the third year after the beginning of the transitional period, negotiations will take place to determine the final status of the West Bank and Gaza and its relationship with its neighbors, and to conclude a peace treaty between Israel and Jordan by the end of the transitional period. These negotiations will be conducted among Egypt, Israel, Jordan, and the elected representatives of the inhabitants of the West Bank and Gaza. Two separate but related committees will be convened, one committee, consisting of representatives of the four parties which will negotiate and agree on the final status of the West Bank and Gaza, and its relationship with its neighbors, and the second committee, consisting of representatives of Israel and representatives of Jordan to be joined by the elected representatives of the inhabitants of the West Bank and Gaza, to negotiate the peace treaty between Israel and Jordan, taking into account the agreement reached on the final status of the West Bank and Gaza. The negotiations shall be based on all the provisions and principles of U.N. Security Council Resolution 242. The negotiations will resolve, among other matters, the location of the boundaries and the nature of the security arrangements. The solution from the negotiations must also recognize the legitimate rights of the Palestinian people and their just requirements. In this way, the Palestinians will participate in the determination of their own future through:

1) The negotiations among Egypt, Israel, Jordan and the representatives of the inhabitants of the West Bank and Gaza to agree on the final status of the West Bank and Gaza and other outstanding issues by the end of the transitional period.

2) Submitting their agreement to a vote by the elected representatives of the inhabitants of the West Bank and Gaza.

3) Providing for the elected representatives of the inhabitants of the West Bank and Gaza to decide how they shall govern themselves consistent with the provisions of their agreement.

4) Participating as stated above in the work of the committee negotiating the peace treaty between Israel and Jordan.

2. All necessary measures will be taken and provisions made to assure the security of Israel and its neighbors during the transitional period and beyond. To assist in providing such security, a strong local police force will be constituted by the self-governing authority. It will be composed of inhabitants of the West Bank and Gaza. The police will maintain continuing liaison on internal security matters with the designated Israeli, Jordanian, and Egyptian officers.

3. During the transitional period, representatives of Egypt, Israel, Jordan, and the self-governing authority will constitute a continuing

committee to decide by agreement on the modalities of admission of persons displaced from the West Bank and Gaza in 1967, together with necessary measures to prevent disruption and disorder. Other matters of common concern may also be dealt with by this committee.

4. Egypt and Israel will work with each other and with other interested parties to establish agreed procedures for a prompt, just and permanent implementation of the resolution of the refugee problem.

B. Egypt-Israel

1. Egypt and Israel undertake not to resort to the threat or the use of force to settle disputes. Any disputes shall be settled by peaceful means in accordance with the provisions of Article 33 of the Charter of the United Nations.

2. In order to achieve peace between them, the parties agree to negotiate in good faith with a goal of concluding within three months from the signing of this Framework a peace treaty between them, while inviting the other parties to the conflict to proceed simultaneously to negotiate and conclude similar peace treaties with a view to achieving a comprehensive peace in the area. The Framework for the Conclusion of a Peace Treaty between Egypt and Israel will govern the peace negotiations between them. The parties will agree on the modalities and the timetable for the implementation of their obligations under the treaty.

C. Associated Principles

1. Egypt and Israel state that the principles and provisions described below should apply to peace treaties between Israel and each of its neighbors — Egypt, Jordan, Syria and Lebanon.

2. Signatories shall establish among themselves relationships normal to states at peace with one another. To this end, they should undertake to abide by all the provisions of the Charter of the United Nations. Steps to be taken in this respect include:

(a) full recognition;

(b) abolishing economic boycotts;

(c) guaranteeing that under their jurisdiction the citizens of the other parties shall enjoy the protection of the due process of law.

3. Signatories should explore possibilities for economic development in the context of final peace treaties, with the objective of contributing to the atmosphere of peace, cooperation and friendship which is their common goal.

4. Claims Commissions may be established for the mutual settlement of all financial claims.

5. The United States shall be invited to participate in the talks on matters related to the modalities of the implementation of the agreements and working out the timetable for the carrying out of the obligations of the parties.

6. The United Nations Security Council shall be requested to endorse the peace treaties and ensure that their provisions shall not be violated. The permanent members of the Security Council shall be requested to underwrite the peace treaties and ensure respect for their provisions. They shall also be requested to conform their policies and actions with the undertakings contained in this Framework.

For the Government of the Arab Republic of Egypt:

A. Sadat

For the Government of Israel:

M. Begin

Witnessed by:

Jimmy Carter
President of the United States of America

## Framework for the Conclusion of a Peace Treaty Between Egypt and Israel

In order to achieve peace between them, Israel and Egypt agree to negotiate in good faith with a goal of concluding within three months of the signing of this framework a peace treaty between them.

It is agreed that:

The site of the negotiations will be under a United Nations flag at a location or locations to be mutually agreed.

All of the principles of U.N. Resolution 242 will apply in this resolution of the dispute between Israel and Egypt.

Unless otherwise mutually agreed, terms of the peace treaty will be implemented between two and three years after the peace treaty is signed.

The following matters are agreed between the parties:

(a) the full exercise of Egyptian sovereignty up to the internationally recognized border between Egypt and mandated Palestine;

(b) the withdrawal of Israeli armed forces from the Sinai;

(c) the use of airfields left by the Israelis near El Arish, Rafah, Ras en Naqb, and Sharm el Sheikh for civilian purposes only, including possible commercial use by all nations;

(d) the right of free passage by ships of Israel through the Gulf of Suez and the Suez Canal on the basis of the Constantinople Convention of 1888 applying to all nations; the Strait of Tiran and the Gulf of

Aqaba are international waterways to be open to all nations for unimpeded and nonsuspendable freedom of navigation and overflight;

(e) the construction of a highway between the Sinai and Jordan near Elat with guaranteed free and peaceful passage by Egypt and Jordan; and

(f) the stationing of military forces listed below.

## STATIONING OF FORCES

A. No more than one division (mechanized or infantry) of Egyptian armed forces will be stationed within an area lying approximately 50 kilometers (km) east of the Gulf of Suez and the Suez Canal.

B. Only United Nations forces and civil police equipped with light weapons to perform normal police functions will be stationed within an area lying west of the international border and the Gulf of Aqaba, varying in width from 20 km to 40 km.

C. In the area within 3 km east of the international border there will be Israeli limited military forces not to exceed four infantry battalions and United Nations observers.

D. Border patrol units, not to exceed three battalions, will supplement the civil police in maintaining order in the area not included above.

The exact demarcation of the above areas will be as decided during the peace negotiations.

Early warning stations may exist to ensure compliance with the terms of the agreement.

United Nations forces will be stationed:

(a) in part of the area in the Sinai lying within about 20 km of the Mediterranean Sea and adjacent to the international border, and (b) in the Sharm el Sheikh area to ensure freedom of passage through the Strait of Tiran; and these forces will not be removed unless such removal is approved by the Security Council of the United Nations with a unanimous vote of the five permanent members.

After a peace treaty is signed, and after the interim withdrawal is complete, normal relations will be established between Egypt and Israel, including: full recognition, including diplomatic, economic and cultural relations; termination of economic boycotts and barriers to the free movement of goods and people; and mutual protection of citizens by the due process of law.

## INTERIM WITHDRAWAL

Between three months and nine months after the signing of the peace treaty, all Israeli forces will withdraw east of a line extending from a point east of El Arish to Ras Muhammad, the exact location of this line to be determined by mutual agreement.

For the Government of the Arab Republic of Egypt:

A. Sadat

For the Government of Israel:

M. Begin

Witnessed by:

Jimmy Carter
President of the United States of America

Note: The texts of the documents were released on September 18.

*Letters Accompanying the Documents Agreed To
at Camp David, September 22, 1978*

September 17, 1978

Dear Mr. President:

I have the honor to inform you that during two weeks after my return home I will submit a motion before Israel's Parliament [the Knesset] to decide the following question:

If during the negotiations to conclude a peace treaty between Israel and Egypt all outstanding issues are agreed upon, "are you in favor of the removal of the Israeli settlers from the northern and southern Sinai areas or are you in favor of keeping the aforementioned settlers in those areas?"

The vote, Mr. President, on this issue will be completely free from the usual Parliamentary Party discipline to the effect that although the coalition is being now supported by 70 members out of 120, every member of the Knesset, as I believe, both on the Government and the Opposition benches will be enabled to vote in accordance with his own conscience.

Sincerely yours,

(signed)

Menachem Begin

[The President, Camp David, Thurmont, Maryland]

September 22, 1978

Dear Mr. President:

I transmit herewith a copy of a letter to me from Prime Minister Begin setting forth how he proposes to present the issue of the Sinai settlements to the Knesset for the latter's decision.

In this connection, I understand from your letter that Knesset approval to withdraw all Israeli settlers from Sinai according to a timetable within the period specified for the implementation of the peace treaty is a prerequisite to any negotiations on a peace treaty between Egypt and Israel.

Sincerely,

(signed)

Jimmy Carter

Enclosure: Letter from Prime Minister Begin
[His Excellency Anwar el-Sadat, President of the Arab Republic of Egypt, Cairo]

September 17, 1978

Dear Mr. President:

In connection with the "Framework for a Settlement in Sinai" to be signed tonight, I would like to reaffirm the position of the Arab Republic of Egypt with respect to the settlements:

1. All Israeli settlers must be withdrawn from Sinai according to a timetable within the period specified for the implementation of the peace treaty.
2. Agreement by the Israeli Government and its constitutional institutions to this basic principle is therefore a prerequisite to starting peace negotiations for concluding a peace treaty.
3. If Israel fails to meet this commitment, the "Framework" shall be void and invalid.

Sincerely,

(signed)

Mohamed Anwar El Sadat

[His Excellency Jimmy Carter, President of the United States]

September 22, 1978

Dear Mr. Prime Minister:

I have received your letter of September 17, 1978, describing how you intend to place the question of the future of Israeli settlements in Sinai before the Knesset for its decision.

Enclosed is a copy of President Sadat's letter to me on this subject.

Sincerely,

(signed)

Jimmy Carter

Enclosure: Letter from President Sadat
[His Excellency Menachem Begin, Prime Minister of Israel]

September 17, 1978

Dear Mr. President:

I am writing you to reaffirm the position of the Arab Republic of Egypt with respect to Jerusalem:

1. Arab Jerusalem is an integral part of the West Bank. Legal and historical Arab rights in the City must be respected and restored.
2. Arab Jerusalem should be under Arab sovereignty.
3. The Palestinian inhabitants of Arab Jerusalem are entitled to exercise their legitimate national rights, being part of the Palestinian People in the West Bank.
4. Relevant Security Council Resolutions, particularly Resolutions 242 and 267, must be applied with regard to Jerusalem. All the measures taken by Israel to alter the status of the City are null and void and should be rescinded.
5. All peoples must have free access to the City and enjoy the free exercise of worship and the right to visit and transit to the holy places without distinction or discrimination.
6. The holy places of each faith may be placed under the administration and control of their representatives.
7. Essential functions in the City should be undivided and a joint municipal council composed of an equal number of Arab and Israeli members can supervise the carrying out of these functions. In this way, the City shall be undivided.

Sincerely,

(signed)

Mohamed Anwar El Sadat

[His Excellency Jimmy Carter, President of the United States]

17 September 1978

Dear Mr. President,

I have the honor to inform you, Mr. President, that on 28 June 1967 — Israel's Parliament [The Knesset] promulgated and adopted a law to the effect: "the Government is empowered by a decree to apply the law, the jurisdiction and administration of the State to any part of Eretz Israel [land of Israel — Palestine], as stated in that decree."

On the basis of this law, the Government of Israel decreed in July 1967 that Jerusalem is one city indivisible, the Capital of the State of Israel.

Sincerely,

(signed)

Menachem Begin

[The President, Camp David, Thurmont, Maryland]

September 22, 1978

Dear Mr. President:

I have received your letter of September 17, 1978, setting forth the Egyptian position on Jerusalem. I am transmitting a copy of that letter to Prime Minister Begin for his information.

The position of the United States on Jerusalem remains as stated by Ambassador [Arthur] Goldberg in the United Nations General Assembly on July 14, 1967, and subsequently by Ambassador [Charles] Yost in the United Nations Security Council on July 1, 1969.

Sincerely,

(signed)

Jimmy Carter

[His Excellency Anwar el-Sadat, President of the Arab Republic of Egypt, Cairo]

September 17, 1978

Dear Mr. President:

In connection with the "Framework for Peace in the Middle East," I am writing you this letter to inform you of the position of the Arab Republic of Egypt, with respect to the implementation of the comprehensive settlement.

To ensure the implementation of the provisions related to the West Bank and Gaza and in order to safeguard the legitimate rights of the Palestinian people, Egypt will be prepared to assume the Arab role emanating from these provisions, following consultations with Jordan and the representatives of the Palestinian people.

Sincerely,

(signed)

Mohamed Anwar El Sadat

[His Excellency Jimmy Carter, President of the United States, The White House, Washington, D.C.]

September 22, 1978

Dear Mr. Prime Minister:

I hereby acknowledge that you have informed me as follows:

A) In each paragraph of the agreed framework document the expressions "Palestinians" or "Palestinian People" are being and will be construed and understood by you as "Palestinian Arabs."

B) In each paragraph in which the expression "West Bank" appears, it is being and will be, understood by the Government of Israel as Judea and Samaria.

Sincerely,

(signed)

Jimmy Carter

[His Excellency Menachem Begin, Prime Minister of Israel]

# Appendix 5

President Reagan's Address to the Nation
on the West Bank and the Palestinians,
September 1, 1982

Today has been a day that should make all of us proud. It marked the
end of the successful evacuation of the P.L.O. from Beirut, Lebanon.
This peaceful step could never have been taken without the good offices of the United States and, especially, the truly heroic work of a
great American diplomat, Ambassador Philip Habib. Thanks to his
efforts, I am happy to announce that the U.S. Marine contingent helping to supervise the evacuation has accomplished its mission. Our
young men should be out of Lebanon within two weeks. They, too,
have served the cause of peace with distinction and we can all be very
proud of them.

But the situation in Lebanon is only part of the overall problem of
conflict in the Middle East. So, over the past two weeks, while events
in Beirut dominated the front page, America was engaged in a quiet,
behind-the-scenes effort to lay the groundwork for a broader peace in
the region. For once, there were no premature leaks as U.S. diplomatic
missions traveled to Mideast capitals and I met here at home with
a wide range of experts to map out an American peace initiative
for the long-suffering peoples of the Middle East, Arab and Israeli
alike.

It seemed to me that, with the agreement in Lebanon, we had an opportunity for a more far-reaching peace effort in the region and I was
determined to seize that moment. In the words of the scripture, the
time had come to "follow after the things which make for peace."

Tonight, I want to report to you on the steps we have taken, and the prospects they can open up for a just and lasting peace in the Middle East.

America has long been committed to bringing peace to this troubled region. For more than a generation, successive U.S. administrations have endeavored to develop a fair and workable process that could lead to a true and lasting Arab-Israeli peace. Our involvement in the search for Mideast peace is not a matter of preference, it is a moral imperative. The strategic importance of the region to the United States is well known.

But our policy is motivated by more than strategic interests. We also have an irreversible commitment to the survival and territorial integrity of friendly states. Nor can we ignore the fact that the well-being of much of the world's economy is tied to stability in the strife-torn Middle East. Finally, our traditional humanitarian concerns dictate a continuing effort to peacefully resolve conflicts.

When our Administration assumed office in January 1981, I decided that the general framework for our Middle East policy should follow the broad guidelines laid down by my predecessors.

There were two basic issues we had to address. First, there was the strategic threat to the region posed by the Soviet Union and its surrogates, best demonstrated by the brutal war in Afghanistan; and, second, the peace process between Israel and its Arab neighbors. With regard to the Soviet threat, we have strengthened our efforts to develop with our friends and allies a joint policy to deter the Soviets and their surrogates from further expansion in the region, and, if necessary, to defend against it. With respect to the Arab-Israeli conflict, we have embraced the Camp David framework as the only way to proceed. We have also recognized, however, that solving the Arab-Israeli conflict, in and of itself, cannot assure peace throughout a region as vast and troubled as the Middle East.

Our first objective under the Camp David process was to insure the successful fulfillment of the Egyptian-Israeli peace treaty. This was achieved with the peaceful return of the Sinai to Egypt in April 1982. To accomplish this, we worked hard with our Egyptian and Israeli friends, and eventually with our friendly countries, to create the multinational force which now operates in the Sinai.

Throughout this period of difficult and time-consuming negotiations, we never lost sight of the next step of Camp David, autonomy talks to pave the way for permitting the Palestinian people to exercise their legitimate rights. However, owing to the tragic assassination of President Sadat and other crises in the area, it was not until January

1982 that we were able to make a major effort to renew these talks. Secretary of State [Alexander] Haig and Ambassador [Richard] Fairbanks made three visits to Israel and Egypt this year to pursue the autonomy talks. Considerable progress was made in developing the basic outline of an American approach which was to be presented to Egypt and Israel after April.

The successful completion of Israel's withdrawal from Sinai and the courage shown on this occasion by Prime Minister Begin and President Mubarak in living up to their agreements convinced me the time had come for a new American policy to try to bridge the remaining differences between Egypt and Israel on the autonomy process. So, in May, I called for specific measures and a timetable for consultations with the Governments of Egypt and Israel on the next steps in the peace process. However, before this effort could be launched, the conflict in Lebanon pre-empted our efforts. The autonomy talks were basically put on hold while we sought to untangle the parties in Lebanon and still the guns of war.

The Lebanon war, tragic as it was, has left us with a new opportunity for Middle East peace. We must seize it now and bring peace to this troubled area so vital to world stability while there is still time. It was with this strong conviction that over a month ago, before the present negotiations in Beirut had been completed, I directed Secretary of State [George] Shultz to again review our policy and to consult a wide range of outstanding Americans on the best ways to strengthen chances for peace in the Middle East.

We have consulted with many of the officials who were historically involved in the process, with members of the Congress, and with individuals from the private sector, and I have held extensive consultations with my own advisers on the principles I will outline to you tonight.

The evacuation of the P.L.O. from Beirut is now complete. And we can now help the Lebanese to rebuild their war-torn country. We owe it to ourselves, and to posterity, to move quickly to build upon this achievement. A stable and revived Lebanon is essential to all our hopes for peace in the region. The people of Lebanon deserve the best efforts of the international community to turn the nightmares of the past several years into a new dawn of hope.

But the opportunities for peace in the Middle East do not begin and end in Lebanon. As we help Lebanon rebuild, we must also move to resolve the root causes of conflict between Arabs and Israelis.

The war in Lebanon has demonstrated many things, but two consequences are key to the peace process:

First, the military losses of the P.L.O. have not diminished the yearning of the Palestinian people for a just solution of their claims; and second, while Israel's military successes in Lebanon have demonstrated that its armed forces are second to none in the region, they alone cannot bring just and lasting peace to Israel and her neighbors.

The question now is how to reconcile Israel's legitimate security concerns with the legitimate rights of the Palestinians. And that answer can only come at the negotiating table. Each party must recognize that the outcome must be acceptable to all and that true peace will require compromises by all.

So, tonight I am calling for a fresh start. This is the moment for all those directly concerned to get involved — or lend their support — to a workable basis for peace. The Camp David agreement remains the foundation of our policy. Its language provides all parties with the leeway they need for successful negotiations.

I call on Israel to make clear that the security for which she yearns can only be achieved through genuine peace, a peace requiring magnanimity, vision and courage.

I call on the Palestinian people to recognize that their own political aspirations are inextricably bound to recognition of Israel's right to a secure future.

And I call on the Arab states to accept the reality of Israel, and the reality that peace and justice are to be gained only through hard, fair, direct negotiation.

In making these calls upon others, I recognize that the United States has a special responsibility. No other nation is in a position to deal with the key parties to the conflict on the basis of trust and reliability.

The time has come for a new realism on the part of all the peoples of the Middle East. The State of Israel is an accomplished fact; it deserves unchallenged legitimacy within the community of nations. But Israel's legitimacy has thus far been recognized by too few countries, and has been denied by every Arab state except Egypt. Israel exists; it has a right to demand of its neighbors that they recognize those facts.

The war in Lebanon has demonstrated another reality in the region. The departure of the Palestinians from Beirut dramatizes more than ever the homelessness of the Palestinian people. Palestinians feel strongly that their cause is more than a question of refugees. I agree. The Camp David agreement recognized that fact when it spoke of the legitimate rights of the Palestinian people and their just requirements. For peace to endure, it must involve all those who have been most deeply affected by the conflict. Only through broader participation in the peace process, most immediately by Jordan and by the Palestinians, will Israel be able to rest confident in the knowledge that its security and integrity will be respected by its neighbors. Only through the process of negotiation can all the nations of the Middle East achieve a secure peace.

These then are our general goals. What are the specific new American positions, and why are we taking them?

In the Camp David talks thus far, both Israel and Egypt have felt free to express openly their views as to what the outcome should be. Understandably, their views have differed on many points.

The United States has thus far sought to play the role of mediator. We have avoided public comment on the key issues. We have always recognized, and continue to recognize, that only the voluntary agreement of those parties most directly involved in the conflict can provide an enduring solution. But it has become evident to me that some clearer sense of America's position on the key issues is necessary to encourage wider support for the peace process.

First, as outlined in the Camp David accords, there must be a period of time during which the Palestinian inhabitants of the West Bank and Gaza will have full autonomy over their own affairs. Due consideration must be given to the principle of self-government by the inhabitants of the territories and to the legitimate security concerns of the parties involved.

The purpose of the five-year period of transition which would begin after free elections for a self-governing Palestinian authority is to prove to the Palestinians that they can run their own affairs, and that such Palestinian autonomy poses no threat to Israel's security.

The United States will not support the use of any additional land for the purpose of settlements during the transition period. Indeed, the immediate adoption of a settlement freeze by Israel, more than any other action, could create the confidence needed for wider participation in these talks. Further settlement activity is in no way necessary for the security of Israel and only diminishes the confidence of the Arabs that a final outcome can be freely and fairly negotiated.

I want to make the American position clearly understood: The purpose of this transition period is the peaceful and orderly transfer of domestic authority from Israel to the Palestinian inhabitants of the West Bank and Gaza. At the same time, such a transfer must not interfere with Israel's security requirements.

Beyond the transition period, as we look to the future of the West Bank and Gaza, it is clear to me that peace cannot be achieved by the formation of an independent Palestinian state in those territories. Nor is it achievable on the basis of Israeli sovereignty or permanent control over the West Bank and Gaza.

So the United States will not support the establishment of an independent Palestinian state in the West Bank and Gaza, and we will not support annexation or permanent control by Israel.

There is, however, another way to peace. The final status of these lands must, of course, be reached through the give-and-take of negotiations. But it is the firm view of the United States that self-government by the Palestinians of the West Bank and Gaza in association with Jordan offers the best chance for a durable, just and lasting peace.

We base our approach squarely on the principle that the Arab-Israeli conflict should be resolved through negotiations involving an exchange of territory for peace. This exchange is enshrined in United Nations Security Council Resolution 242, which is, in turn, incorporated in all its parts in the Camp David agreements. U.N. Resolution 242 remains wholly valid as the foundation stone of America's Middle East peace effort.

It is the United States' position that — in return for peace — the withdrawal provision of Resolution 242 applies to all fronts, including the West Bank and Gaza.

When the border is negotiated between Jordan and Israel, our view on the extent to which Israel should be asked to give up territory will be heavily affected by the extent of true peace and normalization and the security arrangements offered in return.

Finally, we remain convinced that Jerusalem must remain undivided, but its final status should be decided through negotiations.

In the course of negotiations to come, the United States will support positions that seem to us fair and reasonable compromises, and likely to promote a sound agreement. We will also put forward our own detailed proposals when we believe they can be helpful. And, make no mistake, the United States will oppose any proposal — from any party and at any point in the negotiating process — that threatens the security of Israel. America's commitment to the security of Israel is ironclad.

During the past few days, our Ambassadors in Israel, Egypt, Jordan, and Saudi Arabia have presented to their host government the proposals in full detail that I have outlined here tonight.

I am convinced that these proposals can bring justice, bring security and bring durability to an Arab-Israeli peace.

The United States will stand by these principles with total dedication. They are fully consistent with Israel's security requirements and the aspirations of the Palestinians. We will work hard to broaden participation at the peace table as envisaged by the Camp David accords. And I fervently hope that the Palestinians and Jordan, with the support of their Arab colleagues, will accept this opportunity.

Tragic turmoil in the Middle East runs back to the dawn of history. In our modern day, conflict after conflict has taken its brutal toll there. In an age of nuclear challenge and economic interdependence, such conflicts are a threat to all the people of the world, not just the Middle East itself. It is time for us all, in the Middle East and around the world, to call a halt to conflict, hatred and prejudice; it is time for us all to launch a common effort for reconstruction, peace and progress.

It has often been said — and regrettably too often been true — that the story of the search for peace and justice in the Middle East is a tragedy of opportunities missed.

In the aftermath of the settlement in Lebanon we now face an opportunity for a broader peace. This time we must not let it slip from our grasp. We must look beyond the difficulties and obstacles of the present and move with fairness and resolve toward a brighter future. We owe it to ourselves, and to posterity, to do no less. For if we miss this chance to make a fresh start, we may look back on this moment from some later vantage point and realize how much that failure cost us all.

These, then, are the principles upon which American policy towards the Arab-Israeli conflict will be based. I have made a personal commitment to see that they endure and, God willing, that they will come to be seen by all reasonable, compassionate people as fair, achievable, and in the interests of all who wish to see peace in the Middle East.

Tonight, on the eve of what can be a dawning of new hope for the people of the troubled Middle East — and for all the world's people who dream of a just and peaceful future — I ask you, my fellow Americans, for your support and your prayers in this great undertaking.

# Appendix 6

## Excerpt from the Arab League [Fez] Declaration, September 9, 1982

Following is the portion of the Arab League declaration, issued on September 9, dealing with the resolution of the Arab-Israeli conflict. The declaration also dealt with Lebanon, the Persian Gulf war, and the Ethiopia-Somalia conflict:

The summit paid homage to the resistance of the forces of the Palestine revolution, the Lebanese and Palestinian peoples and the Syrian Arab armed forces, and reaffirmed its support to the Palestinian people in the struggle to recover its inalienable national rights.

The summit, convinced of the power of the Arab nation to achieve its legitimate objectives and put an end to the aggression on the basis of the fundamental principles laid down by the Arab summits and in view of the desire of the Arab countries to pursue action by every means for the achievement of a just peace in the Middle East, taking account of the plan of His Excellency President Habib Bourguiba which considers international legality to be the basis for the solution of the Palestinian question, and of the plan of His Majesty King Fahd ibn Abdul Aziz concerning peace in the Middle East, and in the light of discussions and observations made by their majesties, excellencies and highnesses, the kings, presidents and emirs, the summit adopted the following principles:

[1]

The withdrawal of Israel from all Arab territories occupied in 1967 including Arab Al Qods.*

* Jerusalem.

[2]

The dismantling of settlements established by Israel on the Arab territories after 1967.

[3]

The guarantee of freedom of worship and practice of religious rites for all religions in the holy shrines.

[4]

The reaffirmation of the Palestinian people's right to self-determination and the exercise of its imprescriptible and inalienable national rights under the leadership of the Palestine Liberation Organization, its sole and legitimate representative, and the indemnification of all those who do not desire to return.

[5]

Placing the West Bank and Gaza Strip under the control of the United Nations for a transitory period not exceeding a few months.

[6]

The establishment of an independent Palestinian state with Al Qods as its capital.

[7]

The Security Council guarantees peace among all states of the region including the independent Palestinian state.

[8]

The Security Council guarantees the respect of these principles.

# Index

Abd al-Aziz Al Saud (King of Saudi Arabia), 182
Abdullah (crown prince of Saudi Arabia), 180
Abdullah ibn-Hussein (King of Jordan), 36, 136–137
Abraham, 4–6, 7–8, 208; and Damascus, 63; in Egypt, 5, 161; and Middle East, 4
Afghanistan: and Saudi Arabia, 180; Soviet invasion of, 16, 188, 189; Soviet treaty with, 17
Alawite religious sect, and Assad, 83–84
Alexander the Great, and Egypt, 161
Allenby Bridge, 27, 120, 121, 135
Allon, Yigal, 38
Ambiguity: Egyptians' call for, 175; and negotiation, 201, 205
Amman, and Carter visit, 115, 136, 139
Arab conferences. See Conferences, Arab
Arabia (Roman province), 134
Arabian Peninsula: and Assad's

support for Iran, 83; history of, 182; oil reserves in, 4
Arab-Israeli wars. See Wars between Israel and Arabs
Arab League, 162; and Sadat, 165; and Syrian intervention in Lebanon, 95
Arab nations: domestic issues important in, 197; Egypt boycotted by, 169, 175–176; free expression lacking in, 32–33; ineffectiveness of, 3; Israel boycotted by, 72; Israel's emergence misperceived by, 163; Saudis' funding of, 189; in U.S. objectives, 56. See also specific nations and leaders
Arabs: Christian, 32, 91–92, 110, 121; vs. Iranians, 78–79
Arabs, Palestinian. See Palestinians
Arafat, Yasir, 111; and Assad, 71, 82–83, 102, 103; Beirut withdrawal by, 2, 99; in Egyptians' views, 175; goals of, 124; Hussein on, 142; and Mu-

05077086
ISBN 0-395-41498-9